Library of Congress
Subject Headings

RESEARCH STUDIES IN LIBRARY SCIENCE
Bohdan S. Wynar, Editor

No. 1. *Middle Class Attitudes and Public Library Use.* By Charles Evans, with an Introduction by Lawrence Allen.

No. 2. *Critical Guide to Catholic Reference Books.* By James Patrick McCabe, with an Introduction by Russell E. Bidlack.

No. 3. *An Analysis of Vocabulary Control in Library of Congress Classification and Subject Headings.* By John Phillip Immroth, with an Introduction by Jay E. Daily.

No. 4. *Research Methods in Library Science. A Bibliographic Guide.* By Bohdan S. Wynar.

No. 5. *Library Management: Behavior-Based Personnel Systems. A Framework for Analysis.* By Robert E. Kemper.

No. 6. *Computerizing the Card Catalog in the University Library: A Survey of User Requirements.* By Richard P. Palmer, with an Introduction by Kenneth R. Shaffer.

No. 7. *Toward a Philosophy of Educational Librarianship.* By John M. Christ.

No. 8. *Freedom Versus Suppression and Censorship.* By Charles H. Busha, with an Introduction by Peter Hiatt, and a Preface by Allan Pratt.

No. 9. *The Role of the State Library in Adult Education: A Critical Analysis of Nine Southeastern State Library Agencies.* By Donald D. Foos, with an Introduction by Harold Goldstein.

No. 10. *The Concept of Main Entry as Represented in the Anglo-American Cataloging Rules. A Critical Appraisal with Some Suggestions: Author Main Entry vs. Title Main Entry.* By M. Nabil Hamdy, with an Introduction by Jay E. Daily.

No. 11. *Publishing in Switzerland: The Press and the Book Trade.* By Linda S. Kropf.

No. 12. *Library Science Dissertations, 1925-1972: An Annotated Bibliography.* By Gail A. Schlachter and Dennis Thomison.

No. 13. *Milestones in Cataloging: Famous Catalogers and Their Writings; 1835-1969.* By Donald J. Lehnus, with an Introduction by Phyllis A. Richmond.

No. 14. *Weeding Library Collections.* By Stanley J. Slote.

No. 15. *Library of Congress Subject Headings: Principles and Application.* By Lois Mai Chan.

Library of Congress Subject Headings

Principles and Application

Lois Mai Chan

Libraries Unlimited, Inc. - 1978
Littleton, Colo.

LIBRARIES UNLIMITED, INC.
P.O. Box 263
Littleton, Colorado 80160

Library of Congress Cataloging in Publication Data

Chan, Lois Mai.
    Library of Congress subject headings : principles and application.

    (Research studies in library science ; no. 15)
    Bibliography: p. 333
    Includes index.
    1. Subject cataloging. 2. United States. Library of Congress. Subject Cataloging Division. Library of Congress subject headings. I. Title. II. Series.
Z674.R4   no. 15 [Z695]   020'.8s [025.3'3]   78-9497
ISBN 0-87287-187-8

PREFACE

David Judson Haykin's *Subject Headings: A Practical Guide* (1951), which contains a statement of principles and policies and an exposition of subject cataloging practice at the Library of Congress, has served for over a quarter of a century as the guide to the Library of Congress subject headings system. Since 1951, many changes and new developments have taken place which have affected the formation, structure, and application of subject headings. There have been advances in both the theory and the technology of information retrieval through subject analysis. This book attempts to re-examine the underlying principles of *Library of Congress Subject Headings* in light of recent developments and some of the recent theories and to describe current subject cataloging practice as carried out by the Library of Congress.

No attempt was made in this book to formulate any rules. It is an analysis of the principles and a description of current practice. With regard to application, this book is descriptive rather than prescriptive. The need for a code for subject cataloging similar to the one existing for descriptive cataloging has been felt by many for a long time. Such a code, if and when it materializes, must be the concerted effort of many individuals in the field rather than the product of any individual mind.

This book is primarily intended for professional librarians, library instructors, and advanced library science students. Library technicians and beginning students using this book may require the assistance of experienced professionals or instructors.

In the preparation of this work, I am indebted to many individuals and organizations for their assistance. I wish to acknowledge my debt to the following: Barbara B. Mabry, Suzanne Massonneau, John P. Comaromi, Theodora Hodges, for reading parts or all of the manuscript; Patricia A. Boyle for typing the manuscript; and Phoebe Jo Allender for bibliographical assistance. Edward J. Blume, Chief of the Subject Cataloging Division at the Library of Congress, and his staff have been most cooperative and helpful. My special acknowledgment goes to Myrl D. Powell of the Subject Cataloging Division who painstakingly read the entire manuscript.

This study was supported in part by a Council on Library Resources Fellowship.

L.M.C.

To Louis Shores

TABLE OF CONTENTS

PART I

PRINCIPLES, FORM, AND STRUCTURE

CHAPTER 1

INTRODUCTION

HISTORY

The Beginning

The dictionary form was adopted by the Library of Congress for its catalogs in 1898. This decision, augmented by the Library's decision shortly thereafter to make its printed cards available to other libraries in the country, played a major role in the development of the catalog and cataloging practice in American libraries.

Prior to the adoption of the dictionary catalog, the Library of Congress had published in 1869 a subject catalog in the form of an alphabetico-classed catalog. According to Hanson, the first chief of the Catalog Division, among the reasons for adopting the dictionary form was "a desire to be in a position to cooperate with the largest possible number of American libraries."[1]

In the prefaces and introductions to the earlier editions of *Subject Headings Used in the Dictionary Catalogs of the Library of Congress*, Hanson is usually acknowledged as the person who provided the guiding principles:

> The organization of the catalogue to which the list in a measure forms a guide, the determination of the principles and methods to be followed in its construction and their successful application in the development of the subject catalogue are due to Mr. J. C. M. Hanson, chief of the Catalogue Division 1897-1910, assisted by the labors of his associates.[2]
>
> (second and third editions)

> Whatever measure of logic and consistency has been achieved in the headings is due to the continuity of oral tradition which stems from J. M. C. [sic] Hanson, who was Chief of the Catalog Division from 1897 to 1910, Charles Martel, Chief from 1912 to 1930, and their associates in the Catalog Division, and the occasional written instructions issued by them.[3]
>
> (fourth and fifth editions)

In the introduction to the fourth edition of the list, Haykin, then Chief of Subject Cataloging Division of the Library of Congress, presents his view of the beginning of the list:

> There was not, to begin with, a scheme or skeleton list of headings to which additions could be made systematically, completing and rounding out a system of subject headings for a dictionary catalog. Such a scheme

could not have been devised at the time the Library's dictionary catalogs were begun, because there was no solid body of doctrine upon which it could be based; the guiding principles which were then in print for all to read and apply were very meager and concerned themselves with the form of headings and their choice. They did not provide the theoretical basis for a system of headings.[4]

At the time the Library of Congress made its decision, Cutter's *Rules for a Dictionary Catalog*, which is considered by many to have contained the only code for subject headings, was in its third edition. The dictionary form of the catalog was well on its way to becoming the predominant form in American libraries. Haykin obviously did not consider Cutter's rules to have provided sufficient guidance in the forming of the Library of Congress subject headings list. No documented evidence has been found to indicate that Cutter's rules were ever adopted officially by the Library of Congress. In fact, in Haykin's *Subject Headings: A Practical Guide*, which has been acknowledged as the official guide in subsequent editions of the Library of Congress list, there are only a few passing references to Cutter's rules. Cutter was never mentioned in the preface or introduction to any of the editions of the Library of Congress list. Nevertheless, Cutter's influence is quite obvious in Haykin's discussion of the fundamental concepts of Library of Congress subject headings: the reader as the focus, unity, usage, and specificity. Acknowledgment of Cutter's influence comes years later, made by Angell, then chief of the Subject Cataloging Division:

> The final formulation of Cutter's objectives and rules was taking place at the same time that the Library of Congress was expanding and reorganizing the collections at the turn of the century. His work had a considerable influence on the founders of the Library of Congress catalog.[5]

Although never formally acknowledged, Cutter's principles concerning subject headings are reflected in *Library of Congress Subject Headings* in spite of many modifications and compromises for the sake of practicality.

Actual work on the new subject catalog at the Library of Congress began simultaneously with the printing of the first author cards in July 1898.[6] At the same time, it was found necessary to begin an authority list for subject headings. Haykin's statement quoted earlier that there was not a "skeleton list of headings to which additions could be made systematically" might have given the impression that the Library of Congress list was begun *in vacuo*. In fact, the *ALA List of Subject Headings for Use in Dictionary Catalogs* (1895), which was conceived as an appendix to Cutter's rules and designed for the use of small or medium-sized public libraries,[7] had already appeared. In a paper presented at the American Library Association Conference in 1909, Hanson recounts the beginning of the compilation of the Library of Congress list:

> While it was recognized that the A.L.A. list of subject headings had been calculated for small and medium sized libraries of a generally popular character, it was nevertheless decided to adopt it as a basis for subject headings with the understanding, however, that considerable

modification and specialization would have to be resorted to. As a first step preliminary to the real work of compilation, a number of copies of the List were accordingly provided, a number of blank leaves sufficient to treble the size of the original volume were added, and the copies thereupon bound in flexible leather. . . .

New subjects as they came up for discussion and decision were noted on slips and filed. If the subject had already been adopted by the A.L.A. committee, i.e., had appeared as a regular printed heading on the List, a check mark was added to indicate its regular adoption by the Library of Congress.[8]

Hanson also indicates that, in addition to the ALA list, other works consulted included the Decimal and Expansive classifications, the Harvard list of subjects, the New South Wales subject index, Forescue's subject index, and numerous other catalogs, bibliographies, encyclopedias and dictionaries.

Editions

When libraries in the United States began adopting Library of Congress printed cards, a need was felt for the publication of the Library's subject headings list. The printing of the first edition of the list, issued in parts, was begun in the summer of 1909 and completed in March 1914. This edition, followed by fourteen supplementary lists extending to November 1917, was edited by Mary M. Melcher to the end of the letter K, and completed by Mary Wilson MacNair, who also edited the second through fourth editions.

The second edition was published in 1919, followed by three supplements in 1921, 1922, and 1928. The third edition appeared in 1928, followed by cumulative supplements in 1931, 1933, 1935, and 1938. Each of these editions represented a cumulation of the headings in the previous edition and the supplements. The fourth edition, published in 1943, introduced a new feature. Earlier editions had included *see* and *see also* references under the headings, many of which were accompanied by Library of Congress class numbers. However, they lacked the "refer from" tracers, which were available at the Library of Congress only in manuscript or typewritten form.[9] The fourth edition appeared in two volumes, the second being a separate list of the "refer from" tracers. Supplements to this edition were issued quarterly; these were incorporated in a cumulative supplement covering the period from January 1941 through March 1943.

The fifth edition, edited by Nella Jane Martin, appeared in 1948. In this edition the "refer from" tracers were incorporated into the main list under the appropriate headings. There was also a change of format, type size, and use of symbols for references.

The sixth edition, edited by Marguerite V. Quattlebaum, appeared in 1957. The format of this edition was redesigned so as to make it possible to produce the seventh edition by merging linotype slugs from the supplements with the standing type of the sixth edition.

Beginning with the seventh edition, which appeared in 1966 and also edited by Quattlebaum, the list has been printed by photocomposition from computer-produced tape.

The eighth edition was published in 1975. The introduction to this edition has been expanded considerably to include a detailed discussion of subdivision practice. This section, which explains various types of subdivisions and contains a list of the most commonly used subdivisions with elaborate notes explaining their application, offers invaluable information concerning current practice hitherto unavailable to librarians outside of the Library of Congress. The eighth edition also includes *Subject Headings for Children's Literature*, a list which until now had been available only as a separate publication. Another new feature introduced with this edition is the issuance of a microform edition of the list. The list on microfiche now appears quarterly, incorporating all additions and changes occurring since the last issue. This results in virtually a new edition every three months. At the same time, the book-form supplements continue to be published quarterly with annual and biennial cumulations.

LITERARY WARRANT

As in the case of the Library of Congress classification, the Library of Congress subject headings list was developed in close connection with the Library's collection. It was not conceived at the outset and still is not considered a comprehensive system covering the universe of knowledge. It is a subject authority list that has grown with the collection of the Library. This policy of literary warrant is stated in the preface to the second and third editions:

> The list covers subjects in all branches of knowledge so far as the cataloguing of the corresponding classes of books in the Library of Congress progressed.[10]

Haykin comments further in the introduction to the fifth edition:

> [The list] includes only the headings adopted for use in the dictionary catalogs of the Library of Congress in the course of cataloging the books added to the Library's permanent classified collections, and is not, therefore, a list of headings equally complete in all fields of knowledge. Neither is it a skeleton or basic list which could be completed in the course of years of cataloging.[11]

To this pattern of growth, Haykin attributes many failures in logic and consistency:

> The failures in logic and consistency are, of course, due to the fact that headings were adopted as needed, and that many minds participated in their choice and establishment.[12]
>
> (introduction to fourth and fifth editions)

As a result, the development of the list reflects the nature and the growth of the Library's collection. The strong American bias can be attributed to the fact that the *de facto* national library of the United States naturally contains a collection heavily oriented towards American materials.

LACK OF A CODE

The fact that the Library of Congress subject headings list has grown in a process of accretion without the guidance of a specific code or body of rules has been deemed responsible for the many inconsistencies and irregularities which have crept into the system over the years. In the course of the development of the list, while the basic principles of the dictionary catalog as laid down by Cutter and reinforced by Haykin have generally been adhered to, they were often compromised for reasons of practicality. In some cases, the same principle may have been interpreted differently on different occasions, resulting in irregularities. The need for a code for subject headings, corresponding to the one developed for descriptive cataloging, has long been keenly felt but never fulfilled. Interestingly, since Cutter, the only codification of subject headings in a dictionary catalog appeared in Italian in the Vatican rules completed in the 1930s and translated into English in 1948.[13] In essence, the subject headings portion of the Vatican code embodies Cutter's theory as reflected in the practice of Library of Congress.

A surge of interest and an intensified call for a code was apparent in the literature of the 1950s. A serious attempt towards forming a code was undertaken. Frarey's survey of subject catalog use studies[14] and other works on subject headings in the early 1940s provided an impetus and could have laid the groundwork for the code. There is evidence that Haykin did begin work on a code in the late 1950s. Unfortunately, that work was never completed. The remains of that attempt exist in an unpublished document entitled "Project for a Subject Heading Code."[15] Since then, there has not been any renewed effort to continue his project or to begin anew.

As mentioned earlier, over the years the closest thing to a set of rules for subject headings since Cutter was Haykin's *Subject Headings: A Practical Guide* published in 1951. It has been officially acknowledged as the guiding principles for the choice and form of headings and references. Still, it is more a statement and exposition of Library of Congress practice with occasional apologetics, than a code. In the course of a quarter of a century since Haykin's *Guide* was written, many changes have taken place in both the theory and practice of subject analysis. The present study is an attempt to re-examine the basic principles in light of recent developments and changes and to describe current practice at the Library of Congress.

FUNCTIONS OF SUBJECT HEADINGS

In order to design and to maintain a subject catalog which will be useful to the users, an understanding of its functions is essential. Cutter's statement of "objects" is still being frequently quoted as *the* objectives for subject entries:

1. To enable a person to find a book of which the subject is known, and

2. To show what the library has on a given subject and in a given kind of literature.[16]

These two objectives place different demands on the subject catalog. The first objective characterizes the subject catalog as a tool for location (i.e., a finding list), the second as a tool for collocation (i.e., a bibliographic record of considerable scope). As Dunkin states: "The first objective will be best served only if we have entry under the specific subject of the book, the one subject with which it truly tries to deal."[17] The meaning, as well as the means towards achieving the second objective, on the other hand, is open to diverse interpretations and expectations.

Speaking theoretically, Shera and Egan state the following "objectives for any form of subject cataloging":

1. To provide access by subject to *all* relevant material.

2. To provide subject access to materials through all suitable *principles of subject organization*, e.g., matter, process, applications, etc.

3. To bring together references to materials which treat of substantially the *same subject* regardless of disparities in terminology, disparities which may have resulted from national differences, differences among groups of subject specialists, and/or from the changing nature of the concepts with the discipline itself.

4. To show *affiliations among subject fields*, affiliations which may depend upon similarities of matter studied, of method, or of point of view, or upon use or application of knowledge.

5. To provide entry to any subject field at any *level of analysis*, from the most general to the most specific.

6. To provide entry through any *vocabulary* common to any considerable group as users, specialized or lay.

7. To provide a *formal description of the subject content* of any bibliographic unit in the most precise, or specific, terms possible, whether the description be in the form of a word or brief phrase or in the form of a class number or symbol.

8. To provide means for the user to make *selection* from among all items in any particular category, according to any chosen set of criteria such as: most thorough, most recent, most elementary, etc.[18]

Recognizing the idealistic nature of the statement, Shera and Egan continue:

> This list of objectives is a theoretical statement of what a subject catalog could, and possibly should, do if it could be developed without regard to limitations of personnel and finance. Practically, the objectives must always be modified to meet such limitations.[19]

It then becomes a question of what these modifications should be. To what extent should the subject catalog show what the library has on a given subject? Does it really mean *all* the material? Does it mean what books or bibliographic entities the library has on a given subject? Or does it mean also smaller units of information in the library collection, e.g., parts of a book, articles in a journal? With information now contained in mixed media, the questions become even more complex. There is so far no consensus among answers to these questions. Frarey's comment made in the 1950s is still basically valid:

> We do not know whether the subject catalog is doing its job or not; whether it is effective or ineffective; whether it is good or whether it is bad, for it has never been decided what the subject catalog is supposed to be. To some it is, or ought to be, a selected subject bibliography; to some, a subject index; and to still others, the subject catalog is no more than a convenient device for finding some good and useful material on a particular subject.[20]

The frequent criticisms of the subject catalog for being too specific or too general reflect the conflicting demands on the catalog.

Modern writers recognize in general two methods of subject representation: summarization and exhaustive (or depth) indexing. The former aims at displaying the overall subject content of bibliographic entities (books, journals, etc.), while the latter attempts to bring out the content of smaller units of information (e.g., chapters in books, articles in journals, etc.) within bibliographic entities. Many users are content to have the subject catalog fulfill the function of summarization, and leave exhaustive or depth indexing to bibliographies and indexes. Wright speaks to this point of view:

> If a reader really wants "all the material available" on a subject of any size, he is better served by bibliographies than by card catalogs. . . . I believe that, for general library use, subject headings are and will continue to be effective, if we confine them to the task of showing a reasonable display of subject materials for the use of a majority of our readers. The specialist uses bibliographies, for the most part, and we should not attempt to duplicate those bibliographies in the catalog.[21]

Frarey concurs:

> It is [the] failure to define the objective with sufficient precision which has contributed to the long, still unsettled controversy over the most suitable form for the subject catalog to take. It is this same failure which has led in our time to some confusion between the functions of subject cataloging and subject indexing, and to criticisms of the subject catalog because it does not provide the sufficiently deep analysis of the contents of our libraries required or sought by some users of library materials. . . .
>
> There is need to recognize different levels of subject control, and within the hierarchy the bibliography serves one purpose, the subject catalog another, and the subject index still a third.[22]

In a survey of user studies of the subject catalog, Frarey comes to the conclusion that "there is very little use of the subject catalog to find 'all the material the library has,' or to obtain comprehensive coverage of the subject under investigation."[23]

Nevertheless, the Library of Congress subject headings system has often been criticized for its lack of depth in representing the contents of library collections, particularly those of research libraries. The recently developed Subject Access Project at Syracuse University[24] is an experiment in augmenting the depth of subject analysis in on-line library catalogs.

In the course of the development of the Library of Congress subject headings, views on the functions of the subject catalog vary according to the different demands of the users. This lack of consensus and a clear statement of the functions is the cause of many difficulties in defining the basic principles, such as specificity and usage, and in both the construction and the application of subject headings.

REFERENCES

[1] J. C. M. Hanson, "The Subject Catalogs of the Library of Congress," *Bulletin of the American Library Association* 3:389 (July 1, 1909).

[2] United States. Library of Congress. Catalog Division. *Subject Headings Used in the Dictionary Catalogues of the Library of Congress* (3rd ed.; edited by Mary Wilson MacNair; Washington: Government Printing Office, 1928), p. iii.

[3] United States. Library of Congress. Subject Cataloging Division. *Subject Headings Used in the Dictionary Catalogs of the Library of Congress* (4th ed.; edited by Mary Wilson MacNair; Washington: Government Printing Office, 1943), p. iii.

[4] Ibid.

[5] Richard S. Angell, "Library of Congress Subject Headings—Review and Forecast," *Subject Retrieval in the Seventies: New Directions: Proceedings of an International Symposium*; edited by Hans (Hanan) Wellisch and Thomas D. Wilson (Westport, Conn.: Greenwood Publishing Company, 1972), p. 143.

[6] Hanson, p. 387.

[7] Carlyle J. Frarey, *Subject Headings* (The State of the Library Art, vol. 1, part 2; New Brunswick, N.J.: Graduate School of Library Science, Rutgers—The State University, 1960), p. 17.

[8] Hanson, pp. 387, 391.

[9] Robert R. Holmes, "Introduction to the Seventh Edition of Subject Headings Used in the Dictionary Catalogs of the Library of Congress," *Library Resources & Technical Services* 12:324 (1968).

[10] United States. Library of Congress. Catalog Division, 3rd ed., p. iii.

[11] United States. Library of Congress. Subject Cataloging Division. *Subject Headings Used in the Dictionary Catalogs of the Library of Congress* (5th ed.; edited by Nella Jane Martin; Washington, 1948), p. iii.

[12] Ibid.

[13] Vatican Library, *Rules for the Catalog of Printed Books*; trans. from the second Italian edition by Thomas J. Shanahan, Victor A. Schaefer, and Constantin T. Vesselowsky; edited by Wyllis E. Wright (Chicago: American Library Association, 1948), 426pp.

[14] Carlyle J. Frarey, "Studies of Use of the Subject Catalog: Summary and Evaluation," *Subject Analysis of Library Materials*; edited by Maurice F. Tauber (New York: School of Library Service, Columbia University, 1953), pp. 147-65.

[15] David Judson Haykin, "Project for a Subject Heading Code," (Revised; Washington: 1957), 10pp.

[16] Charles A. Cutter, *Rules for a Dictionary Catalog* (4th ed.; Washington: Government Printing Office, 1904), p. 12.

[17] Paul S. Dunkin, *Cataloging U.S.A.* (Chicago: American Library Association, 1969), p. 67.

[18] Jesse H. Shera and Margaret Egan, *The Classified Catalog: Basic Principles and Practices* (Chicago: American Library Association, 1956), p. 10.

[19] Ibid.

[20] Carlyle J. Frarey, "The Role of Research in Establishing Standards for Subject Headings," *Journal of Cataloging and Classification* 10:185 (October 1954).

[21] Wyllis E. Wright, "Standards for Subject Headings: Problems and Opportunities," *Journal of Cataloging and Classification* 10:176, 178 (October 1954).

[22] Carlyle J. Frarey, "Developments in Subject Cataloging," *Library Trends* 2:219, 221 (October 1953).

[23] Frarey, "Studies of Use of the Subject Catalog," p. 162.

[24] "Subject Access Project," *Occasional Newsletter* (Syracuse University School of Information Studies), No. 3, May 1977, pp. 1-4. Project Director: Pauline Atherton.

CHAPTER 2

BASIC PRINCIPLES

THE USER AND USAGE

For Cutter, the foremost principle in cataloging is consideration of the best interest of the user of the catalog. In the preface to the fourth edition of *Rules for a Dictionary Catalog*, he states:

> The convenience of the public is always to be set before the ease of the cataloger. In most cases they coincide. A plain rule without exceptions is not only easy for us to carry out, but easy for the public to understand and work by. But strict consistency in a rule and uniformity in its application sometimes lead to practices which clash with the public's habitual way of looking at things. When these habits are general and deeply rooted, it is unwise for the cataloger to ignore them, even if they demand a sacrifice of system and simplicity.[1]

Haykin calls this guiding principle "the reader as the focus":

> ... the reader is the focus in all cataloging principles and practice. All other considerations, such as convenience and the desire to arrange entries in some logical order, are secondary to the basic rule that the heading, in wording and structure, should be that which the reader will seek in the catalog, if we know or can presume what the reader will look under. To the extent that the headings represent the predilection of the cataloger in regard to terminology and are dictated by conformity to a chosen logical pattern, as against the likely approach of the reader resting on psychological rather than logical grounds, the subject catalog will lose in effectiveness and ease of approach. ...[2]

This principle of "convenience of the public" has played an extremely significant role in the development of subject headings and practice in subject cataloging, to the point that it takes precedence over any systematic or logical considerations. Because logic and consistency were to be sacrificed for the sake of the "convenience of the public," this principle has opened the door to many inconsistent forms and structures of subject headings in the alphabetical subject catalog.

A major problem with this approach has been the difficulty in defining usage and delineating *the user*. Who is the user? Is there such a thing as a "typical user"? A number of writers on the subject catalog have pointed out this difficulty:

Colby: "A general obstacle to putting this principle into practice, is the lack of axiomatic knowledge about readers' habits and of valid methods to study the readers' use of the catalog. With the readers of interest here, there is the additional problem of their heterogeneity."[3]

Metcalfe: "[Cutter] did not see clearly or satisfactorily resolve the conflict of 'usage' with a consistent 'grammar' of headings and sub-headings. . . . Obviously the usage principle is a confusing one for the cataloguer to apply and for the catalogue user to follow"[4]

Olding: "Cutter's admission of the usage principle, or rather his failure to define it adequately, has probably made for more inconsistency in the dictionary catalogue than anything else."[5]

Prevost has asked the most cogent question on this point:

What is the "public" which we, in general libraries, serve through the catalog? Children, young people, adults; the expert, the inept, the illiterate, the savant; scientists, artists, authors, teachers, and— librarians. Once the diverse nature of the users of the catalog is recognized, it becomes a patent absurdity to speak of cataloging according to the "public" mind as if that mind were a single entity.[6]

Dunkin also seriously questions the validity of such an approach:

Is there such a creature as "the public," or are there many publics, each with its individual varieties and needs? Studies will, no doubt, continue as long as cash can be found to pay for them. Suppose some study were to succeed; suppose it were to show that there is only one user and to identify that user and his needs and habits. Would we dare to build a catalog around those habits and needs? Perhaps not. Habits and needs change; this year's man will not be the same man next year. A catalog built on this year's public's habits and needs might hinder next year's public.[7]

In spite of numerous user studies and subject catalog use studies, mostly performed before 1960, it has never been made clear who and what kind of a person this *user* is who is supposed to hold such powerful sway over the form and shape of the catalog. Yet the policy of the "convenience of the public" continues to operate, usually on the premise of the kind of person the catalogers think or assume the user might be and the way he or she might behave. Dunkin's comment on the reason for following such a policy, though a bit harsh, perhaps contains some truth:

On the one hand, it has a noble ring; who can deny that libraries exist to serve? One would as soon attack mother love or home. On the other hand, it is convenient; it gives us an excuse to do almost anything in the catalog.[8]

Thus, there are basically two approaches to the problem. One is to consider the user the supreme arbiter in the choice of form and language, having priority over logic or philosophy. However, the diversity of users and the inability and perhaps impossibility of defining *the user* make codification of cataloging practice extremely difficult. In the case of the Library of Congress subject headings list, part of the difficulty arises from the fact that the list, originally designed for the Library's own collection, must now serve as a general standard. Features and characteristics developed to meet the demands of a large general research collection may not always be suitable to many other types of libraries that also use the list. This makes *the user* even more amorphous and difficult to define.

The second approach is to attempt to develop a system that adheres to logic and strictly formed principles, assuming that a logical and consistent system can be learned by the user. In view of recent developments in cataloging by means of mechanized methods and tools, there is a need for a system that can be easily adapted to machine manipulation. In this regard, there is an increasing demand for consistency and uniformity.

UNIFORM HEADING

The principle of uniform heading is most closely associated with descriptive cataloging. The entry for an author's name is made under a *uniform heading* in order that all works by the same author are grouped together in the catalog. This principle applies to subject entries also. In order to "show what the library has on a given subject," each subject appears in the catalog under one name and one form only. Haykin calls it the principle of *unity*: "A subject catalog must bring together under one heading all the books which deal principally or exclusively with the subject."[9] This principle is also explained in the introduction to *Sears List of Subject Headings*: "One uniform term must be selected from several synonyms and this term must be applied consistently to all works on the topic."[10]

The English language is full of synonyms derived from different linguistic traditions. Many things are called by more than one name, and many concepts can be expressed in more than one way. Different names for the same object or expressions for the same concept often occur in different geographic areas. There are also many near-synonyms which overlap so much that it is impractical to distinguish them and establish them as separate subject headings. In all these cases, one of the several possible names is chosen as the subject heading. If the name chosen appears in different forms, only one form is used.

The main reason stated by Cutter and other authors for grouping all material on a subject under one heading is to prevent the scattering of materials on the same subject. This was considered a remedy for the scattering of materials on the same subject resulting from the earlier practice of catch-word title entry, which depended on the term used by the author of the work being cataloged. A true subject entry lists all works on the same subject together regardless of the authors' choice of terminology.

However, the objective of listing all books on the same subject together also can be fulfilled by listing all works on that subject under each possible name or form. In other words, if the library has twenty books on a subject which can be expressed in five different terms, it is possible to list them repeatedly under each of the five possible headings. However, although this is physically possible, it is not economically feasible in a card or book catalog. It is expensive and it creates a great bulk and congestion in the catalog. Economy, therefore, is the other overriding reason for the adoption of the principle of uniform heading in a dictionary catalog.

Similar to the forming of an author heading in descriptive cataloging, in establishing a subject heading, three choices are often required: name, form, and entry element.

When a subject has more than one name, one must be chosen as the heading to represent all materials on that subject, regardless of the authors' usage. For example, in *Library of Congress Subject Headings*, the heading **Ethics** is chosen among these synonymous terms: "Ethics," "Deontology," "Ethology," "Moral philosophy," "Moral science," "Morality," and "Morals." **Oral medication** is chosen in preference to "Drug by mouth," or "Medication by mouth." Frequently, the same word may be spelled in different ways, e.g., "Esthetics" or "Aesthetics," "Hotbeds" or "Hot-beds," "Marihuana" or "Marijuana." Again, only one of the spellings is used in the heading.

When the name chosen to be the heading can be expressed in different forms, e.g., a phrase heading, a heading with a qualifier, or a subdivided form, only one form is used as the heading. For example, a choice must be made between "Surgical diagnosis" and "Surgery—Diagnosis"; "Cookery (Shrimp)" and "Cookery—Shrimp"; or "Inoculation of plants," "Plant inoculation," and "Plants—Inoculation."

A further choice concerning the entry element is necessary if the form chosen contains two or more elements and both or all could possibly serve as entry elements, for example, "Diagnosis, Surgical" or "Surgical diagnosis"; "Plants, Effect of light on," "Effect of light on plants," or "Light on plants, Effect of."

While in descriptive cataloging, there exist detailed and elaborate rules governing the construction of author headings with regard to the choice of name, form, and entry element, there are no corresponding rules with regard to subject headings. This lack of rules makes consistency and uniformity in the construction of headings extremely difficult to achieve. While the principle of uniform heading is observed in *Library of Congress Subject Headings* in general, there are many exceptions.

The principle of uniform heading renders the *Library of Congress Subject Headings* essentially a single-heading (for each subject) system, as opposed to a multiple-heading (for the same subject) system such as the newly-developed system PRECIS (Preserved Context Index System, used in the *British National Bibliography*). In the PRECIS system, the principle of uniform heading operates with regard to synonyms. However, in the cases of multiple term headings, it allows a separate entry under each significant term. In such a system, the problem of entry element, which is of extreme importance in a single-heading system, does not exist. For example, in *Library of Congress Subject Headings*, we find the heading **Differential equations, Partial** with a *see* reference from "Partial differential equations." The same heading appears in three forms in PRECIS:

Partial differential equations	515'.353
Differential equations	
Partial differential equations	515'.353
Equations	
Partial differential equations	515'.353

Because PRECIS has been developed for a bibliography based on an automated system, the display of multiple forms for the same heading does not entail the same kind of economic burden as in a manually-operated cumulative catalog.

In *Library of Congress Subject Headings*, a heading in the form of a phrase may be entered either in its natural word order or in the inverted form, but not both. In this type of heading, the principle of uniform heading is observed almost without exceptions. In other forms of headings, particularly headings with subdivisions, exceptions to the practice of uniform heading are occasionally made. Haykin mentions several types of duplicate entry.[11] When two components of a heading are equally significant and a reasonable or logical choice of entry element between the two cannot be made, duplicate entries are often made, e.g.,

1. **United States—Foreign relations—France**
2. **France—Foreign relations—United States**

1. **English literature—Translations from Chinese**
2. **Chinese literature—Translations into English**

Another type of duplicate entry, Haykin explains, is used "when a heading for which local subdivision is not provided must be used for a topic which is treated definitely with reference to a place." In this case, a duplicate entry is made under the next broader heading which admits of local subdivision, e.g.,

1. **Gnatcatchers**
2. **Birds—California**

for a work about gnatcatchers in California. As a matter of fact, this practice does not really violate the principle of uniform heading, since these are two different headings which overlap rather than two different forms of the same heading. The following diagrams illustrate the difference between the two types of duplicate entry:

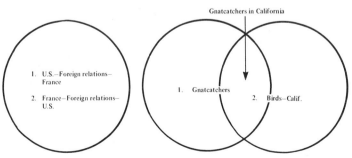

Haykin fails to distinguish the difference between duplicate headings for the same subject, as in the case of the foreign relations headings, and duplicate entries applied to a particular work in order to bring out various aspects. In recent years, there is an increasing use of the latter type of duplicate entries on Library of Congress cataloging records. For example, the practice of assigning duplicate entries to the following categories of works has been announced recently by the Library of Congress:[12]

Bibliography—Bibliography—[topic]

e.g., 1. Bibliography—Bibliography—Outdoor recreation
2. Outdoor recreation—Bibliography

Bibliography—Best books—[topic]

e.g., 1. Bibliography—Best books—Economics
2. Economics—Bibliography

[special language] imprints—[place]

e.g., 1. English imprints—India
2. India—Imprints

Reference books—[topic]

e.g., 1. Reference books—Chemistry
2. Chemistry—Bibliography

Another recent change is the assignment of an additional biographical heading representing the class of persons with appropriate subdivisions to an individual biography.* In cataloging children's materials, duplicate entries are also used frequently. Introducing duplicate or multiple entries into the catalog will no doubt provide additional access points in the catalog. However, it also means multiplication of the number of entries or cards in a card catalog. One must also weigh the implications in terms of economy and congestion. In a computerized catalog, on the other hand, the problem must be viewed differently. The access point is not necessarily the entry or leading word of the bibliographic record. Multiple access points do not entail multiple entries or records. The validity and value of the principle of uniform heading must be viewed in terms of the type of catalog. Different demands in terms of both use and maintenance between a manually-operated catalog and an automated one must be recognized, and as computer-based catalogs begin to predominate, economic barriers to multiple access will diminish.

---

*For a detailed discussion and examples, see Part II, Chapter 10.

TERMINOLOGY

Subject headings are verbal representations of the contents of library materials. A great deal of the effectiveness of the system depends on the choice of terms in forming the headings. The purpose is to effect a perfect match between the term chosen by the user in the search of information and the heading displayed in the catalog. In a system based on the principle of uniform heading, language—or the construction and display of the headings—becomes an extremely important aspect.

With the English language, two problems are of particular significance: 1) choice among synonymous terms, and 2) keeping up with changing usage. An object or concept can often be expressed by more than one term or in more than one way. A subject may acquire different names in different places and at different times. Conversely, the same word often carries different meanings. Both synonyms and homographs are problems that must be dealt with in the construction of subject headings.

Synonyms

When a subject can be represented by more than one term, a choice becomes necessary because the principle of uniform heading requires that each subject be represented by one name and in one form only. The guiding principle in the choice is common usage. This is stated by Cutter:

> General rules, always applicable, for the choice of names of subjects
> can no more be given than rules without exception in grammar. Usage
> in both cases is the supreme arbiter,—the usage, in the present case,
> not of the cataloger but of the public in speaking of subjects.[13]

Haykin phrases the principle of usage in these terms:

> The heading chosen must represent common usage or, at any rate, the
> usage of the class of reader for whom the material on the subject
> within which the heading falls is intended. Usage in an American
> library must inevitably mean current American usage. Unless this
> principle is adhered to faithfully most readers will not find the mate-
> rial they desire under the heading which first occurs to them, if they
> find it at all.[14]

How does one determine common usage? In each of the following categories, Cutter, Haykin, and other writers offer general guidelines:*

---

*In the choice of proper names, the problem involves more than usage alone. Since most of the proper names, particularly of persons, places, and corporate bodies, also serve as main and added entries, a coordination between descriptive cataloging and subject cataloging is necessary. The choice and forms of proper names will be discussed in a later chapter.

Choice among synonymous terms. Cutter's rule no. 169 states:

In choosing between synonymous headings prefer the one that—
(a) is most familiar to the class of people who consult the library.
(b) is most used in other catalogs.
(c) has fewest meanings other than the sense in which it is employed.
(d) comes first in the alphabet, so that the reference from the other can be made to the exact page of the catalog.
(e) brings the subject into the neighborhood of related subjects.[15]

(a) and (b) concern usage. (c) aims at providing a distinctive term for a subject. (d) concerns mainly the printed catalog and has been generally ignored in card catalogs. (e) betrays Cutter's desire to achieve, whenever possible, subject collocation in an alphabetical subject catalog. An example which conforms to Cutter's rule is the choice of **Church history** in preference to "Ecclesiastical history" in the Library of Congress list.

There is also the problem of near-synonymous terms, as Eaton points out:

Much more of a problem than synonyms are the near-symonymous terms. . . . There are other subjects that are not exactly the same, but they are closely related and it is easy to put them together under one heading.[16]

Cutter's instruction concerning near-synonymous terms is:

In choosing between two names not exactly synonymous, consider whether there is difference enough to require separate entry; if not, treat them as synonymous.[17]

There are many examples in the Library of Congress list of near-synonyms treated as synonymous terms. For example, "Religious history" is treated as a synonym of **Church history** and "Freedom" is treated as a synonym of **Liberty**.

Choice between variant spellings. Needless to say, a current spelling is preferred to an obsolete one at the time of establishing the heading. The existence of some obsolete spellings in the Library of Congress list is due to the fact that the spelling changed after the heading was established and the heading has not yet been updated. For variant spellings that are in use concurrently, American spellings are preferred, e.g., **Labor** instead of "Labour," **Catalog** instead of "Catalogue." In other cases, the choice follows *Webster's Third New International Dictionary*, e.g., **Aesthetics** instead of "Esthetics," and **Archaeology** instead of "Archeology."

Choice between English and foreign terms. The choice would appear to be obvious. A catalog designed to serve English-speaking users should naturally rely on English terms. Yet there are exceptions. Cutter's rule concerning language states:

> When possible let the heading be in English, but a foreign word may
> be used when no English word expresses the subject of a work.[18]

Haykin states the rule in the following terms:

> Foreign terms should be used only under the following conditions:
> (1) when the concept is foreign to Anglo-American experience and
> no satisfactory term for it exists, e.g., *Reallast, Précieuses*; and (2)
> when, especially in the case of scientific names, the foreign term is
> precise, whereas the English one is not, e.g., *Ophiodon elongatus*,
> rather than *Buffalo cod*, or *Blue cod; Pityrosporum ovale*, rather than
> *Bottle bacillus.* Terms of foreign origin, which retain their foreign
> form, but which have been incorporated into the English vocabulary
> are, of course, to be regarded as English words, e.g., *Terrazzo,
> Sauerkraut.*[19]

Following the principle of common usage, the Library of Congress chooses
English terms as a matter of general policy. However, in a case where a foreign term
has been well established in English works and accepted by English speaking people,
it is chosen, as for example, **Laissez-faire**. Another exception is made when there is
no English equivalent to a foreign term which expresses precisely and accurately
the subject to be represented, e.g., **Bonsai**.

Choice between technical (or scientific) and popular terms.   Cutter states:

> A natural history society will of course use the scientific name, a town
> library would equally of course use the popular name—*Butterflies*
> rather than *Lepidoptera*, *Horse* rather than *Equus caballus*. But the
> scientific may be preferable when the common name is ambiguous or
> of ill-defined extent.[20]

Haykin echoes Cutter's principle:

> Whether a popular term or a scientific one is to be chosen depends on
> several considerations. If the library serves a miscellaneous public,
> it must prefer the popular to the scientific term. It may even prefer
> it, if the popular term is commonly used in the professional or
> scientific literature; in speaking of the genus bee in general, for
> example, even the scientist will use the term "bee" rather than *Apis*.
> However, the popular term must be precise and unambiguous.[21]

On another occasion, Haykin further explains:

> The choice is not difficult because, obviously, in a catalog intended for
> a miscellaneous public the popular term must be used as the kind most
> likely to be resorted to by the largest group of users, whereas scientific
> terms, although usually more precise in their meanings, will be sought

by the specialist in each field and are, therefore, suitable for a special library catalog.[22]

The focus in both Cutter's and Haykin's statements is the user. Both allow that the choice must be different in a general library serving a general public from that in a special library serving specialists. In the Library of Congress list, popular terms are preferred in most cases, e.g., **Cockroaches** instead of "Blattariae" and **Lizards** instead of "Lacertilia." In some cases, scientific terms are used instead of popular ones, e.g., **Ascorbic acid** instead of "Vitamin C" and **Bioflavonoids** instead of "Vitamin P."

Choice between obsolete and current terms. In establishing a new heading, the choice between an obsolete term and a current term presents no problem, provided that one term is clearly more current than the other(s). The only problem is, how does one recognize an obsolete term? Personal knowledge of the language is a help but not always a reliable guide. Frequently, outside sources must be consulted. Dictionaries seem to be the natural tool, but Haykin expresses reservations about the use of dictionaries as the source of subject headings:

> Dictionaries record both older terms no longer in use and terms in use at the time of the compilation of the dictionary. They do not usually indicate a choice on the basis of currency.[23]

He considers periodicals to be the "surest sources" of usage since they carry the most current literature on various subjects. However, in dealing with new subjects, a heading is needed immediately, often before its terminology is settled. A new invention or concept is sometimes called different names by different people, and the cataloger is in the position of having to choose among several possible names without much help or guidance from outside sources. One example was the choice of **Electronic calculating-machines** as the heading for computers.

A further problem is that common usage does not remain stable. Many terms once in common usage become obsolete. Others acquire different meanings. For example, "Negroes" and "Blacks" refer to the same ethnic group, but the former term, which was once the standard term used in subject headings, has acquired a pejorative connotation in the social context and has become an objectionable term. It has recently been replaced by the terms **Blacks** and **Afro-Americans**.

Theoretically, an established heading consisting of a term which has become obsolete should be replaced by the more current term. Haykin points out the need for constant revision:

> [The cataloger] must use the term in the sense in which it is currently used, regardless of the older literature in and out of the catalog. This leads inevitably to a policy of constant change in order to maintain the catalog up to date. To put this policy into effect the cataloger must substitute the latest heading for the one which is obsolescent or obsolete and must refer the reader to the current heading from the headings which have fallen into disuse.[24]

However, in practice, economic consideration plays an important role. It is costly to change existing subject entries in a manually-operated catalog, especially when there is a large number of works already cataloged under the heading. In the case of the Library of Congress list, the consideration is not only the Library's own catalog, but also all the libraries that use the list. This is the reason that, until recently, the Library of Congress had been rather conservative in revising obsolete headings. This is why **Electronic calculating-machines** and **Aeroplanes** remained in the Library of Congress list long after the terms went out of common usage. As a result, many obsolete terms remain in the list and it is under constant fire. Berman has made a thorough analysis of this problem.[25] In recent years, the currency of terminology has become the most criticized aspect of the list, much more so than structural aspects.

For a period between 1975 and 1977, the Library of Congress updated a large number of obsolete terms. The changes are reflected in the supplements to the eighth edition of the printed list. In 1977, in anticipation of the closing of the card catalog within a few years when many changes are expected, the Subject Cataloging Division of the Library of Congress declared a temporary halt on major or large-scale changes among existing headings.

The problem must be viewed in a different light with regard to computerized catalogs. In a computerized catalog, replacing old headings with new ones does not create the same kind of economic burden as in a manual system. In a computerized catalog, it is possible that the change of the form of a heading would need to be done only once, and all bibliographic records previously linked to the old form of the heading would automatically be linked to the new form of the heading.[26]

Homographs

As a corollary to the rule that the same subject cannot be represented by more than one term, there is also the rule that each heading cannot represent more than one subject. A problem arises when dealing with homographs. Cutter's rule states:

Carefully separate the entries on different subjects bearing the same name, or take some other heading in place of one of the homonyms.[27]

Frequently, "some other heading" may not be available. In such a case, a modifier is added to differentiate between the homographs, e.g., **Cold** and **Cold (Disease)**.

SPECIFIC ENTRY

Specific and Direct Entry

In the *Rules for a Dictionary Catalog*, Cutter claims that the rule of specific entry is the main distinction between the dictionary catalog and the alphabetico-classed catalog. His explanation of the rule of specific entry is: "Enter a work under its subject-heading, not under the heading of a class which includes the subject. . . . Put Lady Cust's book on 'The Cat' under **Cat**, not under **Zoology** or **Mammals**, or

Domestic animals; and put Garnier's 'Le fer' under **Iron**, not under **Metals** or **Metallurgy**."[28]

The Vatican code of 1948 states the principle of specific entry in these terms: "Works are recorded under their specific subjects, and not under the names and designations of the classes and disciplines to which they belong, e.g., **Poll-tax**, not **Taxation** or **Finance**."[29]

From these statements and examples, it would appear that the difference between the alphabetico-classed catalog and the dictionary catalog in the treatment of the subject "cats" represents a choice between **Zoology** and **Cats** as the subject heading. Such is, in fact, not the case. In an alphabetico-classed catalog, the heading for a book on cats would presumably be

Zoology—Vertebrates—Mammals—Domestic animals—Cats

and not **Zoology** alone. In terms of the degree of specificity, this heading is as specific as the heading **Cats**. The real difference is in the choice of the entry element, or the access point in the catalog. In the alphabetico-classed catalog, in order to find the subject "cats," the user must look under **Zoology**, while in the dictionary catalog, the subject is listed under **Cats** without intervening elements. This is what is meant by direct entry: the patron looks directly under the term that specifically describes the topic rather than finding that term as a subdivision of a broader term. Coates has analyzed the problem in these terms:

> The difficulty and confusion in Cutter's thinking about subject headings arises from his intermittent failure to distinguish between the criteria applicable to a complete subject heading on the one hand and to an entry word on the other. . . . He fails to distinguish two separate stages in subject cataloguing a work for the alphabetico-specific catalogue. The first stage is the naming of the work's specific subject, the second is the selection of a particular part of a compound name to serve as entry word.[30]

With regard to the first stage, i.e., the naming of the work's specific subject, there is no real difference between the alphabetico-classed catalog and the dictionary catalog. The main difference lies in the arrangement of the headings in the catalog resulting from different entry elements for the same heading in these two kinds of catalogs. In the alphabetico-classed catalog, headings are arranged to a large extent according to their subject relationships. Each heading begins with the broadest term and contains a hierarchical chain of terms leading to the specific subject. In the dictionary catalog, subject relationships are abandoned in favor of the alphabetical arrangement for the sake of ready or direct access. Haykin clarifies this point by stating:

> In effect the headings for a given topic in an alphabetico-classed and a dictionary catalog are equally specific. The difference lies in the fact that in the former the specific topic is the last element in a complex heading, whereas in the latter it is named directly; what distinguishes the subject heading in a present-day dictionary catalog from other forms is that it is both specific and direct.[31]

The arrangement of entries in an alphabetico-classed catalog results in grouping related subjects together. In the dictionary catalog, on the other hand, the collocation of related subjects is abandoned in order to provide the advantage of direct access, or what Cutter calls the "facility of reference," which he considers the primary object of the dictionary catalog. In using an alphabetico-classed catalog, the user usually requires the assistance of an alphabetical index. The dictionary catalog combines the subject headings list and the index, thereby saving the user the extra effort of consulting a separate index. But in doing so, the advantage of subject collocation is sacrificed.

The question may be raised regarding the relative merits and drawbacks of each kind of catalog. Cutter claims that the objective of the dictionary catalog is "to show at one view all the sides of each object; the classed catalog shows together the same side of many objects."[32] At the same time, Cutter also recognizes some of the disadvantages of the alphabetical arrangement:

> The systematic catalog undertakes to exhibit a scientific arrangement
> of the books in a library in the belief that it will thus best aid those
> who would pursue any extensive or thorough study. The dictionary cata-
> log sets out with another object and a different method. . . . Its sub-
> ject entries, individual, general, limited, extensive, thrown together
> without any logical arrangement, in most absurd proximity, . . . are
> a mass of utterly disconnected particles without any relation to one
> another, each useful in itself but only by itself.[33]

Cutter's views are echoed by Pettee:

> The superiority of the alphabetical subject catalog over the classed
> catalog rests not only upon its direct access to specific subject matter
> without the intermediary of an index to a classification scheme, but
> also upon its ability to collect material from different fields under a
> topical name, and this is its supreme claim to distinction.
>   Its disadvantage is, of course, that the alphabetical dispersion of
> topics makes it impossible to assemble logically related material
> brought together in a linear classification scheme.[34]

In order to achieve the benefit of direct access in the catalog, the advantages of subject collocation must be abandoned. However, in the course of the development of the dictionary catalog in this country, there seems to have been a constant desire to have the best of both worlds, especially in the earlier stages when the users as well as makers of subject headings were still accustomed to the classed catalog. The recognition of the advantage of direct access has often been accompanied by the desire to maintain as well the advantage of the classed catalog of grouping related subjects together. As a result, many headings which are characteristic of an alphabetico-classed catalog have been introduced into the dictionary catalog over the years. This phenomenon is manifested in *Library of Congress Subject Headings*. The source of this development has been analyzed by Angell:

> For the most part, the subject headings used in these catalogs [of the
> Library of Congress] derive from statements of "objects" and "means"

formulated by Charles Ammi Cutter in his *Rules for a Dictionary Catalog.* . . . While the early officers were in accord with Cutter and the majority of United States libraries in rejecting the classified or alphabetico-classed catalog in favor of the dictionary catalog, they were unwilling to contemplate the dispersion of headings that could follow from full adherence to Cutter's rule of specific entry, at least in its application to compound headings. They preferred to combine elements of a dictionary and a classified arrangement. The fact that the Library's subject headings began as a mixed system opened the door to inconsistent decisions as the catalog grew.[35]

The cost of the compromise has been the loss of consistency and predictability of the forms of headings. There is a basic difference between the forms of headings in the alphabetico-classed and those in the dictionary catalogs. When a heading is entered under a broader term leading toward the specific term for the subject involved, then it is no longer direct. Coates has pointed out this basic difference:

Specific alphabetical entry designed to give the enquirer immediate access to his subject . . . is incompatible with the assembly of entries on related subjects. The alphabetico-specific catalogue arranges headings by their affinities of spelling, the classified and the alphabetico-classed forms arrange their entries by affinities of meaning.[36]

To intersperse alphabetico-classed headings in a dictionary catalog is to invite inconsistency, particularly when there are no rigorous rules or guidelines concerning the extent to which such headings can be introduced. Such has been the case with the *Library of Congress Subject Headings*, particularly among the inverted headings and certain headings with subdivisions. (These will be discussed in detail in later chapters.)

The Concept of Specificity

In the application of the principle of specific entry, the greatest difficulty has been the definition of the very concept of specificity. There have been various attempts at defining the term "specific entry," for example:

Cutter: "Enter a work under its subject-heading, not under the heading of a class which includes that subject."[37]

Haykin: "The heading should be as specific as the topic it is intended to cover. As a corollary, the heading should not be broader than the topic."[38]

Sears List of Subject Headings: "The rule of specific entry is to enter an item under the most specific term, i.e., subject heading, which accurately and precisely represents its content. This word serves as a succinct abstract of the work."[39]

Lilley, in an inquiry into the meaning and nature of specificity, identifies at least four types of relationships which determine the nature of specificity:

1. Specificity is in part a function of a particular subject area.
2. Specificity is in part a function of a particular library.
3. Specificity is in part a function of a particular book.
4. Specificity is in part a function of a searcher's exact need at a particular moment of time.[40]

These attempts, however, do not get at the heart of the problem: the nature of specificity. What does one mean when one says an entry is specific? It should be recognized first that a specific heading is not necessarily a narrow one, nor a general heading always a broad one. In respect to subject headings, "general" is not synonymous with "broad," nor "specific" with "narrow." The heading **Zoology** is generally considered a broad one, and the heading **Cats** a narrow one. Whether either term is general or specific depends on the context of application. The heading **Zoology** is general when applied to a work about cats. On the other hand, for a work of zoology, the heading **Zoology** is as specific as the heading **Cats** is to a work about cats. However, the heading **Cats** when applied to a work about Siamese cats becomes a general heading. In other words, specificity is a relative term which must be viewed in a particular context. A specific heading is one which represents the content of the document to which it is applied, while a general heading is one which represents the class to which the subject content of the document is subordinate. As a result, within a given context, a general heading is always broader than a specific heading.

Degree of Precision

In practice, there is also the problem of determining the extent to which specific entry should be applied. The choices range from using extremely broad headings for works on both broad and narrow topics to using headings which cover no more than the content of the work, i.e., headings that are co-extensive with the content of the document. The use of extremely broad headings is to be avoided, as argued by Haykin:

> If the subject catalog were to consist of a predetermined number of more or less broad headings, a work on a specific topic would have to be entered under the broader one. The broader heading would thus be used for works as comprehensive as the heading, as well as for works on all the topics comprehended by it. To find out whether the library possesses a book on a specific topic, the reader would, in the first place, need to know how broad a heading might be used for it, and, in the second place, would have to scan all the entries under the broader heading in order to select those which are of interest to him. Even then, he would be able to identify only those of which the titles clearly indicate the subject; conceivably the titles might be cryptic, even misleading.[41]

The other extreme, i.e., using headings that are co-extensive with the subject content of the document, appears to be the ultimate in carrying out the principle of specific entry. The statements made by Cutter and Haykin with regard to specificity quoted above seem to imply precisely that. However, in practice, this has not always been the case. Haykin feels that "there are limits to the principle of specificity . . . beyond which its application does not appear to serve the best interest of the reader."[42] Angell expresses a similar view:

> Specificity has at least two aspects. The first is the specificity that is possible. This is determined by the document in hand that is being analyzed; in other words, the document itself determines the degree of precision with which its own content can be described. The second aspect is the specificity that is desirable. This specificity is not determined by the document but by the characteristics of the demands which are made upon an information system in a particular application or installation.[43]

Writers, including Cutter, Haykin, and Pettee, differentiate the needs of small libraries from those of large libraries, and the needs of general libraries from those of specialized libraries. In a small general library, for example, would it be in the best interests of the users to enumerate very specific subjects in the catalog? Even if they were enumerated, would the readers be likely to consult these very specific headings? In practice, precision is often sacrificed for the "convenience of the public." Scheerer summarizes the practice and its consequence:

> Specificity is . . . determined upon a "pragmatic" basis with reference to outside factors. These are the number of books upon the subject, the size of the collection, the size of the catalog, the specialist demands of the library's clientele, and the personal experience of the librarian. The result is a relative state of affairs that nullifies the advantages of a standard subject heading list for all types of libraries and evidences a lack of method.[44]

The question then becomes: How specific is specific? Should a book about storm petrels be entered under **Storm petrels**; **Petrels**; **Sea birds** or **Birds**? Should a book about the Volkswagen Rabbit be entered under **Rabbit automobile**; **Volkswagen automobile**; or **Automobiles**? The answers must necessarily vary with regard to the nature and extent of the collections and the users. Even in the PRECIS system which aims at co-extensive entries, the most specific term is not always considered the most useful. For example, the string created for a work entitled *Disruptive Behaviour in Schools: The Report of a Working Party of the Essex County Teachers' Association* is:

Schools. Students. Behaviour problems. Essex. Reports, surveys

The particular kind of behavior is not specified.

Lancaster feels that the retention of a specific term in a subject retrieval system should be justified by its use:

However often a term is used in indexing, it is unjustified if, for instance, over a two-year period it has never been used in searching. This would indicate fairly clearly that the term is unnecessarily specific. Indexers use it because it is available and documents exist on the specific topic. However, requests are never made this specifically in this particular subject area so that a term at this level of specificity is redundant.[45]

The determination of the degree of precision creates a unique problem for those responsible for the development of the Library of Congress subject headings list. Because the list, although originally designed for the Library's own collection, has become a standard list for all but the very small libraries and some specialized libraries, it must try to be all things to all people, an all but impossible task. The needs of different sizes, functions, clientele, of the libraries place demands on the system which are often incompatible or even conflicting. As a result, there is considerable variation in the degree to which Library of Congress catalogers apply the rule of specific entry. In most cases, headings applied to works being cataloged are co-extensive with their content. In other cases, headings broader than the topics of the documents are often used.

Pre-Coordination and Synthesis

In general, the content of a document falls into one of the following categories:

1)   a single subject or concept, or single subjects or concepts (in works of multiple topics treated separately), e.g., flowers; or flowers and shrubs;
2)   aspect(s) of a subject or concept, e.g., fertilization of flowers; arrangement of flowers;
3)   two or more subjects treated in relation to each other, e.g., flowers in art; flowers in religion, folklore, etc.

In a system of subject headings based on the principle of specific entry, devices must be provided to represent precisely and accurately the specific content of the document being cataloged. Taube identifies two methods of attaining specificity: "the specificity of a specific word or phrase and whatever degree of subdivision is allowed" and "the specificity achieved by the intersection, coordination, or logical product of terms of equal generality."[46]

In order to represent the first category of materials mentioned above, a single term denoting the subject or concept is usually sufficient. However, as discussed earlier, in Library of Congress practice, there is variation in the degree to which terms and content match in specificity. It has not been found desirable always to use the *most* specific term.

Frequently with the second category and always with the third category, a single term is not sufficient. In order to achieve the specificity required, two or more terms must be used. In many cases, specificity is achieved by combining two or more general terms, either of which is broader than the resulting heading, e.g.,

Fertilization of flowers
Flowers in art
Effect of light on plants

For example, for a document on the "fertilization" of "flowers," both terms will
be required in representing the subject. This is also true in the case of the subject
"flowers in art." However, the methods of display vary in different systems of subject headings and indexing. The subject relationship may be expressed at the stage
of input, a system called pre-coordination as in the case of PRECIS. Or, the terms
may be coordinated at the point of retrieval, a system referred to as coordinate or
post-coordinate indexing, an example being the Uniterm system. In this respect, the
Library of Congress system lies somewhere between a system in which no pre-
coordination is used at all and a system which requires a tailor-made heading with
all the terms coordinated in appropriate relationships for each document being
analyzed. In other words, pre-coordination is allowed but not insisted upon.

With regard to Cutter's treatment of aspects of a subject, Harris comments:

> Nowhere in his rules does Cutter define specific entry explicitly
> enough to show whether he thought of it as including the aspect or
> point of view from which a subject is treated.[47]

Cutter's classic example of Lady Cust's book entitled *The Cat* has the subtitle: *Its
History and Diseases*; but these aspects are not reflected in Cutter's subject heading.
Nevertheless, there is scattered evidence that Cutter recognized the need for specifying aspects of a subject. Although he provides no explicit rules concerning subdivision, it is assumed in his rules for filing. The *Catalogue of the Library of the
Boston Athenaeum*, for which Cutter was responsible, includes headings of the type
Cattle–Diseases. In his rule for "compound subject-names" provisions are made by
means of phrase headings for expressing aspects of a subject and relationships
between two or more subjects. His rule 174 reads:

The name of a subject may be –

(a) a single word, as *Botany*, *Economics*, *Ethics*. Or several words
taken together, either –

(b) a noun preceded by an adjective, as *Ancient history*, *Capital
punishment*, *Moral philosophy*, *Political economy*.

(c) a noun preceded by another noun used like an adjective, as
Death penalty, *Flower fertilization*.

(d) a noun connected with another by a preposition, as *Penalty of
death*, *Fertilization of flowers*.

(e) a noun connected with another by "and," as *Ancients and
moderns*.

(f) a phrase or sentence, as in the titles "Sur la regle *Paterna
paternis materna maternis*" and "De usu paroemiae juris
Germanici, *Der Letzte thut die Thüre zu*," where the whole
phrase would be the subject of the dissertation.[48]

Although Cutter fails to distinguish between headings representing single concepts
and those indicating complex relationships, it is clear from the rule that he

recognizes the need for combining terms, or coordination, in order to represent specific subjects.

Since the early editions of the *Library of Congress Subject Headings*, combination of terms for the purpose of denoting aspects of subjects and complex subjects has existed. The increasing number of coordinated headings introduced into each subsequent edition of the list is a reflection of the increasingly complex nature of modern knowledge and the way it is presented. However, because of the lack of rules regulating the degree of precision, the device of pre-coordination has not been applied consistently. In many cases, a complex subject is represented by several headings, each of which indicates one part of the subject. For example, the Library of Congress list contains the heading **Nuns as public school teachers**, but no single heading for "public school teachers." Until such a heading is established, two headings, **Public schools** and **Teachers** will be required to represent a work on public school teachers.

There are two approaches to representing a complex subject in the catalog: by using a complex heading which reflects all elements and facets of the subject or by using several headings, each of which brings out one or more of the elements or aspects. When a complex heading required by the document does not exist, the subject cataloger at the Library of Congress may propose a new heading as required by the work. However, because there are no rules concerning specificity or co-extensivity, the cataloger may and often does choose the second approach. For example, highly complex and specific headings such as

Opening of the eyes of one blind at Bethsaida (Miracle)

Church maintenance and repair (Ecclesiastical law)

Suites (Clarinets (2), horns (2), violins (2), viola, double bass)

have been introduced into the Library of Congress list. On the other hand, for the work entitled *The Military Satellite Communications Market*, instead of creating a specific heading, the Library of Congress cataloging record shows three separate headings:

1. **Artificial satellites in telecommunication**
2. **Communication**
3. **Defense contracts—United States**

In dealing with a complex subject for which no single heading exists, it is difficult to predict which approach will be taken by the Library of Congress. In original cataloging, not knowing whether the Library of Congress will create a specific heading for the complex subject and, if so, which form it will take, catalogers outside of the Library of Congress have the tendency to follow the second approach by using several existing, more general, headings in order to bring out the various elements and/or aspects covered in the document.

Means of Pre-Coordination

The device used to express complex subjects is the combination of terms, also called synthesis. Synthesis takes several forms in the Library of Congress subject headings list:

Adjectival phrases, e.g.,
  Plant inspection
  Plant diseases
  Engineering research

Phrases containing conjunctions, e.g.,
  Church and education
  Boats and boating

Phrases containing prepositions, e.g.,
  Pantomimes with music
  Italians in foreign countries
  Fertilization of plants
  Cookery for allergics
  Deficiency diseases in plants
  Flowers in literature

Headings with qualifiers, e.g.,
  Cookery (Chicken)
  Flowers (in religion, folklore, etc.)

Headings with subdivisions, e.g.,
  Church architecture—Italy
  Plants—Identification
  Physics—Research

Headings containing a series of terms, e.g.,
  Hotels, taverns, etc.

Combinations of the forms above, e.g.,
  Church and education in Connecticut
  Church and labor—Italy
  Piano, trumpet, viola with orchestra—Scores
  Clocks and watches in art

There are no fixed rules or practice concerning which form to choose in order to express a specific relationship. Usage, or what may appear to be the form most likely to be consulted by the user, generally determines the choice of form. For example, the geographic aspect may be expressed either by the phrase [subject] in [location], or the subdivided form [subject]—[location].

With regard to the use of the subdivided form, one must also consider its purpose. If, as Haykin[49] and Mann[50] claim, subdivision is a device for subarrangement, then it is required only when there is a considerable file under a given heading. But if the purpose of subdivision is to render the headings more specific, then the subdivision is justified even if there is only one document under the subdivided term.

Another problem with pre-coordinated headings is that when two or more terms are combined, there is no fixed citation order. Because of the principle of uniform heading, only one term in a compound or complex heading is used as the entry element. The lack of a predictable order and consistency among similar headings limits retrieval effectiveness.

There are indications that in some areas, the Library of Congress subject headings system is moving towards a greater degree of specificity and co-extensivity. In music headings particularly, recent trends are towards more formularized coordination with fixed citation orders. As a result, many headings of similar types previously printed in the list have been removed because catalogers can now easily formulate the required heading according to the established patterns or citation formulae. The increasing use of free-floating subdivisions (see discussion in a later chapter) also provides a greater degree of synthesis than was allowed previously.

REFERENCES

[1] Charles A. Cutter, *Rules for a Dictionary Catalog* (4th ed.; Washington: Government Printing Office, 1904), p. 6.

[2] David Judson Haykin, *Subject Headings: A Practical Guide* (Washington: Government Printing Office, 1951), p. 7.

[3] Robert A. Colby, "Current Problems in the Subject Analysis of Literature," *Journal of Cataloging and Classification* 10:20 (Jan. 1954).

[4] John W. Metcalfe, *Information Indexing and Subject Cataloging: Alphabetical: Classified: Coordinate: Mechanical* (New York: Scarecrow, 1957), pp. 73, 77.

[5] R. K. Olding, "Form of Alphabetico-Specific Subject Headings, and a Brief Code," *Australian Library Journal* 10:128 (July 1961).

[6] Marie Louise Prevost, "An Approach to Theory and Method in the Library of Congress Subject Headings," *Library Quarterly* 16:140 (April 1946).

[7] Paul S. Dunkin, *Cataloging U.S.A.* (Chicago: American Library Association, 1969), pp. 141-42.

[8] Ibid., p. 141.

[9] Haykin, p. 7.

[10] "Principles of the *Sears List of Subject Headings*," *Sears List of Subject Headings* (11th ed., edited by Barbara M. Westby; New York: H. W. Wilson Company, 1977), p. xiv.

[11] Haykin, pp. 57-60.

[12] "Additional Subject Assignments for Special Categories of Bibliography," *Cataloging Service* 118:10-11 (Summer 1976).

[13] Cutter, p. 69.

[14] Haykin, p. 8.

[15] Cutter, p. 70.

[16] Thelma Eaton, *Cataloging and Classification: An Introductory Manual* (4th ed.; Ann Arbor: Edwards Brothers, 1967), p. 156.

[17] Cutter, p. 70.

[18] Ibid., p. 69.

[19] Haykin, p. 9.

[20] Cutter, p. 70.

[21] Haykin, p. 9.

[22] David Judson Haykin, "Subject Headings: Principles and Development," *The Subject Analysis of Library Materials*, ed. by Maurice F. Tauber (New York: School of Library Service, Columbia University, 1953), p. 50.

[23] Haykin, *Subject Headings*, p. 8.

[24] Ibid.

[25] Sanford Berman, *Prejudices and Antipathies: A Tract on the LC Subject Heads Concerning People* (Metuchen, N.J.: Scarecrow, 1971), 249pp.

[26] Mary Kay Daniels Ganning, "The Catalog: Its Nature and Prospects," *Journal of Library Automation* 9:55 (March 1976).

[27] Cutter, p. 71.

[28] Ibid., p. 66.

[29] Vatican Library, *Rules for the Catalog of Printed Books*; trans. from the second Italian edition by Thomas J. Shanahan, Victor A. Schaefer, and Constantin T. Vesselowsky; ed. by Wyllis E. Wright (Chicago: American Library Association, 1948), p. 250.

[30] E. J. Coates, *Subject Catalogues: Headings and Structure* (London: Library Association, 1960), p. 37.

[31] Haykin, *Subject Headings*, pp. 3-4.

[32] Cutter, p. 68.

[33] Ibid., p. 79.

[34] Julia Pettee, *Subject Headings: The History and Theory of the Alphabetical Subject Approach to Books* (New York: H. W. Wilson, 1947), p. 59.

[35] Richard S. Angell, "Library of Congress Subject Headings—Review and Forecast," *Subject Retrieval in the Seventies: New Directions: Proceedings of an International Symposium*; ed. by Hans (Hanan) Wellisch and Thomas D. Wilson (Westport, Conn.: Greenwood Publishing Company, 1972), pp. 143-44.

[36] Coates, p. 26.

[37] Cutter, p. 66.

[38] Haykin, *Subject Headings*, p. 9.

[39] "Principles," *Sears List of Subject Headings*, p. xii.

[40] Oliver Linton Lilley, "How Specific Is Specific?" *Journal of Cataloging and Classification* 11:4-5 (1955).

[41] Haykin, *Subject Headings*, pp. 9-10.

[42] Ibid., p. 10.

[43] Richard S. Angell, "Standards for Subject Headings: A National Program," *Journal of Cataloging and Classification* 10:193 (October 1954).

[44] George Scheerer, "Subject Catalog Examined," *Library Quarterly* 27:190 (July 1957).

[45] F. W. Lancaster, *Vocabulary Control for Information Retrieval* (Washington: Information Resources Press, 1972), p. 104.

[46] Mortimer Taube, "Specificity in Subject Headings and Coordinate Indexing," *Library Trends* 1:222 (October 1952).

[47] Jessica Lee Harris, *Subject Analysis: Computer Implications of Rigorous Definition* (Metuchen, N.J.: Scarecrow, 1970), p. 22.

[48] Cutter, pp. 71-72.

[49] Haykin, *Subject Headings*, p. 27.

[50] Margaret Mann, *Introduction to Cataloging and the Classification of Books* (2nd ed.; Chicago: American Library Association, 1943), p. 146.

CHAPTER 3

FORMS OF HEADINGS

INTRODUCTION

Subject headings in the Library of Congress system represent a mixture of natural language and an artificial language. Single nouns, adjectival phrases, and prepositional phrases are based on the natural forms and word order of the English language. On the other hand, headings with qualifiers, headings with subdivisions, and inverted headings are forms especially designed, not forms used in everyday speech.

Traditionally, forms of subject headings have been viewed in terms of their grammatical or syntactical structure, i.e., the way words are put together to form phrases or sentences. Cutter names the following categories of subject headings in a dictionary catalog:

(a)   a single word

(b)   a noun preceded by an adjective

(c)   a noun preceded by another noun used like an adjective

(d)   a noun connected with another by a preposition

(e)   a noun connected with another by "and"

(f)   a phrase or sentence.[1]

Haykin identifies seven forms used in *Library of Congress Subject Headings*: noun headings; adjectival headings; inverted adjectival headings; phrase headings; inverted phrase headings; compound headings; and composite forms.[2]

Angell categorizes the forms as follows:

Headings proper have the grammatical form of noun or phrase, the principal types of the latter being adjective-noun, phrases containing a preposition, and phrases containing a conjunction. Phrases may be in normal direct order of words, or inverted.

Headings are amplified as required by 1) the parenthetical qualifier, used principally to name the domain of a single noun for the purpose of resolving homographs; and 2) the subdivision, of which there are four kinds: topic, place, time, and form.[3]

In the Library of Congress system, the sentence form mentioned by Cutter is not used.

Daily,[4] in a thorough morphological and syntactical study of the forms of subject headings, divides them into the following categories: one-word headings, two-word headings; headings consisting of three or more words without function words; and those with function words. Variations within each group are also identified.

Non-verbal symbols used in conjunction with the words in a heading are relatively simple in the Library of Congress system. The comma is used to separate a series of parallel terms and to indicate an inverted heading. Parentheses are used to enclose qualifiers. The dash is the signal for subdivisions, e.g., **United States—Air defenses**. The period is used to separate a subheading from the main heading and only appears in an author heading used as a subject heading, e.g., **United States. Air Force**.

Another way of categorizing headings is in terms of semantic aspects. Most headings represent single concepts or objects. Compound headings contain more than one concept or object, some expressing an additive relationship, others representing phase relationships (such as cause and effect, influence, bias, etc.) between concepts and objects. There are still other headings which represent a particular aspect of a subject, such as form, space, time, process, or property.

In the Library of Congress subject heading system, there does not seem to be a relationship between the grammatical forms and the semantic functions. A heading representing an aspect of a subject is usually in the form of a subdivided heading, but may also appear in the form of an adjectival phrase (direct or inverted), a prepositional phrase (direct or inverted), or a heading with a qualifier, e.g.,

> **Factor tables**
> **Multiplication—Tables**
> **Squares, Tables of**
> **Plant inspection**
> **Fertilization of plants**
> **Plants, Protection of**
> **Cookery (Squash)**

The problem is then how to determine or predict the choice of a particular form in a given situation. Both Cutter and Haykin attempt to deal with the problem, but fail to provide specific guidelines.

Choice Between Nouns and Phrases

When a choice is to be made between a noun and a phrase which represent the same object or concept, Cutter proposes that phrases "shall when possible be reduced to their equivalent nouns, as Moral philosophy to Ethics or to Morals; Intellectual or Mental philosophy to Intellect or Mind."[5] However, he also recognizes the difficulty in applying such a rule:

> In reducing, for instance, Intellectual philosophy or moral philosophy, will you say Mind or Intellect, Morals or Ethics? And the reader will not always know what the equivalent noun is,—that Physics=Natural

philosophy, for example, and Hygiene=Sanitary science. Nor does it help us at all to decide whether to prefer Botanical morphology or Morphological botany.[6]

No satisfactory solution to the problem has been offered.

Choice Among Different Types of Phrases

In his rules, Cutter[7] gives examples of the same subject named in different ways, e.g.,

Capital punishment
Death penalty
Penalty of death

Floral fertilization
Flower fertilization
Fertilization of flowers

He feels that there is no way to formulate an absolute rule to ensure consistency in the choice, and that the best course to follow is, "When there is any decided usage (i.e., custom of the public to designate the subjects by one of the names rather than by the others) let it be followed." The difficulty is, as Cutter recognizes immediately, "As is often the case in language, usage will be found not to follow any uniform course." As a result, there is no uniformity in the choice among different types of phrases.

Choice Between Phrases and Headings with Subdivisions

The problem of choice among several possible forms is compounded by the use of subdivisions, which adds another possible form to choose from. Although headings with subdivisions are covered in Cutter's rules for filing, his rules for subject entry do not mention subdivided headings. Haykin recognizes the problem of having to choose among forms which have equal standing in current usage, such as **Stability of ships; Ships' stability**; and **Ships—Stability**, but offers no solution. In *Library of Congress Subject Headings*, any of the three forms may have been chosen with regard to individual headings, e.g.,

Squares, Tables of
Factor tables
Multiplication—Tables

Recent practice favors headings with subdivision over phrase headings. According to a recent policy decision, unless the proposed phrase heading is very well known by the informed public in exactly that form, it is considered more useful to establish the proposed new concept as a topical subdivision under the generic heading, e.g.,

> Butterfat—Fat globules
> [*instead of* Milk fat globules]

> Greenhouses—Climate
> [*instead of* Greenhouse climate]

Because of the lack of specific rules regulating the choice of forms over the years and because of the fact that many people have participated in establishing headings, many inconsistencies exist in *Library of Congress Subject Headings*. Nonetheless, there are certain predominant patterns in the usage and function of each form of headings. Recent efforts at establishing specific guidelines will ensure greater consistency in newly formed headings. Following is a discussion of the problems and recent guidelines regarding various forms of headings.

SINGLE NOUN OR SUBSTANTIVE

A single noun is chosen as the heading when it represents the object or concept precisely, e.g.,

Chapels
Economics
Forgery
Humanism
Railroads
State, The
Success

When adjectives and participles are chosen, they are used as substantives or noun equivalents, e.g.,

Advertising
Aged
Comic
Poor
Sick
The West

In the past, as Daily has pointed out, the article was used in some cases but not others even when grammatical usage would require it.[8] A recent decision was made that, because of machine filing, no new subject heading is to be established with a "The" in the initial position. Many of the existing headings with an initial "The" have been converted to the required form,* e.g.,

---

*The headings **The West** and **State, The** remain in their original form, because the article is necessary for their meaning. **The West** is uninverted because it is a name.

Original Form	Converted Form
The arts	Arts
The Many (Philosophy)	Many (Philosophy)
The One (Philosophy)	One (The One in philosophy)

On the whole, the plural form of a noun is used for denoting a concrete object or a class of people, e.g., **Airplanes**; **Churches**; **Florists**; **Teachers**. This is not a rigid rule and there are many exceptions. A deliberate exception is made for names of fruits for which the singular noun is used for both the fruit and the tree, e.g., **Peach**; **Pear**. Headings which represent biological species are generally in the singular, e.g., **Japanese macaque**; **Rhesus monkey**; headings for larger taxa are almost always in the plural, e.g., **Macaques**; **Monkeys**. In cases where both the singular and the plural forms of a noun were used as headings, they represent different subjects. Usually the singular form represents a concept or abstract idea and the plural a concrete object, e.g., **Essay** [as a literary form] and **Essays** [for a collection of specimens of this literary form]. However, in newly established headings, this distinction is no longer made.

In headings for art, the former practice of using the singular, e.g., **Painting**, to represent the activity and the plural, e.g., **Paintings**, for the objects has been discontinued. Currently, the singular noun denoting activity, e.g., **Watercolor painting**, is used to represent both the activity and the objects.[9] Another way of distinguishing between the art and the specimens is to add a qualifier to one of the headings, e.g.,

Biography [for collective biographies] and **Biography (as a literary form)**.

ADJECTIVAL HEADINGS

An adjectival heading consists of an adjectival modifier followed by a noun or noun phrase. The modifier takes one of the following forms:

Common adjective, e.g.,

>**Military supplies**
>**Rural churches**
>**Nuclear physics**

Ethnic, national, or geographic adjective, e.g.,

>**Jewish etiquette**
>**American drama**
>**European newspapers**

Other proper adjective, e.g.,

>**Brownian movements**

Present or past participle, e.g.,

>**Laminated plastics**
>**Mining machinery**

Common noun in the possessive case, e.g.,

> **Carpenters' square**
> **Children's art**

Proper noun in the possessive case, e.g.,

> **Carleton's Invasion, 1776**

Common noun, e.g.,

> **Ocean currents**
> **Lake steamers**
> **Landscape gardening**
> **Milk contamination**

Proper noun, e.g.,

> **Norton motorcycle**
> **Norway pine**
> **Lakeland terriers**

Combination, e.g.,

> **Real estate office buildings**
> **Gold-platinum alloys**
> **California Railroad Strike, 1894**

Haykin points out the importance of recognizing the distinctions between various types of adjectival headings, because the kind of *see* references needed varies with the type of heading:

> In general, no reference need be made if the generic term, that is, the noun, serves merely as the vehicle for the modifier which gives meaning to the phrase. Conversely, a reference is needed if the adjective, or adjectival noun, serves primarily to modify or qualify.[10]

The following examples illustrate Haykin's statement:

Electric capacity
[no reference]

Electric cables
> *x*   Cables, Electric

In current practice, new headings of the second type would be established in the inverted form to begin with.

In the past, no distinction was recognized between adjectival phrases which represent specific concepts such as **Nuclear physics** and phrases which represent aspects or facets of a subject and can be easily turned into a subdivided form, e.g., **Milk contamination** (instead of "Milk–Contamination"); **Mining machinery** (instead of "Mining–Mechanical equipment"). As a result, different forms were often used for similar headings. Current practice favors the subdivided form.

CONJUNCTIVE PHRASE HEADINGS

This type of heading which consists of two or more nouns, with or without modifiers, connected by the word "and" or ending with "etc." is used for one of two purposes:

1) The subjects or topics contained in the heading are affinitives or sometimes opposites which are usually treated together in works. The conjunction expresses an additive feature. Examples of this type of heading are:

> **Good and evil**
> **Libel and slander**
> **Crime and criminals**
> **Reporters and reporting**
> **Boats and boating**
> **Lamp-chimneys, globes, etc.**
> **Hotels, taverns, etc.**
> **Law reports, digests, etc.**
> **Libel and slander (Roman-Dutch law)**
> **Library institutes and workshops**
> **Literary forgeries and mystifications**
> **Emigration and immigration**
> **Emerald mines and mining**
> **Children's encyclopedias and dictionaries**
> **College and school periodicals**
> **Mines and mineral resources**
> **Open and closed shelves**

Haykin calls these "compound headings" or "composite forms." By a recent Library of Congress policy decision, no new headings of this type are to be established. Current policy requires the establishment of separate headings for each element. Many previously established headings of this type have been replaced by separate headings, e.g., **Textile industry and fabrics** being replaced by **Textile fabrics** and **Textile industry**.

2) The conjunctive phrase form is also used in compound headings which represent relationships, such as cause and effect, influence, etc., between objects or concepts, e.g.,

> **Religion and international affairs**
> **Literature and society**
> **Television and children**

The relationship in these headings is implied and distinguished by context rather than by form.

PREPOSITIONAL PHRASE HEADINGS

This type of heading consists of two or more nouns, with or without modifiers, connected by preposition(s), e.g.,

Children as musicians
Community mental health services for children
Grooming for men
Photography of animals
Radar in speed limit enforcement
Television in health education
Transplantation of organs, tissues, etc.

Some of these headings express a single concept which cannot be named by a single noun, e.g.,

Divine right of kings
Spheres of influence

Some represent a relationship between distinctive and otherwise independent subjects, e.g.,

Communication in birth control
Discrimination in housing
Federal aid to community development

Many of the prepositional phrase headings represent an aspect or facet of a subject (such as locality or an action), and could equally be represented by a subdivided heading, e.g.,

Cataloging of art
    [*instead of* Art—Cataloging]

Taxation of aliens
    [*instead of* Aliens—Taxation]

[topic] in art
    [*instead of* [Topic] —Art]

Church and state in Wales*
    [*instead of* Church and state—Wales]

---

*Current policy requires that new headings of this type be established in the subdivided form.

QUALIFIERS

A qualifier in the form of a noun or phrase enclosed within parentheses placed after a main heading (in either single-noun or phrase form) is used to distinguish between homographs, e.g., **Pool (Game)**; **Cold (Disease)**; **Rape (Plant)**; or to clarify the meaning of a heading which is obscure, e.g., **Polyps (Pathology)**; **Extra Hungariam non est vita (The Latin phrase)**. It is also used to limit the meaning of a heading in order to render it more specific, e.g., **Olympic games (Winter)**.

The qualifier may be a generic term added to a proper name in order to indicate the nature of the name, e.g., **Queen Mary (Steamship)**; **Banabans (Oceanian people)**; **Oświęcim (Concentration Camp)**.

In some cases, the qualifier is used as an alternative for a subdivided form, e.g.,

> **Cookery (Chicken)**
> [*instead of* Cookery—Chicken
> *or* Chicken—Cookery]

> **Marches (Voice with piano)**
> *but* **Symphonies—Vocal scores with piano**

In still other cases, it is not clear why the qualifying form instead of the phrase form was used, or why it was used at all, e.g.,

> **Profession (in religious orders, congregations, etc.)**

> **Light and darkness (in religion, folk-lore, etc.)**
> *but* **Light and darkness in literature**

> **Programming languages (Electronic computers)**

In order to insure greater consistency in newly established headings, the Library of Congress has recently developed the following guidelines with regard to qualifiers. The parenthetical qualifier is used for the purpose of resolving homographs. It is no longer added to a general concept for the purpose of designating a special application of that concept. In other words, qualified headings of the following types will no longer be established: **Vibration (Marine engineering)**; **Error analysis (Linguistics)**; **Cookery (Frozen foods)**; **Excavations (Archaeology)**; **Symmetry (Biology)**. In cases similar to these, one of the following forms is now used instead:

1) an "in" phrase heading, e.g., **Debugging in computer science**;
2) a phrase heading, e.g., **Combinatorial enumeration problems**;
3) a subdivided heading, e.g.,   **Blood groups—Lewis system**
                                         Photography—Scientific applications

The third type is preferred whenever it is practical to subdivide the principal topic.

INVERTED HEADINGS

When a subject heading contains only a noun, there is no question about entry element. When the heading contains more than one word, then the question arises as to which of the terms is to be used as the entry word. Strictly speaking, subject headings in a dictionary catalog based on the principle of specific entry should be entered directly according to the natural word order, e.g., **Life insurance** or **Theory of Knowledge**. However, such has not always been the case. From the earliest stage of the development of the dictionary catalog, it has been found desirable to invert certain headings so that they will be filed under a term other than the first in the phrase according to natural word order. In *Library of Congress Subject Headings*, many headings are inverted, with the noun brought forward, e.g.,

Insurance, Life
Knowledge, Theory of

However, not all adjectival or phrase headings are inverted. There is no specific guideline, nor discernible pattern, for inverted headings. In many cases, there is no way to predict the form of a heading in *Library of Congress Subject Headings*, e.g.,

Bessel functions
Functions, Abelian
Abelian Groups
Groups, Continuous

In adjective-noun headings containing national adjectives, certain patterns based on subject categories have been discovered.[11] However, the same patterns do not seem to hold for the majority of headings containing other kinds of adjectives, e.g.,

Agricultural chemistry
Biological chemistry
Physiological chemistry

but

Chemistry, Clinical
Chemistry, Medical and pharmaceutical
Chemistry, Organic

The rationale for inverted headings has been explained by Haykin:

When it is desired to bring the noun in an adjectival heading into prominence, either in order that it may appear in the catalog next to other headings beginning with that noun, or because the adjective is used simply to differentiate between several headings on the same subject the inverted type of adjectival heading is used.[12]

Mann advises using inverted headings "only when necessary," and offers the rationale for this form:

A problem arises if a term such as pathological psychology is used. The general heading *Psychology* will lose all the books which deal with this subject in its application to medicine, because the two groups will not be filed together. In such a case, the term may be changed to bring the new subject into relation with the main subject heading to which it belongs; in other words, a term must be found which will allow the special application of the topic to be grouped with the main subject. Such headings are called "inverted headings." They are adopted when it seems desirable to keep classes together to maintain a somewhat logical arrangement. . . .

Several good reasons for grouping the various aspects of a subject in the dictionary catalog warrant the use of inverted headings. Such an arrangement (1) brings books on related aspects of a subject together; (2) it results in a grouping that is frequently different from the classified arrangement on the shelves; and (3) it relieves readers of the trouble of searching in a number of places in the catalog to find related topics.[13]

The reason given in these statements for inverted headings is to bring related subjects together. Wright comments succinctly: "The use of inverted phrases is usually a mark of attempted classification."[14] In practice, because some but not all of the phrase headings are inverted, the advantage of subject collocation is only partially realized, e.g.,

Insurance, Disaster
Insurance, Life
Insurance, Social

but

Disaster relief
Life insurance trusts [cf. also **Trusts, industrial**]
Social insurance courts

While different kinds of insurance are grouped together by means of the inverted form, various aspects of the same kind of insurance are separated.

Looking back, one finds that this practice has been sanctioned by Cutter[15] himself: "Enter a compound subject-name by its first word, inverting the phrase only when some other word is decidedly more significant or is often used alone with the same meaning as the whole name." The advantage of this "noun rule" is subject collocation. Cutter recognizes that "to adopt the noun (the class) as the heading is to violate the fundamental principle of the dictionary catalog" and that "the specific-entry rule is one which the reader of a dictionary catalog must learn if he is to use it with any facility; it is much better that he should not be burdened with learning an exception to this, which the noun rule certainly is." To invert a phrase heading in order to bring the noun forward is a concession to the alphabetico-classed catalog. Nonetheless, Cutter's misgivings about violating the principle of specific entry were evidently overruled by his policy of the "convenience of the public."

Since not all headings containing more than one word are to be inverted, there remains the question of when to invert. Cutter has attempted to provide some guidelines. Concerning the order of words in headings containing more than one word, he discusses three options:

1) "We can consider the subject to be the phrase *as it reads*, as *Agricultural chemistry*, *Survival of the fittest*."

Cutter's objection to this form is that "it may be pushed to an absurd extent" in headings containing a noun preceded by an adjective. He offers an example:

A man might plausibly assert that Ancient Egypt is a distinct subject from Modern Egypt, having a recognized name of its own, as much so as Ancient history, and might therefore demand that the one should be put under *A* (Ancient) and the other under *M* (Modern) and similar claims might be made in the case of all subject-names to which an adjective is ever prefixed, which would result in filling the catalog with a host of unexpected and therefore useless headings.

The interesting words in this statement are "unexpected" and "useless." They are evidently used in reference to users who were accustomed to the classified arrangement. A user acquainted with the rule of specific and direct entry should not find these headings unexpected. In the same paragraph, Cutter hastens to add: "Nevertheless the rule seems to me the best if due discrimination be used in choosing subject-names."

2) "We can make our entry . . . under what we consider the most significant word of the phrase, inverting the order of the words if necessary; as . . . *Species*, Origin of the, the word Origin here being by itself of no account; *Alimentary* canal, Canal being by itself of no account."

This form is reminiscent of the catchword titles. The objection to it, Cutter sees immediately, "is that there would often be disagreement as to what is 'the most important word of the phrase,' so that the rule would be no guide to the reader. But in connection with (1) and as a guard against its excesses (2) has its value."

3) "We can take the phrase as it reads . . . but make a special rule for a noun preceded by an adjective . . . *first*, that all such phrases shall when possible be reduced to their equivalent nouns . . . ; and *secondly*, that in all cases where such reduction is impossible the words shall be inverted and the noun taken as the heading, as *Chemistry*, Agricultural; *Chemistry*, Organic."

The objection to this rule is that "it would put a great many subjects under words where nobody unacquainted with the rule would expect to find them," e.g., works on the **Alimentary canal** would hardly be looked for under "Canal."

As a final solution, Cutter offers his noun-rule quoted earlier: "Enter a compound subject-name by its first word, inverting the phrase only when some other word is decidedly more significant or is often used alone with the same meaning as the whole name." Nonetheless, he recognizes immediately that this "combined rule" will not solve all the problems. On the contrary, it often compounds them. Cutter concedes that "this rule is somewhat vague and that it would be of doubtful application." Subsequent application of the noun rule in *Library of Congress Subject Headings* bears out Cutter's misgivings.

Cutter distinguishes between the adjective-noun headings in which the noun is the name of a class and the adjective indicates a subdivision (e.g., "Comparative anatomy" and "Capital punishment"), and the adjective-noun heading where the adjective implies a subject and the noun indicates the aspect in which the subject is viewed, e.g., "Ancient history" or "Medieval history" (i.e., a historical study of the ancient world or the middle ages). However, in determining the forms of headings, this distinction has not always been used as a criterion.

Entering a heading under the "more significant" word has always been, and is still, followed as a general guideline in the Library of Congress system. However, because this guideline allows a great deal of subjective judgment on the part of the catalogers with regard to the determination of the "significant" word, many inconsistencies in form have resulted over the years.

In spite of repeated efforts of writers since Cutter, no rigorous, objective criteria for determining entry elements have yet been developed. This is an area on which much literature has been written. Following is a summary of some of the discussions and proposals.

The Vatican code offers the following guidelines for adjective-noun headings:

> The adjective usually precedes the noun in English when it conveys the specific sense, while it follows the noun when it only qualifies a concept that is already specific in itself or indicates a minor variety or division.[16]

In practice, it is difficult to perceive how this rule would apply in the formation of the group of headings related to chemistry cited above.

The Vatican code also provides rules for inverting prepositional phrase headings. Its rule 384 states:[17]

1) Prepositional phrases which represent a distinct concept are usually retained in their common form.

Conflitto di leggi	Conflict of laws
Piante nell'arte	Plants in art
Padri della chiesa	Fathers of the church

2) The words are inverted when the first word represents a vague and indistinct concept, while the second term indicates a specific topic.

Animali, Leggende e racconti di	Animals, Legends and stories of
Discendenza reale, Famiglie di	Royal descent, Families of

It is not clear why the word "families" in the last example should be considered to represent "a vague and indistinct concept." Nor do these rules provide clearcut guidance in determining the form of a heading such as "Directors of corporations."

Conceding that "uninverted phrase headings are to be preferred since they represent the normal order of words and it can be reasonably assumed that most readers would not look under the inverted form," Haykin offers this criterion for inverting headings:

> However, phrase headings in inverted form are used when the first element in effect qualifies the second and the second is used in the catalog as an independent heading. The inversion is then equivalent to subdivision, but is used in place of subdivision to preserve the integrity of the commonly used phrase.[18]

In practice, Haykin's statement has failed to provide a clearcut guideline to the extent of ensuring a reasonable degree of consistency in form. For example,

Knowledge, Theory of

but

Profession of faith [in spite of the fact that **Faith** is an independent heading in the list]

Prevost[19] proposes a "noun rule" which reduces all phrase headings to the "Noun—Subdivision" form, e.g.,

Libraries—Branches
    —Centralization
    —Chemical
    —History
    —Librarians—Interchange of
    —Loans—Interlibrary
    —Medical
    —(relations with) School
    —Science (of)—Schools

However, critics usually wince at this proposal when they see the heading **International relations** reduced to "Nations—Inter-relations."

Granting that inverted headings are necessary, Coates[20] proposes a criterion for choosing the most significant term as the entry element based on "the word which evokes the clearest mental image." He concludes that "images of things are simpler, more readily formed, more accessible to memory than images of actions." However, he immediately recognizes the difficulty in applying this criterion to headings containing two or more equally concrete things as in the case of double noun phrases.

Harris proposes the criterion of word-frequency, suggesting that in an adjective-noun combination, "the less common of the two words might be regarded as best specifying the subject."[21] Unfortunately, it has not been demonstrated how this criterion is to be applied in establishing new subject headings.

In order to ensure consistency in form, much more rigorous rules concerning when, or whether, to invert phrase headings must be developed. In most of the discussions on this subject in print, the linguistic and semantic criteria play the major role. In practice, the subject criterion seems to also play a significant role in *Library of Congress Subject Headings*.

FUNCTIONS OF HEADINGS

In terms of functions of headings—what they indicate about the works they are applied to—the headings in the alphabetical subject catalog may be divided into the following categories.

Topical or Subject Headings

A topical heading represents the subject content of the work. The overwhelming majority of subject headings assigned to works fall into this category. For example, a work about clinical chemistry is assigned the heading **Chemistry, Clinical**; a work on the process of arriving at decisions for action is assigned the heading **Decision-making**; etc.

Bibliographic Form Headings

Some headings indicate the bibliographic form rather than the subject content of the work. Most of these are assigned to works not on any particular subject or on very general, broad subjects, e.g., **Encyclopedias and dictionaries**; **Almanacs**; **Yearbooks**; etc. These are relatively few in number. The same headings are assigned to works discussing the particular forms, e.g., a work about compiling almanacs. In these cases, no attempt is made to distinguish works in and works about the forms.

However, many headings representing bibliographic forms are used only as topical headings and are not assigned to individual specimens of the form. For example, the heading **American periodicals** is assigned to a work about American periodicals, but not to a publication such as *Atlantic Monthly*.

Artistic and Literary Form Headings

Many headings indicate the artistic or literary genre of the work. These generally occur in fields in which the forms of the works are considered of greater importance than their subject content. They are used extensively in three fields in particular: literature, art, and music. Examples of this type of headings are:

Essays
Painting, Dutch
Suites (Wind ensemble)

In some cases, a distinction is made between works in a particular genre and works about it, e.g., **Essay** [as a literary form] and **Essays** [a collection]. Detailed discussions on headings for literature and music will be presented in later chapters.

REFERENCES

[1] Charles A. Cutter, *Rules for a Dictionary Catalog* (4th ed.; Washington: Government Printing Office, 1904), pp. 71-72.

[2] David Judson Haykin, *Subject Headings: A Practical Guide* (Washington: Government Printing Office, 1951), pp. 21-25.

[3] Richard S. Angell, "Library of Congress Subject Headings—Review and Forecast," *Subject Retrieval in the Seventies: New Directions: Proceedings of an International Symposium*; ed. by Hans (Hanan) Wellisch and Thomas D. Wilson (Westport, Conn.: Greenwood Publishing Company, 1972), p. 144.

[4] Jay E. Daily, "The Grammar of Subject Headings: A Formulation of Rules for Subject Headings Based on a Syntactical and Morphological Analysis of the Library of Congress List," (Diss.: New York: Columbia University, 1957), 234pp.

[5] Cutter, p. 72.

[6] Ibid., p. 74.

[7] Ibid.

[8] Daily, p. 56.

[9] "Art Headings," *Cataloging Service* 121:13-14 (Spring 1977).

[10] Haykin, p. 21.

[11] Lois Mai Chan, " 'American Poetry' but 'Satire, American': The Direct and Inverted Forms of Subject Headings Containing National Adjectives," *Library Resources & Technical Services* 17:330-39 (Summer 1973).

[12] Haykin, p. 22.

[13] Mann, p. 144.

[14] Wyllis E. Wright, "The Subject Approach to Knowledge: Historical Aspects and Purposes," *The Subject Analysis of Library Materials*; ed. by Maurice F. Tauber (New York: School of Library Service, Columbia University, 1953), pp. 10-11.

[15] Cutter, pp. 72-74.

[16] Vatican Library, *Rules for the Catalog of Printed Books*; trans. from the second Italian edition by Thomas J. Shanahan, Victor A. Schaefer, and Constantin T. Vesselowsky; ed. by Wyllis E. Wright (Chicago: American Library Association, 1948), p. 257.

[17] Ibid., p. 260.

[18] Haykin, pp. 23-24.

[19] Marie Louise Prevost, "An Approach to Theory and Method in the Library of Congress Subject Headings," *Library Quarterly* 16:140-51 (April 1946).

[20] E. J. Coates, *Subject Catalogues: Headings and Structure* (London: Library Association, 1960), p. 50.

[21] Jessica Lee Harris, *Subject Analysis: Computer Implications of Rigorous Definition* (Metuchen, N.J.: Scarecrow, 1970), p. 67.

CHAPTER 4

SUBDIVISIONS

INTRODUCTION

Subdivisions are used extensively in *Library of Congress Subject Headings.* According to Haykin, the rationale for subdividing a heading is that it serves as a device for subarranging a large number of works sharing the same main heading:

> Subdivision is distinguished from qualification in that it is ordinarily used not to limit the scope of the subject matter as such, but to provide for its arrangement in the catalog by the form which the subject matter of the book takes, or the limits of time and place set for the subject matter.[1]

Mann has also stated earlier:

> The tendency to group under one subject heading all books in a given field is desirable up to a certain point, but such a procedure will lead to a day of reckoning when the entries under that caption become so numerous that it is difficult to differentiate between titles. When this happens the subject must be subdivided.[2]

Coates, on the other hand, disagrees with this reasoning. He calls Haykin's argument of subdivision as a device for subarrangement "a mere play upon words." Coates explains:

> . . . in the alphabetical subject catalogue the degree of subject specification and the mechanics of arrangement are simply two aspects of a single operation. One decides upon a particular heading and by the same token determines the position of the entry in the catalogue.[3]

The decision on whether to subdivide a subject or not depends to a large extent on one's perception of the purpose of subdivision. If subdivision is used solely as a means of subarrangement, it is called for only if there is a substantial amount of material on a subject. But if subdivision is used for the purpose of rendering a subject more specific, which is by and large the current philosophy of the Library of Congress, a heading is subdivided when there are documents that focus on a specific aspect of the subject. The subdivided heading thus serves to maintain coextensivity between the heading and the document.

In *Library of Congress Subject Headings*, there are four types of subdivisions: topical, geographic, period, and form. Topical subdivisions have always been used to achieve specificity as well as to provide for subarrangement. On the other hand, period subdivisions have been used mainly as a device for subarrangement of large files. Many subjects which lend themselves to chronological treatment are not subdivided by period, e.g., **English essays**. Likewise, the histories of many small countries are not divided chronologically. In the past, form and geographic subdivisions were also used mainly as a means of subarrangement. This is the reason why many headings have not been subdivided by place, even though there were library materials on the subject limited to a certain locality. Current policy requires the use of form subdivisions when applicable and appropriate. Newly established headings indicate a trend towards greater use of geographic subdivision, even where the size of the file would not require it; the criterion followed now is suitability of geographic qualification to the literature of the subject.[4]

TOPICAL SUBDIVISION

A main subject heading subdivided by a topical subdivision resembles an entry in an alphabetico-classed catalog. Both Cutter and Haykin feel that classed entries should be avoided in a dictionary catalog. Cutter provides no specific rules for subdivision. Haykin's feelings about subdivisions are expressed in the following statement:

> The use of topics comprehended within a subject as subdivisions under it is to be avoided. It is contrary to the principle of specific entry, since it would, in practice, result in an alphabetico-classed catalog.
> That subject catalogs, as a matter of fact, contain headings subdivided by topics is evidence of a lack of a clear understanding of the purpose of the alphabetical subject catalog and of the distinction between a specific heading of the direct type and an alphabetico-classed heading.[5]

A subdivision that represents a kind or a part of the main subject (forming a genus-species, thing-part, or class-inclusion relationship) is characteristic of an entry in a classed catalog. A classed heading usually consists of a string of terms beginning with the broadest term, with each term subordinate to the one preceding it and containing the one following it. The heading represents a hierarchy based on the genus-species or thing-part relationship which indicates a class-inclusion unit. Haykin feels that this type of heading should not be introduced into a dictionary catalog:

> If alphabetico-classed headings are to be avoided, limitations must be set on methods of subdivision. In the case of alphabetico-classed headings, by definition, subdivision is by areas, elements, and phases of the main subject. In other words, subordination is by topic. In subject headings proper; that is, headings which name the topic directly, without subordination, subdivision can only serve as a convenient shorthand for long phrases and a means of desirable, logical grouping of material recorded under the heading. In other words, subdivision

should usually be limited to the form organization and bibliographic character of the material (for instance such subdivisions as HISTORY, DICTIONARIES, YEARBOOKS), the geographic area covered by it, and the time of publication or period covered. In effect these subdivisions are extensions or modifications of the subject heading, and not more specific subject areas within those covered by the main heading.[6]

However, there are different types of topical subdivisions, some of which are not of the genus-species or class-inclusion type, and resemble alphabetico-classed entries in their outward form only. For example, the relationship between the main heading and the topical subdivision in the headings **Heart—Diseases** or **Agriculture—Taxation** is not that of genus-species or thing-part type. The example used by Haykin is: "CONSTRUCTION INDUSTRY—TAXATION is another way of saying 'taxation of the construction industry', and obviously not 'taxation as a division of the subject CONSTRUCTION INDUSTRY'."[7] He states that the topical subdivision is used "only where the broad subject forms part of the name of the topic and a convenient phrase form sanctioned by usage is lacking, or, for the purpose of the catalog, where it is desirable to conform to an existing pattern."[8] For example, "chemical research" is a commonly accepted phrase while "physical research" is not. Therefore, the headings used for these similar subjects are **Chemical research** *but* **Physics—Research**. As a result, aspects of a subject may be represented in several different ways: by topical subdivisions, phrase headings, or, in some cases, by headings with qualifiers. In order to ensure greater uniformity among newly established headings, current policy requires the use of the form **[topic]—Research**.

In *Library of Congress Subject Headings*, topical subdivisions are most often used to bring out aspects or facets of the main subject, rather than to indicate its kinds or parts. Nonetheless, a small number of headings characteristic of the classed entries (i.e., hierarchically-divided headings) have been introduced into the list.

The following examples are of the genus-species type:

Shakespeare, William, 1564—1616—Characters—Children
Shakespeare, William, 1564—1616—Characters—Fathers

Wages—Minimum wage

In the first two examples, the genus-species relationship is most obvious between the subdivision and the sub-subdivision, e.g., **—Characters—Children**.

While these headings bring together all types of characterization in Shakespeare's works, an advantage of the classed catalog, this practice results in inconsistency because this form is not used regularly with similar or related headings, e.g.,

Children in literature
     [*and not* Literature—Characters—Children]

Retirement income
     [*and not* Income—Retirement income]

In these cases, the principle of specific entry is observed.

Examples of the thing-part type of headings are:

Airplanes–Motors–Carburetors
Airplanes–Motors–Mufflers
Airplanes–Wings

The purpose of this form, again, is subject collocation, i.e., to group different parts of the airplane together. Again, the problem is in maintaining consistency and predictability in similar headings. Although **Motors** and **Wings** are entered as subdivisions under **Airplanes**, ailerons, flaps, and tabs–also parts of the airplane–are entered in the direct form:

Ailerons
Flaps (Airplanes)
Tabs (Airplanes)

Fortunately, *see* references are made from the forms not used and the reader will be guided to the forms used, e.g.,

Airplanes–Motors–Carburetors
    x   Aircraft carburetors

Flaps (Airplanes)
    x   Airplanes–Flaps

GEOGRAPHIC SUBDIVISION*

Many subjects lend themselves to geographic treatment. When the geographic aspect of the subject is of significance, geographic (also called place, or local) subdivisions are provided. Principles concerning geographic subdivision are stated by Haykin:

> When the data of the subject treated are limited to a geographic or
> political area, the heading may be subdivided by the name of the place.
> This method of subdivision is variously called place, local, or geographic.
> It is applicable to such subjects as possess a geographic connotation.[9]

Subjects which can be divided geographically are indicated in *Library of Congress Subject Headings* by one of two designations, *(Direct)* or *(Indirect)*, which referred to the two different methods (used until recently) of dividing a subject geographically. As explained in the introduction to the eighth edition of the *Library of Congress Subject Headings*, the designation *(Direct)* meant that the local subdivision follows directly after the subject heading, e.g., **Banks and banking–Cleveland**, while the designation *(Indirect)* indicated that, with certain exceptions,

---

*Source documents for this discussion: Introduction to 8th ed. of *LCSH; Cataloging Service* bulletins nos. 114, 116, 118, 120, 121. For forms of geographic names, see Chapter 6.

the name of the relevant country was to be interposed between the subject heading and the name of any subordinate political, administrative, or geographical division within the country, e.g., **Music—Switzerland—Zurich.**

A recent policy[10] was made to discontinue direct geographic subdivision except in a few cases. All subject headings with a designation of either *(Direct)* or *(Indirect)* are now subdivided in the same manner. There are at least two reasons for discontinuing the use of direct geographic subdivisions. The use in the past of direct and indirect subdivisions without clearly defined criteria has been a source of confusion for both users and catalogers. Another reason is that the geographic code developed as part of the Library of Congress MARC format has a built-in hierarchy, with the result that, on the MARC records, all subject headings to which the geographic code has been assigned in effect contain "indirect" subdivision.[11]

This recent change in policy has rendered most of the discussion concerning local subdivision in the introduction to the eighth edition of *Library of Congress Subject Headings* obsolete. Based on recent documents, the following is a summary of current practice.

In subdividing a subject geographically, the name of the relevant country or island groups in some instances is to be interposed between the subject heading and the name of any subordinate political, administrative, or geographical division within the country. No geographic name higher than the level of a country is to be used as an interposing element. No subject heading contains more than two geographic elements, e.g.,

Music—Europe
Music—Germany, West
[*not* Music—Europe—Germany, West]

Music—Germany, West—Bavaria
Music—Germany, West—Munich
[*not* Music—Germany, West—Bavaria—Munich]

The following statements which appear in *Cataloging Service* Bulletins 116 (Winter 1976) and 120 (Winter 1977) have now replaced the section on local subdivision in the introduction to the eighth edition of *Library of Congress Subject Headings:*

1) When a heading is coded *(Indirect)* or *(Direct)*, subdivide locally by interposing the name of the country (or island groups in some instances) between the topical heading and the name of any entity falling wholly within that country's territorial limits, including subordinate political jurisdictions (e.g., provinces, counties, cities), historic kingdoms, geographic features and regions, and islands, as shown:

Agriculture—France—Saône-et-Loire (Dept.)
Music—Switzerland—Zürich
Geology—Caroline Islands—Truk Islands

2) When subdividing locally, always use the latest name of any entity whose name has changed during the course of its existence, regardless of the form of the name used in the work cataloged, e.g.:

Title: *The Banks of Leopoldville, Belgian Congo.* 1950.
    1.   Banks and banking—Zaire—Kinshasa.

3) Subdivide locally only in accordance with the present territorial sovereignties of existing nations, regardless of the past territorial divisions described in the work cataloged. For a region or jurisdiction which existed in the past under various sovereignties, always interpose the name of the country now in possession regardless of the political situation existing during the period covered by the work, as long as the region or jurisdiction is located wholly within that country, e.g.:

Title: *The Present State of Education in Alsace.* 1910.
    1.   Education—France—Alsace.

Title: *Educational Conditions in Leipzig in 1900.*
    1.   Education—Germany, East—Leipzig.

Title: *Educational Conditions in Breslau, Germany, in 1900.*
    1.   Education—Poland—Wrocław.

4) Exceptions:
    (a)   Assign directly first order political subdivisions of the following countries:*

Country	Divisions
Canada	Provinces
Great Britain	Constituent countries
Soviet Union	Republics
United States	States

Subdivide these entities further, if required, by names of counties, cities, or other subordinate units, e.g.:

Music—Québec (Province)—Québec
Sports—England—London metropolitan area
Nursing—Ukraine—Kiev (Province)
Education—California—San Joaquin Valley

For Great Britain, subdivide the heading in each case by the name of the pertinent constituent country, and add as a further subdivision the name of the county, city, or other subordinate unit, e.g.:

---

*The exceptions previously made for the states, provinces, or major divisions of Australia, Austria, France, Germany, Italy, and Netherlands (cf. p. xiii of introduction to *Library of Congress Subject Headings*) have been removed.

> Medicine—England—London
> Geology—Northern Ireland—Ballycastle region
> Heraldry—Scotland—Forfar
> Mines and mineral resources—Wales—Merionethshire

Do not further subdivide the jurisdiction of Great Britain itself to bring out any specific locality of Great Britain. If the subordinate unit needed is larger than any one constituent country, assign that unit directly.

In the LC catalogs, as far as a few dozen headings were concerned, local subdivision practice was formerly deliberately altered by the use of a *see* reference, e.g.:

> Boards of trade—England
> *see*   **Boards of trade—Great Britain**

For the Soviet Union:

i) For subject headings requiring indirect subdivision, assign the appropriate constituent republic of the Soviet Union after the topical subject heading followed by the name of the province, city, or other subordinate unit as a further subdivision, e.g.:

> **Geology—Ukraine—Kiev (Province)**
> **Sports—Russian Republic—Moscow**

ii) Do not subdivide the heading **Russia** (i.e., the Soviet Union) to bring out any specific locality. Either go through the constituent republic or, if the entity is larger than any one of these, assign the entity directly. Examples of the latter:

> **Zoology—Siberia**
> **Folk dancing—Dnieper Valley**

iii) For the constituent republics, use the following name forms as subject headings—all are existing subject headings except **Russian Republic** which replaces **Russia** (1917-   R.S.F.S.R.), although the latter is still in use as a corporate heading:

> **Armenia**
> **Azerbaijan**
> **Estonia**
> **Georgia (Transcaucasis)**
> **Kazakhstan**
> **Kirghizistan**
> **Latvia**
> **Lithuania**
> **Moldavian S. S. R.**
> **Russian Republic**
> **Tajikistan**
> **Turkmenistan**

(Example continues on next page.)

Ukraine
Uzbekistan
White Russia

(b)   Assign directly the name of any jurisdiction or region which does not lie wholly within a single existing country or first order political subdivision of the four countries of (a) above. Such jurisdictions or regions may include: the names of the four countries of (a) above; historic kingdoms, empires, etc.; geographic features and regions, such as continents and other major regions, bodies of water, mountain ranges, etc., e.g., **Europe; Siberia; Great Lakes; Mexico, Gulf of; Rocky Mountains; Nile Valley.**

(c)   Assign directly names of islands or groups of islands which are situated some distance from land masses, even if they do not represent autonomous political units, e.g., **Geology–Bermuda Islands.**

Assign indirectly islands which lie close to a large land mass (usually within the territorial limits of a country) and are politically a subdivision of the country, e.g., **Agriculture–Italy–Sicily.**

Assign indirectly an individual island within an island group situated some distance from a land mass, even if the group is not an independent nation, e.g., **Water-supply–Canary Islands–Teneriffe.**

(d)   Assign directly the names of the following cities: Berlin, Jerusalem, New York, Washington, D.C.

5) When subdividing locally, if the geographic qualifier of the subordinate entity is identical to the name of the country or the name of the first-order political subdivision of the countries in 4(a) above, omit the geographical qualifier to avoid redundancy, e.g.:

Sill River, Austria
but
Stream measurements–Austria–Sill River

Amazonas, Brazil (State)
but
Transportation–Brazil–Amazonas (State)

Do not delete the qualifier when the qualifier and the country subdivision are not identical, e.g.:

Stone age–Yugoslavia–Porodin, Macedonia

PERIOD SUBDIVISION

Period, or time, subdivision is used most frequently with headings in the fields of history, literature, and the arts. Not all headings in these fields are subdivided by period; the general guide is the amount of material on the subject. Period subdivision appears most frequently under names of places. Not all period subdivisions used on Library of Congress cataloging records appear in the printed list. A separate publication, *LC Period Subdivisions Under Names of Places*[12] provides a full list of period subdivisions under geographic names adopted by the Library of Congress through January 1975. Period subdivisions established since that date have been and will be listed in *Library of Congress Subject Headings*.

Division

The division of historical periods varies from place to place and from subject to subject. The general rule stated by Haykin is:

> The period subdivisions used should either correspond to generally recognized epochs in the history of the place or should represent spans of time frequently treated in books, whether they possess historic unity or not.[13]

In other words, scholarly consensus is the general guide. The period subdivisions under the history of a given country are not always mutually exclusive. As Haykin points out:

> The presence in the catalog of broad subdivisions does not preclude the use of subdivisions covering events or lesser epochs falling within the broad period.[14]

In application, a broad period subdivision and a more specific period subdivision falling within it are not usually used together for the same work. Prior to the eighth edition, the arrangement of period subdivisions beginning with the same date was to place greater periods before lesser periods, e.g.,

France—History—Revolution, 1789-1900
 —Revolution, 1789-1815
 —Revolution, 1789-1799
 —Revolution, 1789-1793
 —Revolution, 1789.

In the eighth edition, to facilitate computer filing, a strictly numerical arrangement is adopted, resulting in filing shorter periods before broad periods, e.g.,

France—History—Revolution, 1789
 —Revolution, 1789-1793
 —Revolution, 1789-1799
 —Revolution, 1789-1815
 —Revolution, 1789-1900

Period subdivisions under other subjects are usually mutually exclusive, e.g.,

English literature—To 1100
    —Middle English, 1100-1500
    —Early modern, 1500-1700
    —18th century
    —19th century
    —20th century

Corporate headings for chiefs of state, which are used as main or added entries, e.g.,

Great Britain. Sovereigns, etc., 1558-1603 (Elizabeth)

are not used as subject headings except in the case of an author-title subject entry. For a work about the reign or administration of a chief of state, a counterpart in the form of [name of jurisdiction]—History—[period subdivision] is used, e.g.,

Title: *An Humble Supplication to Her Maiestie*
  1. Great Britain. Sovereigns, etc., 1558-1603
    (Elizabeth) Declaration of great troubles
    pretended against the realme.

Title: *Elizabethan Backgrounds: Historical Documents of the*
     Age of Elizabeth I.
  1. Great Britain—History—Elizabeth, 1558-1603—Sources.

One peculiarity in the treatment of wars and battles has been pointed out by Haykin.[15] Wars, other than civil wars, are entered under their own names with references from the names of participating countries followed by the appropriate periods of their history and variant terms applied to the wars.

Austro-Prussian War, 1866
  x Austria—History—Austro-Prussian War, 1866
    Austro-German War, 1866
    Prussia—History—Austro-Prussian War, 1866
    Seven Weeks' War

Spain—History—Civil War, 1936-1939.

Exceptions are made for wars, other than those of world-wide scope, in which the United States (or the American colonies) participated; these are entered under **United States.**

United States—History—King George's War, 1744-1748
  x Governor Shirley's War
  x King George's War, 1744-1748

(Example continued on page 72.)

United States—History—War of 1898
    x   American Spanish War, 1898
    x   Hispano-American War, 1898
    x   Spain—History—War of 1898
    x   Spanish American War, 1898

European War, 1914-1918
    x   United States—History—European War, 1914-1918
         War of 1914
         World War, 1914-1918

Battles, on the other hand, are entered under their own names rather than the war heading, with *see also* references from the latter.

Berlin, Battle of, 1945
    x   Berlin—Siege, 1945
    xx   World War, 1939-1945—Campaigns—Germany

Lenino, Battle of, 1943
    xx   World War, 1939-1945—Campaigns—White Russia

Forms of Period Subdivision

Period subdivisions appear in various and sundry forms.
1)   An inverted "noun, adjective" heading:

Art, Ancient
Art, Baroque
Art, Gothic
Art, Medieval
Art, Renaissance
Art, Rococo
Art, Romanesque

Modifiers such as "Ancient," "Renaissance," and "Medieval" denote both period and subject characteristics. Such headings are not true period subdivisions, and therefore are interfiled alphabetically with other headings that have no period connotation.
    2)   A main heading with a subdivision containing beginning and ending dates or the beginning date alone (also called an open-ended date):

English language—Grammar—1800-1870
English language—Grammar—1950-

Egypt—Economic conditions—332 B.C.-640 A.D.
France—Politics and government—1589-1610

    3)   A main heading with a subdivision containing the name of a monarch, a historical period, or an event, followed by dates:

English drama—Restoration, 1660-1700
German poetry—Middle High German, 1050-1500

China—History—Ming dynasty, 1368-1644
Germany—History—Ferdinand I, 1556-1564
Japan—History—Meiji period, 1868-1912
United States—History—Colonial period, ca.1600-1775
United States—History—Revolution, 1775-1783

This form is mostly used with the subdivision, —**History** under names of places.
The same periods, when applied under other topical subdivisions such as
—**Foreign relations**; —**Politics and government,** usually appear without the descriptive terms or phrases, e.g.,

Great Britain—History—Puritan Revolution, 1642-1660
Great Britain—Politics and government—1642-1660

Great Britain—History—Victoria, 1837-1901
Great Britain—Foreign relations—1837-1901

Headings with period subdivisions established previously in the form of a descriptive term or phrase alone, e.g.,

United States—History—Civil War

have recently been revised by adding the appropriate dates in order to simplify computer filing in a chronological sequence.

4)   A main heading with the name of the century as a subdivision:

Italian poetry—15th century
Netherlands—Church history—17th century

This form of period subdivision is usually adopted when there is a lack of a distinctive name for the period or event, when a longer period of time than a single event or movement has to be covered, or when only very broad period subdivisions are required.

The designation for a century may also take the form of beginning and ending years of the century, e.g.,

Great Britain—Description and travel—1701-1800

This form is used most frequently with the subdivision —**Description and travel.**
In fact, the designation —**18th century** is filed as if written —**1701-1800.**

5)   A main heading with a period subdivision constructed with the preposition "to" followed by a date, e.g.,

Great Britain—Civilization—To 1066
Rome—History—To 510 B.C.

This type of period subdivision usually appears as the first of the period subdivisions under a subject or place. It is used when the beginning date is uncertain or cannot be determined.

The different forms of period subdivision may appear under the same heading, depending on which type is the most appropriate in expressing a particular period.

6)   A main heading with a subdivision in the form of —**Early works to** [**date**]. While period subdivisions usually indicate the periods covered in works, this type of period subdivision represents the date of publication rather than indicating periods covered within the works, e.g.,

Algebra—Early works to 1800.

FORM SUBDIVISION

Haykin explains the nature and the function of the form subdivision:

Form subdivision may be defined as the extension of a subject heading based on the form or arrangement of the subject matter in the book. In other words, it represents what the book is, rather than what it is about, the subject matter being expressed by the main heading.[18]

Form subdivisions include those indicating the physical or bibliographical forms of the works, such as

—**Maps**
—**Periodicals**

—**Collected works**
—**Bibliography**
—**Dictionaries**

Traditionally, certain subdivisions which indicate the authors' approaches to their subjects are also considered form subdivisions, occasionally referred to as "inner forms," e.g.,

—**History**
—**Juvenile literature**
—**Study and teaching**

Certain form subdivisions imply a non-comprehensive treatment of the subject. For these, the readers are referred to the introduction to the eighth edition of *Library of Congress Subject Headings.*

One area which is still in the developmental stage is treatment of audio-visual or non-book materials. In the treatment of the subject content, there should not be any difference between book and non-book materials. The main difference lies in the physical format or media. It would appear that a form subdivision indicating the medium added to a subject heading would bring out the differences.

However, in practice, only a few subdivisions representing the media have appeared in *Library of Congress Subject Headings*, e.g., **—Juvenile films** and **—Juvenile phonorecords**, but there are no parallel subdivisions for adult non-book materials.

FREE-FLOATING SUBDIVISIONS*

At the Library of Congress, each time a subdivision is used in a heading for the first time, the usage must be established editorially in the same manner that a new heading is established. (This procedure is described in Chapter 7.)

To this pattern of practice, there are certain exceptions. A number of subdivisions, generally of wide application, have been designated as "free-floating" subdivisions. The term refers to certain form and topical subject subdivisions which Library of Congress subject catalogers are authorized to use, whenever appropriate, for the first time under a particular subject or name heading without establishing the new usage editorially. The various combinations of free-floating subdivisions with subject headings, therefore, appear in the subject tracings on Library of Congress cataloging records, but not necessarily so listed in the printed list.

In a way, these subdivisions are analogous to the standard subdivisions in the Dewey Decimal Classification system, which reflect the principle of facet analysis and provide for freedom of synthesis. The term "free-floating" is also used with a group of auxiliary tables in the Library of Congress Classification scheme, which can be used from schedule to schedule whenever appropriate.

The designation by the Library of Congress of certain categories of form and topical subdivisions as free-floating subdivisions began in 1974. It has resulted in a significant increase in productivity among subject catalogers, has reduced the cost of editorial processing, and has allowed for significant reduction in the size of the printed list of subject headings. Consequently, the Library of Congress recently declared all of the subdivisions listed in the section entitled "Most Commonly Used Subdivisions" in the introduction to the eighth edition of *Library of Congress Subject Headings* free-floating.** This decision allows much more synthesis in the formation of headings than ever before.

Although there is no restriction on the application of free-floating subdivisions, they should not be used indiscriminately without regard for appropriateness and any previously established principles governing the use of a particular subdivision.

In determining the appropriateness of using a free-floating subdivision for the first time under a subject heading, the following considerations should be borne in mind.

---

*Source documents: *Cataloging Service* 111:9 (Fall 1974); 114:9-10 (Summer 1975).

**Cataloging Service* 123:11 (Fall 1977).

Correct usage. The cataloger should consider the compatibility of the subdivision with the subject heading to which it is being attached. Any limitations in scope and application stated in scope notes in the introduction to the printed list should be observed.

Conflict. Before assigning a free-floating subdivision, the cataloger should first determine whether the use under consideration conflicts with previously established headings, in which case the subdivision should not be assigned. Frequently, a phrase heading already exists which means the same as the heading with subdivision being considered. For example, since the heading **Psychological research** already exists as a valid heading, the subdivision —**Research** then should not be used under **Psychology**. Further examples are **School management and organization** instead of **Schools—Management,** and **Electronic apparatus and appliances** instead of **Electronics—Equipment and supplies.**

Reconciling entries in the catalog. When using a combination for the first time, the cataloger should check existing entries consisting of the same subject headings in the catalog in order to reconcile any inconsistencies or conflicts resulting from the use of the new combination.

The free-floating subdivisions appear in the following categories:
1) Free-floating form and topical subdivisions of general application.
All of the subdivisions listed in the section entitled "Most Commonly Used Subdivisions" in the introduction to the eighth edition of *Library of Congress Subject Headings* are free-floating subdivisions, with the exceptions of a few obsolete subdivisions (see Appendix B). A number of other subdivisions have also been added to the list (see Appendix B).
2) Free-floating subdivisions under geographical headings.
Any standard topical subdivision normally used under a place name is a free-floater as long as the usage has been specifically provided for under the generic heading in the basic list of subject headings. For example, in the eighth edition under the heading **Altitudes** is found the general reference:

see also subdivision Altitudes *under names of countries, states, etc.,*
e.g., United States—Altitudes; New York (State)—Altitudes

Additional topical or chronological subdivisions under the first topical subdivision are generally not free-floaters, however, and each instance of new usage must be established editorially.
a) Subdivisions used under names of regions, countries, etc. (For a complete listing of these subdivisions, see Appendix C.)

b) Subdivisions used under names of cities.* (A complete listing of these subdivisions is included in Appendix C.)

---

*Note that headings for city districts or sections, e.g., **Georgetown, D.C.,** cannot be subdivided topically, nor are they used as geographic subdivisions.

3) Free-floating topical subdivisions controlled by pattern headings.

Certain standardized sets of topical subdivisions have been developed by the Library of Congress in connection with particular categories of subject headings or author headings used as subject headings. In order to avoid repeating these subdivisions under each heading to which they are applicable, they are listed under one, or occasionally several, representative headings in each category. These subdivisions then become free-floating within each category and can be used under all headings of that category when appropriate and when there is no conflict. These representative headings are called "pattern" or "model" headings.

The list of pattern or model headings which appears in the introduction to the eighth edition of *Library of Congress Subject Headings* (p. xiv) has been updated:

a) Free-floating subdivisions under personal names.*

Categories	*Model Headings*
Founders of religion	**Jesus Christ**
Philosophers	**Thomas Aquinas, Saint**
Statesmen, politicians	**Lincoln, Abraham (preferred)** **Napoleon** **Washington, George**
Musicians	**Wagner, Richard**
Literary authors	**Shakespeare, William**

b) Free-floating subdivisions controlled by model headings.**

Subject Field	*Category*	*Pattern Headings*
Philosophy and religion	Monastic and religious orders	**Jesuits**
	Religions	**Buddhism**
	Christian denominations	**Catholic Church; Baptists**
	Sacred works (including parts)	**Bible**
	Special theological topics	**Salvation**
The Arts	Groups of authors	**Authors, English; Poets, English; Dramatists, English; etc.**

(Listing continues on page 78.)

---

*For complete lists of these subdivisions, see Appendix D.

**This list (updated as of January 1978) replaces the one on page xiv of *Library of Congress Subject Headings*. Consult the eighth edition of *Library of Congress Subject Headings* and its supplements for complete lists of subdivisions under the model headings. Appendix E of this book includes a number of updated lists.

Subject Field	Category	Pattern Headings
The Arts (cont'd)	Philology	English philology
	Languages	English language
	Literatures (including particular genres)	English literature; English poetry; Short stories, English; English periodicals; etc.
	Newspapers of particular countries, e.g., Canadian newspapers	Newspapers
History and geography	Legislative bodies (including individual chambers)	United States. Congress.
	Military services (including armies, navies, marines, etc.)	United States. Army; United States. Navy; United States–Armed Forces
	Wars	World War, 1939-1945; United States–History–Civil War, 1861-1865
	Indians (including specific tribes)	Indians of North America
Education	Types of institutions	Universities and colleges
	Universities	Harvard University
Social sciences	Industries	Retail trade; Construction industry
Science and technology	Land vehicles	Automobiles
	Materials	Concrete; Metals
	Chemicals	Copper
	Organs and regions of the body	Heart; Foot
	Diseases	Cancer; Tuberculosis
	Plants and crops	Corn
	Animals	Fishes
	Livestock	Cattle

4)   Free-floating period subdivisions.*

The following period subdivisions are used under the subdivision —History:

—History—16th century
—History—17th century
—History—18th century
—History—19th century
—History—20th Century

They may be used under topical headings to which the free-floating subdivision —History can be assigned appropriately. However, they are not used with headings which begin with the name of a region, country, etc., e.g., "America—History—19th century." Period subdivisions under each heading of this type are printed in *Library of Congress Subject Headings.*

5)   Subjects or topics as free-floating subdivisions.

According to Library of Congress practice, under certain headings, names of subjects may be assigned as subdivisions whenever appropriate without establishing the usage editorially. These headings are indicated in the printed list either with a note, e.g.,

Reference books
        Subdivided by subject, e.g., **Reference books—Chemistry**;
        Reference books—Journalism

Bibliography—Best books
        Subdivided by subject, e.g., **Bibliography—Best books—
        Economics**

or by means of a "multiple" subdivision, e.g.,

Baptism—Anglican Communion [Catholic Church, etc.]

Mysticism—Brahmanism [Judaism, Nestorian Church, etc.]

ORDERING OF SUBDIVISIONS

The practice of subdividing a subject in *Library of Congress Subject Headings* comes closest to manifesting the modern theory of facet analysis and synthesis. In general, the subdivisions bring out various aspects or facets of the main subject.

In the earlier stages of development, subdivisions were fairly simple. Usually, a subject was divided by form, period, place, or topical aspect. Gradually, more and more subdivisions were introduced and various kinds of subdivisions were allowed to be combined and applied to the same heading, forming a string or chain. In many cases, more than one subdivision of the same kind may be used together with a particular heading. The combination in some cases is quite elaborate, for example:

Cataloging Service 124:19 (Winter 1978).

> United States–History–Civil War, 1861-1865–
> Secret service–Juvenile literature
>
> Mathematics–Study and teaching (Secondary)–
> Illinois–Chicago–Addresses, essays, lectures

In the formation of headings with numerous subdivisions, the order of the string should be an important issue. Interestingly, one looks in vain for stated instructions concerning the arrangement of elements in the string, something similar to the citation formula that are part of modern classification schemes. In most cases, one follows the arrangement already established in the subject headings list, and new headings are generally established according to existing patterns. Because there are no guidelines for establishing them, however, the patterns one finds are often inconsistent and sometimes even incompatible. Following is a discussion of some of the areas with regard to the order of subdivisions.

Order of Main Heading and Subdivision

When a heading contains a topical element and a form, place, period, or another topical aspect, it must first be determined which is to be the main heading and which the subdivision.

Topic vs. topic. In the Library of Congress system, the term representing a concrete subject generally serves as the main heading, and the term indicating an action is used in the subdivision, similar to the key system/action arrangement in PRECIS.

> **Kidneys–Surgery**
> **Kidneys–Diseases–Diagnosis**
>
> **Automobiles–Taxation**

However, there are exceptions, e.g.,

> **Advertising–Cigarettes**
> **Classification–Books**

Topic vs. form. On the whole, the topic serves as the main heading with the form as a subdivision, e.g.,

> **Chemistry–Bibliography**
> **Library science–Periodicals**

There are a few exceptions to this pattern, e.g.,

> **Reference books–Chemistry**

Topic vs. period. Like the form subdivision, the period division does not usually stand alone without first conceding the subject. Rather, topics are divided by time periods, e.g.,

Drama—18th century

There is, however, an exception to this pattern: widely-used names of historical periods may appear as main headings. When they do, they are not usually subdivided by topic, although they are often subdivided by form of material, e.g.,

Renaissance—Juvenile literature

Topic vs. place. Like form and period subdivisions, place names are usually used as subdivisions under a topic to indicate the locality for the study of the subject. However, unlike form or period, the place often is the main subject of a work, particularly in history and geography. In many areas of social sciences, the place is considered of greater significance than the topic. In these cases, the name of the place is used as the main heading subdivided by topical or other elements, e.g.,

United States—History
United States—Social life and customs

However, in some cases, the distinction or emphasis is not so obvious, as in works on geology. In still other cases, in order to bring out materials on local places, many topics are arbitrarily used as subdivisions under names of cities, e.g.,

San Francisco—Hospitals
but
Hospitals—California

Because of the principle of uniform heading, either the place or the topic appears as the main heading, or the entry element, but not both. There must be some way to determine which should be the case. Both Cutter and Haykin have attempted to deal with this problem.

Cutter's rules do not provide for subdivisions. His rules with regard to topic versus place concern mainly the choice between the subject and the place as the heading:

164. The only satisfactory method is double entry under the local and the scientific subject—to put, for instance, a work on the geology of California under both *California* and *Geology*, ... But as this profusion of entry would make the catalog very long, we are generally obliged to choose between country and scientific object.

165. A work treating of a general subject with special reference to a place is to be entered under the place, with merely a reference from the subject.[17]

Obviously, this rule was found to be unsatisfactory and in practice compromises have been found to be necessary. As a result, some headings have topics subdivided by place, while others are in the form of place names subdivided by topics.

Although it is difficult for a user to predict whether in a given case, the form [topic–place] or the form [place–topic] is used, the inclusion of the lists of "Subdivisions Under Place Names" (see Appendix C) contributes to the maintenance of consistency.

In practice, it has been found desirable to provide a modified form of duplicate entry in some cases in which it is felt that users are likely to approach the catalog through either the topic or the place. For example, in cataloging materials of interest to genealogists and historians dealing with a particular place, a heading in the form of [place–broader topic] is assigned in addition to the [topic–place] heading normally assigned, e.g.,

> Title: *Wills and Their Whereabouts*
> 1.   **Wills–Great Britain.**
> Add: 2.   **Great Britain–Genealogy.**

This practice does not violate the principle of uniform heading because the second heading consists of a topic broader than the one contained in the first. This type of [place–topic] is called a "generic heading."

Order of Subdivisions under the Same Main Heading

When more than one subdivision is used with the same main heading, the ordering of the string becomes an important issue, because it determines the context of the statement. One of the superior features of the PRECIS system is precisely the very rigorous formula dictating the order of the elements in the string (cf. International PRECIS Workshop. *The PRECIS Index System: Principles, Applications, and Prospects: Proceedings.* Edited by Hans H. Wellisch. New York: H. W. Wilson Company, 1977. 211pp.) In *Library of Congress Subject Headings*, no stated formula exists, except in the case of music headings. Based on current practice, the following arrangements are generally used:

1)   Form subdivision is usually the last element in a string.

2)   When the words *(Direct)* or *(Indirect)*, both of which now mean "Indirect," follow the main heading, the geographic name is interposed between the main heading and the subdivision, e.g.,

> **Construction industry** *(Indirect)*
>   **–Finance**
> **Construction industry–Poland–Finance**

When the words *(Direct)* or *(Indirect)* follow the subject subdivision, the local subdivision is placed at the end, e.g.,

> **Construction industry** *(Indirect)*
>   **–Law and legislation** *(Direct)*
> **Construction industry–Law and legislation–Poland**

A list of "Subdivisions Further Subdivided by Place" appears in Appendix F.

Different ordering of the same elements in a heading may result in different meanings. For example, the following headings containing the same elements,

Labor supply—Research—United States
Labor supply—United States—Research

have different meanings. The first implies research conducted in the United States on labor supply in general, and the second means research on labor supply in the United States. In the Library of Congress subject headings system, the distinction is not always made. In the case of the history of a discipline in a place, for instance, a heading in the form of [**name of discipline**]—[**place**]—**History**, e.g., **Agriculture— United States—History**, denotes both the history of the discipline in a place and the history of conditions in a place.

On the other hand, in many cases, the distinction is made. In the case of subdivisions listed below, the geographic aspect of a work may be brought out either by interposition of geographic subdivision, by further subdividing the topical or form subdivision by place, or by both methods, as appropriate:

—**Collectors and collecting**
—**Conservation and restoration**
—**Documentation**
—**Forgeries**
—**Information services**
—**Library resources**
—**Mutilation and defacement**
—**Private collections**
—**Research**
—**Study and teaching** [and all parenthetically qualified forms of this heading]
—**Teacher training**
—**Vocational guidance**

Examples:

Postage-stamps—United States—Collectors and collecting
[refers to the collecting of U.S. postage stamps without regard to where the collecting is done]

Postage-stamps—Collectors and collecting—United States
[refers to the collecting of any postage stamps which is done in the United States]

Postage-stamps—Russia—Collectors and collecting—United States
[refers to the collecting of Russian postage stamps done in the United States]

Blacks—Latin America—Study and teaching—United States
[refers to the study and teaching in the United States about the blacks in Latin America]

In a few special cases, the history of a discipline in a place and conditions are represented by different headings, e.g.,

Economics—United States—History
[means history of the discipline economics in the United States]

United States—Economic conditions
[means economic conditions of the United States]

In such instances, scope notes are provided in the printed list, e.g.,

Economics *(Indirect)*
Here and with local subdivision are entered works on the discipline of economics. Works on the economic conditions of particular countries, regions, cities, etc., are entered under the name of the place subdivided by Economic conditions.

Economics—United States
Here are entered works on the discipline of economics in the United States. Works on the economic history or conditions of the United States are entered under the heading United States—Economic conditions.

Economics—History
Here are entered works on the history of economics as a discipline. Works on economic history or conditions are entered under the heading Economic history or the subdivision Economic conditions under names of countries, regions, cities, etc.

REFERENCES

[1] David Judson Haykin, *Subject Headings: A Practical Guide* (Washington: Government Printing Office, 1951), p. 27.

[2] Margaret Mann, *Introduction to Cataloging and the Classification of Books* (2nd ed.; Chicago: American Library Association, 1943), p. 146.

[3] E. J. Coates, *Subject Catalogues: Headings and Structure* (London: Library Association, 1960), p. 75.

[4] Richard S. Angell, "Library of Congress Subject Headings—Review and Forecast," *Subject Retrieval in the Seventies: New Directions: Proceedings of an International Symposium* (edited by Hans (Hanan) Wellisch and Thomas D. Wilson; Westport, Conn.: Greenwood Publishing Company, 1972), p. 151.

[5] Haykin, pp. 35-36.

[6] David Judson Haykin, "Subject Headings: Principles and Development," *The Subject Analysis of Library Materials* (edited by Maurice F. Tauber; New York: School of Library Service, Columbia University, 1953), p. 51.

[7] Ibid.

[8] Haykin, *Subject Headings: A Practical Guide*, p. 36.

[9] Ibid., p. 29.

[10] *Cataloging Service* 114:7 (Summer 1975); 121:14 (Spring 1977).

[11] Angell, p. 151.

[12] Marguerite V. Quattlebaum, comp., *LC Period Subdivisions under Names of Places* (2nd ed.; Washington: Library of Congress, 1975), 111pp.

[13] Haykin, *Subject Headings: A Practical Guide*, p. 33.

[14] Ibid., p. 34.

[15] Ibid., pp. 34-35.

[16] Ibid., p. 27.

[17] Charles A. Cutter, *Rules for a Dictionary Catalog* (4th ed.; Washington: Government Printing Office, 1904), p. 68.

CHAPTER 5

CROSS REFERENCES

INTRODUCTION

In an alphabetical subject catalog, cross references carry a great deal of the burden of leading users to wanted material. Under the principle of uniform heading, a given subject is represented by only one term; users, however, cannot be expected to always know which of several synonymous or near synonymous terms or which of several possible forms will have been used as the heading. Furthermore, under the principle of specific entry, material will be listed under a specific term even though many users may look for it under a more general term. Finally, the principle of alphabetical arrangement has the effect of dispersing headings for related subjects.

It is considered to be in the interest of users to lead them from terms that are not used in the catalog to those that are, and, in addition, to lead them to terms used for related subjects. Both objectives are achieved by means of cross references.

Four types of cross references are used in *Library of Congress Subject Headings*: *see* references, *see also* references, general references, and subject-to-name references. These are discussed below.

SEE REFERENCES

A *see* reference guides the user from a term which is not used as a heading to the one which is. Circumstances which require such references are synonymous terms, variant spellings, alternative forms, different entry elements, opposite terms, and "overly" narrow terms. *See* references from synonymous terms and variant spellings are generally made in most of the indexing systems. The other kinds of *see* references are provided in the Library of Congress system because of the principle of uniform heading and the unique features of specific entry discussed earlier.

Synonymous Terms

When a heading has been chosen from two or more synonymous terms, *see* references are made from the unused terms to the heading. Cutter's rule states: "Of two exactly synonymous names choose one and make a reference from the other."[1] In practice, this kind of reference is extended to near-synonymous terms when it is considered impractical to distinguish between them. Haykin notes that the basic significance of such references is that "the subject matter is entered not under the heading which occurred to the reader, but under the one chosen by the cataloger even when the terms are not completely synonymous."[2] Examples of *see* references* from synonymous and near-synonymous terms are:

Archaeology
 x Ruins
    Prehistory

Color-sense
 x Color discrimination
    Color perception

Dogma
 x Doctrines

Genealogy
 x Genealogical research

Government lending
 x Government loans

Greenhouses
 x Conservatories
    Hot-houses

Stuffed foods (Cookery)
 x Filled foods (Cookery)

Liberty
 x Freedom

Variant Spellings

See references are made from different spellings and different grammatical structures of the same term, e.g.,

Aeolian harp
 x Eolian harp

Airplanes
 x Aeroplanes

Archaeology
 x Archeology

Dialing
 x Dialling

Dogs
 x Dog

(List is continued on page 88.)

---

*The symbol *x* means a *see* reference is to be made from the term that follows.

Fishing nets
    x   Fish nets
          Fishnets

Coffee-houses
    x   Coffeehouses

Goeduck
    x   Goeduck
          Gooeyduck

Microcrystalline polymers
    x   Microcrystal polymers
          Polymer microcrystals

Different Language Terms

Colliberts
    x   Coliberti

Laissez-faire
    x   Free enterprise

Popular and Scientific Terms

Androids
    x   Robots

Prosencephalon
    x   Forebrain

Ascorbic acid
    x   Vitamin C

Cockroaches
    x   Blattariae

Alternative Forms

Because of the principle of uniform heading which requires that a heading appear in the catalog in only one form, other forms of the same heading likely to be consulted by users are referred to the one chosen as the heading. It should be pointed out, however, that in *Library of Congress Subject Headings*, this is true in principle, but not always consistent in practice. Examples:

Cataloging of manuscripts
    x   Manuscripts–Cataloging

Glass research
  x   Glass–Research

Education of the aged
  x   Aged–Education

Deaf–Education
  x   Education of the deaf

Foreign exchange–Accounting
  x   Foreign exchange accounting

Galaxies–Evolution
  x   Galactic evolution

Schools–Accounting
  x   School accounting

Advertising research
  [No *see* references]

Cataloging of rare books
  [No *see* references]

Handicapped–Education
  [No *see* references]

Hospitals–Accounting
  [No *see* references]

Different Entry Elements

When a heading is inverted, a *see* reference is generally provided from the direct form, e.g.,

Chemistry, Inorganic
  x   Inorganic chemistry

Exclusion, Right of
  x   Right of exclusion

In cases where the first word in the direct form is non-distinctive and therefore not likely to be consulted by the users, the reference is often omitted or made in a different form, e.g.,

Plants, Effect of ultra-violet rays on
  x   Ultra-violet rays–Effect on plants

Plants, Effect of music on
  [No *see* references]

See references are only occasionally made from inverted forms to direct headings. Some examples are:

Cataloging of anonymous classics
    x   Anonymous classics (Cataloging)

Cataloging of special collections in libraries
    x   Special collections in libraries, Cataloging of

Catalyst poisoning
    x   Poisoning of catalysts

Choice by lot
    x   Lot, Choice by

Chronic diseases
    x   Diseases, Chronic

Electronics in biology
    x   Biology, Electronics in

Previously, when a compound heading expressed relationship between two objects or concepts, a *see* reference was made from the form with the terms reversed, e.g.,

Education and state
    x   State and education

Current policy is to make a *see also* reference from the second term if it exists as an independent heading, e.g.,

Religion and civilization
    xx   Civilization

When a compound heading connects two parallel or opposite objects or concepts which are often treated together, but not necessarily in relationship to each other, a *see* reference is made from the second term in the heading, e.g.,

Encyclopedias and dictionaries
    x   Dictionaries

Cities and towns
    x   Towns

Emigration and immigration
    x   Immigration

Opposite Terms Not Used as Headings

In the past, when a term was chosen between two opposite ones as the heading, a *see* reference was made from the other, e.g.,

Temperance
    x   Intemperance

Railroads—Evaluation
    x   Railroads—Depreciation

This is rarely done now. Current policy is to establish both terms as separate headings when required.

Narrow Terms Not Used as Headings

When a term is considered too narrow to be established as a separate heading, a *see* reference, also called an "upward" reference, is sometimes made from the narrow term to a broader one which is used as a heading, e.g.,

Children as authors
    x   Children as poets

Church management
    x   Parish management

Pollution
    x   Pollution—Control
          Pollution—Prevention

Russia—Economic policy
    x   Five-Year Plan (Russia)

Schools—Accounting
    x   High schools—Accounting
          Public schools—Accounting

Occasionally, a *see* reference is made from a narrow term not used as a heading to a broader heading and to other related headings at the same time, e.g.,

Christmas books
    See   Christmas
           Christmas plays
           Christmas stories
           Gift-books (Annuals, etc.)

In recent years, there has been a decreasing number of such references being added to the list. Recent policies prefer establishing the narrow terms as separate headings.

Broad Terms Not Used as Headings

It is rarely the case that a broad term is not used as a heading while narrower terms representing its kinds or aspects are. When this occurs, *see* references are made from the broad term to the narrower headings, e.g.,

Cowboys
    x   Herdsmen

Gauchos
    x   Herdsmen

Shepherds
    x   Herdsmen

SEE ALSO REFERENCES

The primary objective of the dictionary catalog is direct access at the expense of subject collocation. In terms of subject relationship, the entries in a dictionary catalog appear in what Cutter calls the "most absurd proximity."[3] Yet the advantages of the classed catalog are not to be abandoned. As Cutter observes: "The dictionary catalog sets out with another object and a different method, but having attained that object—facility of reference—is at liberty to try to secure some of the advantages of classification and system in its own way."[4] Cutter seeks to combine the advantages of the dictionary catalog with those of an alphabetico-classed catalog by means of *see also* references, or syndetic devices: "By a well-devised net-work of cross-references, the mob becomes an army, of which each part is capable of assisting many other parts."[5] It is the *see also* references that impose a logical structure on the alphabetical subject catalog.

A *see also* reference connects terms which are both used as subject headings. It usually expresses certain kinds of subject relationship. Cutter's rule states:

> Make references from general subjects to their various subordinate subjects and also to coordinate and illustrative subjects.[6]

Haykin rephrases the rule in these terms:

> In binding related headings together the basic rule is that a "see also" reference be made from a given subject: 1) to more specific subjects or topics comprehended within it, or to an application of the subject; and 2) to coordinate subjects which suggest themselves as likely to be of interest to the user seeking material under the given heading, because they represent other aspects of the subject, or are closely related to it.[7]

Broad to Narrow

In modern indexing terms, a *see also* reference is made from a broad term (BT) to a narrow term (NT). In a hierarchy of subjects, each level is led to the one immediately subordinate to it, thus forming what Cutter calls a "pyramid of references."

In the Library of Congress system, each term in a chain of subjects from a hierarchical structure is connected to the one immediately below it by means of the *see also* reference,* e.g.,

Chordata
　　sa　Vertebrates

Vertebrates
　　sa　Mammals

Mammals
　　sa　Primates

Primates
　　sa　Monkeys

Monkeys
　　sa　Baboons

Baboons
　　sa　Hamadryas baboon

Using the subject "cats" as an example, Richmond[8] has demonstrated the "hidden classification" in the cross reference structure. Even though the structure is imperfect and could be improved, the potential is there.

Figure 1 (page 94) illustrates part of a classificatory structure based on the *see also* references in *Library of Congress Subject Headings*. The hierarchical structure is embodied in the references, with only occasional irregularities. In this case, a *see also* reference which circumvents a level in the hierarchy was made. For the chain **Monkeys–Macaques–Japanese macaque**, the following references have been made:

Monkeys
　　sa　Japanese macaque
　　　　Macaques

Macaques
　　sa　Japanese macaque

As a result, **Japanese macaque**, which is a subordinate subject to **Macaques**, appears also on the same level of the hierarchy with the latter. Furthermore, the subject **Chordata** is not connected to any subject superordinate to it, e.g., **Animals**.

An alphabetical subject catalog with a thorough, systematically constructed network of cross references can provide the best of both worlds by combining the advantages of both the alphabetical and classified approaches. However, in practice, it has been questioned whether the labor required for the construction of such a system of references is justified. Cutter experimented with "a synoptical

---

*The symbol *sa* means a *see also* reference is to be made *to* the term that follows.

Figure 1

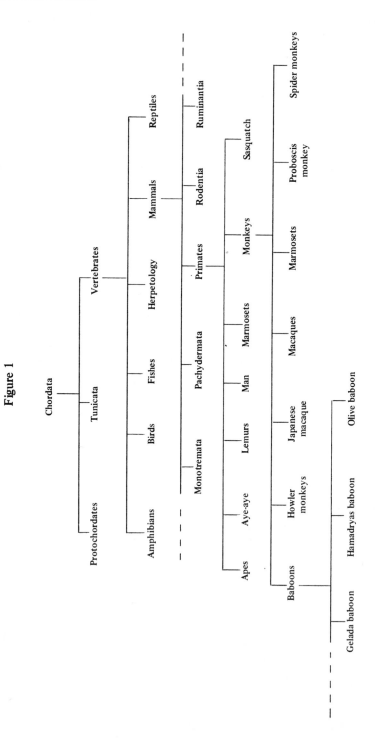

table of subjects" for the Catalogue of the Library of the Boston Athenaeum. However, the Library's committee voted not to include the table, and Cutter conceded that the immense labor required was probably not justified after all:

> My experience then disposes me to adhere to the phrase "immense labor" and my observation since of the way in which catalogs are used makes me think that little practical utility was lost to the catalog by the Committee's vote. Such a table would be infrequently consulted, and it would be incomplete, as new headings are continually added to the catalog of a growing library.[9]

He was content to leave it to the tables and indexes of the Decimal and Expansive classification systems to satisfy the rare reader who wishes "to push his investigations into every ramification of his subject."

Haykin has also expressed his thoughts on this topic:

> Subject references have been described in the literature of subject headings as a kind of substitute for the systematic arrangement of the classed catalog, in the sense that they make it possible for a reader to find in the alphabetical catalog the material on a subject and all of its ramifications. However, this claim for the alphabetical subject catalog is worth little since the reader could find all the material only with the great effort involved in following up all the references. In any case, the need for a comprehensive approach, whether through the classed catalog or syndetic features of the alphabetical subject catalog, has been overplayed: it is very rarely that a catalog can supply a sufficiently complete record of the literature of a subject, and the user who wants a comprehensive view of the literature of a subject would be better advised to resort to a bibliography.[10]

Narrow to Broad

The question is often raised as to why *see also* references are not made from narrow headings to broad ones. Dunkin sees the advantage of references going up and down. He feels that upward *see also* references will help the subject catalog to fulfill a third objective: "To show what books the library has on broader subjects which include the narrow topic the user specifically wants."[11]

Wright also feels that the lack of such upward references represents a loss on the part of the user:

> The practice of referring from the general to the particular but not vice versa means that a large segment of the available material on any subject may be lost, since it is generally true that more useful material on a topic is usually to be found in sections of works on larger subjects than in any of the books on more specific subjects.[12]

In fact, Cutter has a rule dealing with this aspect: "Make references occasionally from specific to general subjects." While recognizing that "much information about limited topics is to be found in more general works; the very best description of a single plant or of a family of plants may perhaps be contained in a botanical encyclopaedia," Cutter concedes that it is out of the question to make all possible references of the ascending kind. He explains the reason with an example:

> From *Cathedrals*, for example, one would naturally refer to *Christian art* and to *Ecclesiastical architecture*, because works on those subjects will contain more or less on cathedrals. But so will histories of architecture and histories of English, French, German, Italian, or Spanish architecture; so will travels in England, France, Germany, Italy, Spain. And anyone who desired to take an absolutely complete survey of the subject, or who was willing to spend unlimited time in getting information on some detail, would have to consult such books. Yet the cataloger may very excusably not think of referring to those subjects, or if he thinks of it may deem the connection too remote to justify reference, and that he should be overloading the catalog with what would be generally useless.[13]

Dunkin appears to accept Cutter's argument:

> Perhaps it is just as well. If the system of "see also" references were complete both going up and coming down, it is likely that the user would never bother to follow the directions hither and yon. Even if he did bother, he would soon grow weary.[14]

Haykin also agrees:

> References from the specific to the broader heading would have the effect of sending the reader on a wild goose chase. . . . Furthermore, if references from all topics comprehended within a given subject were to be made, on the assumption that the reader would find in treatises on that subject material on these topics, the catalog would be cluttered up with a plethora of references.[15]

In practice, upward *see also* references are seldom ever made in *Library of Congress Subject Headings*.

Coordinate Subjects

See also references are made between terms which are related other than hierarchically, i.e., related terms which do not constitute a genus-species or thing-part relationship. In this case, since neither term is broader than the other, the *see also* references* are made both ways, e.g.,

---

*The symbol *xx* means that a *see also* reference is to be made *from* the term that follows.

Religion
    sa   Theology
    xx   Theology

Memory
    sa   Comprehension
    xx   Comprehension

In most indexing systems, the symbols BT (broad term), NT (narrow term), and RT (related term) are used to indicate the relationships between subjects connected by the references. In *Library of Congress Subject Headings, sa* and *xx* are used for both types of *see also* references. The only way one can tell the relationship is by the directions of the references. *See also* references between broad and narrow terms are made in one direction—from broad to narrow—only, while those between related coordinate terms are made both ways.

GENERAL REFERENCES

See references and *see also* references which are directed to individual headings are called specific references. Frequently, a *see also* reference is directed to a group or category of headings instead of individual members of the group or category. This is called a general reference. By way of example, one or more of the individual members is usually included in the reference, e.g.,

Tools
    sa   *specific tools, e.g.* Files and rasps, Saws

Science
    sa   *headings beginning with the word* Scientific

Muscles
    sa   *names of muscles, e.g.* Tensor tympani muscle

Museums
    sa   *subdivision* Museums *under subjects, or names of wars, cities, or institutions, e.g.* Indians of North America—Museums; World War, 1939-1945—Museums; New York (City)—Museums; Harvard University—Museums; *and subdivision* Museums, relics, etc. *under names of persons or families, e.g.* Lincoln, Abraham, Pres. U.S. 1809-1865—Museums, relics, etc.

Brass trios
    sa   Suites, Variations, Waltzes, *and similar headings with specification of instruments*

The major advantage of general reference is economy of space. They obviate the need of long lists of specific references and bring to the attention of the user the most direct method of finding the material desired.

SUBJECT-TO-NAME REFERENCES

References from subject headings to author headings, previously called "Red-to-Black References," direct the user's attention from his or her particular field of interest to names of individuals or corporate bodies that are active or associated in some way with the field. These references, with a few exceptions, are not included in the printed list.

The reason for making such references is, as Haykin points out:

> It avoids the multiplication of subject entries in instances where the author, or inevitable added entries, are sufficient to bring the material to the attention of the reader.[16]

Subject-to-Personal Names

According to Haykin,[17] references from subject headings to personal headings were generally made from headings representing occupations, e.g.,

Architects, British

see also

Wren, *Sir* Christopher, 1632-1723.

However, this practice has been discontinued by the Library of Congress. Likewise, references from subject headings to uniform titles of anonymous classics have also been abandoned, except in the case of sacred books.

Subject-to-Corporate Names

References from subject headings to corporate bodies associated with the particular subjects are very useful because of the numerous publications issued by the bodies which deal with their activities or their special fields of interest. Current practice at the Library of Congress is to provide such references to the following kinds of corporate headings: societies, institutions, firms, and governmental agencies. Congresses are excluded. Such references are made from the most specific subject heading in each case, in accordance with the same principle in making specific *see also* references. In general, the most specific heading is a generic heading subdivided by place. In some cases, references may be required from several generic headings divided by place in order to bring out all aspects of the corporate body. (For examples see pages 112-15 discussing corporate names as subject headings.)

CONCLUSION

The cross references in the alphabetical subject catalog provide a useful structure of subject relationships. In practice, however, it has not been demonstrated how much of the effectiveness and usefulness of these references have been realized in actual use. In many libraries, it is a question whether all necessary references have been provided in the catalog. To ensure that all the suggested references are made and placed in a catalog requires a great deal of effort and time. At a time when fast cataloging is of first priority and on-line cataloging is often performed by technicians at the terminals, it is a question of how many libraries are actually able to follow up on all the references each time a new heading is introduced into the catalog or a new reference has been suggested by the Library of Congress. On the other hand, both the principle of specific entry and the principle of uniform heading place a great burden on the cross references for subject collocation. Omission or negligence of provision of cross references must mean a great loss in terms of the effectiveness of the alphabetical subject catalog as a tool for subject retrieval.

REFERENCES

[1] Charles A. Cutter, *Rules for a Dictionary Catalog* (4th ed.; Washington: Government Printing Office, 1904), p. 70.

[2] David Judson Haykin, *Subject Headings: A Practical Guide* (Washington: Government Printing Office, 1951), p. 14.

[3] Cutter, p. 79.

[4] Ibid.

[5] Ibid.

[6] Ibid.

[7] Haykin, p. 14.

[8] Phyllis Allen Richmond, "Cats: An Example of Concealed Classification in Subject Headings," *Library Resources & Technical Services* 3:102-112 (Spring 1959).

[9] Cutter, p. 80.

[10] David Judson Haykin, "Subject Headings: Principles and Development," *The Subject Analysis of Library Materials* (edited by Maurice F. Tauber; New York: School of Library Service, Columbia University, 1953), p. 52.

[11] Paul S. Dunkin, *Cataloging U.S.A.* (Chicago: American Library Association, 1969), p. 81.

[12] Wyllis E. Wright, "Standards for Subject Headings: Problems and Opportunities," *Journal of Cataloging and Classification* 10:175-76 (October 1954).

[13] Cutter, p. 80.

[14] Dunkin, p. 81.

[15] Haykin, "Subject Headings: Principles and Development," p. 51.

[16] Haykin, *Subject Headings: A Practical Guide*, p. 16.

[17] Ibid.

CHAPTER 6

PROPER NAMES IN SUBJECT HEADINGS

Proper names frequently appear as subject headings, parts of subject headings, or as subdivisions. They are generally omitted from the printed list, with a few exceptions which are included as models or in order to show unique references or subdivisions. In order to ensure consistency, there are general guidelines for the formation of these name headings.

PERSONAL NAMES

Names of Individual Persons

Names of individual persons are used as subject headings for biographies, eulogies, festschriften, criticisms, bibliographies, and literary works in which the persons figure. At the Library of Congress, in order that the same form of a personal name is used as author and subject entries, headings consisting of names of persons are established by the Descriptive Cataloging Division. In general, the forms of personal headings are established according to the *Anglo-American Cataloging Rules*, except, in many cases, because of the policy of superimposition, the forms established according to earlier codes persist.

A number of personal name headings have been included in the printed list as patterns for subdivisions: Thomas Aquinas (philosopher); William Shakespeare (literary author); Richard Wagner (musician); Abraham Lincoln, George Washington, and Napoleon (statesmen and rulers); and Jesus Christ (founder of religion).* Subdivisions listed under these names may be used with any personal heading in the same category, e.g.,

Mozart, Johann Chrysostom Wolfgang Amadeus, 1756-1791 –
    Iconography

**Kennedy, John Fitzgerald, Pres. U.S., 1917-1963–
    Assassination

Nixon, Richard Milhous, 1913-   **–Inauguration**

---

*For complete lists of these subdivisions, see Appendix D.

**Form of the personal name heading was established according to the *ALA Cataloging Rules for Author and Title Entries*.

Because the personal headings included in the list serve as patterns, there may be subdivisions which are not appropriate for the person under whose name the subdivisions are listed, but are needed for other people in the same category, e.g.,

Shakespeare, William, 1564-1616—Political career

Family Names*

The heading for a family name appears in the form of [**proper name**] **family**, e.g., **Rockefeller family**. The older form with qualifier, e.g., **Smith family (William Smith, 1669-1743)** has been discontinued. No effort is made to distinguish between families with the same surname. The heading **Kennedy family**, for example, is used for works about any family with the surname Kennedy.

See references are made from each known variant of the family name, e.g.,

> **Adams family**
>   *x*   Adam family
>   Addam family
>   Addams family

Variants are usually determined from the work being cataloged and from standard reference works. Individual entries in the catalog often serve as a source for name variants based on surnames found there.

Similar names from different ethnic backgrounds are established as separate headings, connected by *see also* references, e.g.,

> **Koch family**
>   *see also* Cook family
>
> **Cook family**
>   *see also* Koch family

Topical *see also* references are not made for family names.

Names of Legendary Characters

These names are not covered by the *Anglo-American Cataloging Rules.* However, they are often required as subject headings. As Haykin comments,

> Beings whose existence belongs in the realm of myth or pure literary invention may achieve identity to a point where books are written about them. Names of such beings may be used as subject headings exactly as those of real persons. The same rules apply with respect to the choice of form of name and references. The best-known English form should be given preference and references made from other, including vernacular, forms.[1]

---

*Cf. *Cataloging Service* 123:12-13 (Fall 1977).

Examples of headings for legendary characters are:

Arthur, King

Robin Hood

Odysseus
     x   Ulysses

Legendary characters include literary characters which appear in more than one work. Characters which exist in one literary work only are established in a different form, e.g.,

Shakespeare, William, 1564-1616–Characters–Falstaff

Names of Gods and Goddesses

Until recently, names of gods and goddesses of classical mythology were usually established in the Latin form only with *see* references from the names of their Greek counterparts. Cutter defends the use of the Latin form for the reasons:

> (1) that the Latin names are at present more familiar to the majority of readers; (2) that it would be difficult to divide the literature, or if it were done, many books must be put both under *Zeus* and *Jupiter*, *Poseidon* and *Neptune*, etc., filling considerable room with no practical advantage.[2]

A new policy* announced recently requires that the heading be established in the form according to the usage in the work being cataloged, e.g.,

Aphrodite
Venus (Goddess)

Zeus
Jupiter

Qualifications are added when there is a conflict, e.g.,

Nike (Greek goddess)

Eros (Greek god)

Past practice had not been consistent, so other kinds of qualifiers may be found in older headings.

---

*Cataloging Service 121:18 (Spring 1977).

When equivalencies can be determined between Greek and Roman gods and goddesses, *see also* references are made between them, e.g.,

Juno
  see also
 Hera

Hera
  see also
 Juno

The following pattern shows the complete set of references made for the heading of a god:

[name of god]
  sa [equivalent god]
  xx [equivalent god]
     Gods, Greek [*or* **Roman**]
     Mythology, Greek [*or* **Roman**]

Example:

Persephone
  sa Proserpine
  xx Gods, Greek
     Mythology, Greek
     Proserpine

For deities from other religions, a qualifier designating the religion is usually added to the heading, e.g.,

Kamakshi (Hindu deity)
  xx Gods, Hindu

Sekhmet (Egyptian deity)

NAMES OF CORPORATE BODIES

Works related to the origin, development, activities, and functions of corporate bodies are assigned subject entries under their names. Because corporate bodies, like individuals, also serve as authors, the headings for corporate bodies are established by descriptive catalogers at the Library of Congress. With few exceptions, the same headings are used as subject entries for works about the corporate bodies.

Corporate bodies include public and private organizations, societies, associations, institutions, government agencies, commercial firms, churches, and other groups identified by a name, such as conferences, exploring expeditions. Examples of corporate names used as subject headings are:

American Society of Mechanical Engineers
American Library Association
Columbia University. Dept. of Mechanical Engineering
Kommunisticheskaĭa partiĭa Ukrainy
France. Armée. Légion étrangère
Center for the Study of Democratic Institutions
United Nations. Secretary-General
Carnegie Steel Company
Confédération générale du travail
Conference on Security and Cooperation in Europe
Canadian Arctic Expedition, 1913-1918
Lewis Cass Expedition, 1820
New York. World's Fair, 1964-1965

Name Changes in Corporate Bodies

When the name of a corporate body is changed, successive entries are established as in descriptive cataloging. However, for subject cataloging purposes, successive entries for the same corporate body are not assigned to the same work even if it covers the history of the body under different names.* Explanatory references, also called history cards or information cards, are provided under the various headings established.

Information Cards (History Cards)

An information card consists of a corporate heading (one of the variant names of a corporate body under consideration), an explanatory text, often a list of headings in catalog-entry form, and a subject entry statement. The explanatory text includes histories of the organizations in question, indicating dates of founding, name changes, connection with other bodies, dates of dissolution, etc. Multiple copies of the individual card are made, and each body mentioned in the text or listed below, if it is a bona fide author heading, becomes in turn a main entry on the card. The purpose of the card is to indicate at a useful point in the catalog the facts about a corporate body, its precise relationship with other bodies, the respective author headings in use, and under what conditions they may be used as subject headings. Such cards are made only for more complex situations, i.e., involving at least three names with two changes.

The subject entry statement consists of one or more formula sentences, depending upon the kind of name change described. All restate in one form or another the principles announced above. A few formula sentences are provided below as examples:

---

*For the assignment of subject headings to works about a corporate body, see Chapter 10.

Linear name change. Works about these bodies are entered under the name used during the latest period covered.

Linear name change with superimposition. Works about these bodies are entered under the name used during the latest period covered. In the case where the required name is represented in this catalog only under a later form of the name, entry is made under the later form.

Merger. Works about these bodies are entered under the name resulting from the merger. Works limited in subject coverage to the pre-merger period are entered under the name of one or more of the original bodies.

Separation. Works about these bodies are entered under one or more of the names resulting from the separation. Works limited in coverage to the pre-separation period are entered under the name of the original body.

Complex series of name changes with superimposition. Works about these bodies are entered under the name or names in existence during the latest period for which subject coverage is given. In the case where the required name is represented in this catalog only under a later form of the name, entry is made under the later form.

Examples:

Linear

Alcalá de Henares, Spain. Universidad.

The Universidad de Alcalá de Henares, also known as the Universidad Complutense, was founded in 1508. It was transferred to Madrid in 1836 with the name Universidad Central. The name was changed in 1971 (?) to Universidad Complutense de Madrid.

Works by these bodies are found under the following headings according to the name used at the time of publication:

Alcalá de Henares, Spain. Universidad.
Madrid. Universidad.
Universidad Complutense de Madrid.

SUBJECT ENTRY: Works about these bodies are entered under the name used during the latest period covered.

72–224909

Library of Congress 72 ₍2₎

(An information card is made under each of the variant names)

Linear with Superimposition

Tennessee Valley Authority. Division of Forestry.

The Division of Forestry of the Tennessee Valley Authority was created in 1933. In 1938 the name was changed to Dept. of Forestry Relations; in 1948, to Division of Forestry Relations; in 1962, to Division of Forestry Development; and on Dec. 19, 1969, to Division of Forestry, Fisheries, and Wildlife Development.

Works by this body published before the change of name in 1938 are found under

Tennessee Valley Authority. Division of Forestry.

Works published between the change of name in 1938 and that in 1969 are found under

(Continued on next card)

72 ₍2₎

72–213831

Tennessee Valley Authority. Division of Forestry. (Card 2)

Tennessee Valley Authority. Division of Forestry Development.

Works published after the change of name in 1969 are found under

Tennessee Valley Authority. Division of Forestry, Fisheries, and Wildlife Development.

SUBJECT ENTRY: Works about this body are entered under the name used during the latest period covered. In the case where the required name is represented in this catalog only under a later form of the name, entry is made under the later form.

72–213831

Library of Congress   72 ₍2₎

Merger

Kensington and Chelsea Public Libraries.

After the London boroughs of Kensington and Chelsea joined to form the Royal Borough of Kensington and Chelsea, the Kensington Public Library and its branches, and the Chelsea Public Library became part of the Kensington and Chelsea Public Libraries.

Works by these bodies are found under the following headings according to the name used at the time of publication:

Kensington, Eng. Public Libraries.
Chelsea, Eng. Public Libraries and Museums.
Kensington and Chelsea Public Libraries.

SUBJECT ENTRY: Works about these bodies are entered under the name resulting from the merger. Works limited in subject coverage to the pre-merger period are entered under the name of one or more of the original bodies.

74–236474

Library of Congress 75 [2]

Separation

Catholic Church.   Congregatio Sacrorum Rituum.

The Congregatio Sacrorum Rituum (established in 1588) was divided in 1969 to form the Sacra Congregatio pro Cultu Divino and the Sacra Congregatio pro Causis Sanctorum.

Works by these bodies are found under the following headings according to the name used at the time of publication:

Catholic Church.   Congregatio Sacrorum Rituum.
Catholic Church.   Congregatio pro Cultu Divino.
Catholic Church.   Congregatio pro Causis Sanctorum.

SUBJECT ENTRY: Works about these bodies are entered under one or more of the names resulting from the separation. Works limited in coverage to the pre-separation period are entered under the name of the original body.

73–210400

Library of Congress   73 [2]

Complicated Changes

U. S. Bureau of Occupational Safety and Health.

The U. S. Office of Industrial Hygiene and Sanitation was organized in the Public Health Service in 1914. In Feb. 1937 it merged with the Office of Dermatoses Investigations to form the Division of Industrial Hygiene of the National Institute of Health. In Dec. 1943 the Division of Industrial Hygiene was transferred to the Public Health Service, but its research activities were retained in the Industrial Hygiene Research Laboratory of the National Institute of Health. The name of the Division of Industrial Hygiene was changed to Division of Occupational Health in 1951. In Apr. 1954 the Division of Occupational Health became the Occupational Health Program. In 1960 the program was reorganized to reestablish the Division of Occupational Health. In 1966 the division was again designated Occupational Health Program. In Dec. 1968 the name of

(Continued on next card)

72–213769

72 [2]

U. S. Bureau of Occupational Safety and Health. (Card 2)

the Occupational Health Program was changed to Bureau of Occupational Safety and Health.

Works by the Division of Occupational Health and by the Division of Industrial Hygiene during the period 1943–51 when it was part of the Public Health Service are found under

U. S. Public Health Service. Division of Occupational Health.

Works by the other bodies are found under the following headings according to the name used at the time of publication:

U. S. Office of Industrial Hygiene and Sanitation.
U. S. Office of Dermatoses Investigations.
U. S. National Institutes of Health. Division of Industrial Hygiene.

(Continued on next card)

72–213769

72 [2]

(This card continues on page 110.)

Complicated Changes (cont'd)

U. S. Bureau of Occupational Safety and Health. (Card 3)

U. S. Industrial Hygiene Research Laboratory, Bethesda, Md.
U. S. Occupational Health Program.
U. S. Bureau of Occupational Safety and Health.

SUBJECT ENTRY: Works about these bodies are entered under the name or names in existence during the latest period for which subject coverage is given.

72-213769

Library of Congress   72 [2]

Complicated Changes (cont'd)

McNeese State University.

Lake Charles Junior College was founded in 1938 as a division of Louisiana State University. In 1940 the name was changed to John McNeese Junior College. In 1950 the college was separated from Louisiana State University and renamed McNeese State College. In 1970 this name was changed to McNeese State University.
Works by this body published before the change of name in 1950 are found under

Louisiana. State University and Agricultural and Mechanical College. John McNeese Junior College, Lake Charles.

Works published after that change of name are found under the following headings according to the name used at the time of publication:

(Continued on next card)
72-214004

72 [2]

(Card 2 of this example is on page 111.)

Complicated Changes (cont'd)

McNeese State University. (Card 2)

McNeese State College.
McNeese State University.

SUBJECT ENTRY: Works about this body are entered under the name used during the latest period covered. In the case where the required name is represented in this catalog only under a later form of the name, entry is made under the later form.

72-214004

Library of Congress   72 [2]

Information cards involving political jurisdictions do not normally make use of formula sentences. The wording of each subject entry statement is customized to fit the facts of the case in hand.

Examples:

Jurisdiction, with Territorial Changes

Papua New Guinea.

British New Guinea, a British protectorate since 1884, became a territory of Australia in 1901. In 1906 its name was changed to the Territory of Papua, and in 1945 it was joined to the Territory of New Guinea to form the administrative unit of the Territory of Papua-New Guinea. The Papua New Guinea act of 1949 provided for the administration by Australia of the United Nations Trust Territory of New Guinea in an administrative union with the Territory of Papua under the name of Papua New Guinea. On Dec. 1, 1973 Papua New Guinea became self-governing.
Works by these jurisdictions published before 1945 are found under

New Guinea (Ter.)
Papua.

(Continued on next card)
74-224028
74 [2]

(Card 2 of this example is on page 112.)

Jurisdiction, with Territorial Changes (cont'd)

Papua New Guinea. (Card 2)

Works published after 1945 are found under

Papua New Guinea.

SUBJECT ENTRY: Works about these jurisdictions, **regardless** of period covered, are entered under Papua New Guinea. Works limited in subject coverage to historical, political or cultural aspects of Papua New Guinea for the pre-1945 period are entered under Papua and/or New Guinea (Ter.) Works on other subjects relating to Papua and/or New Guinea (Ter.) for the pre-1945 period are entered under the name of the present jurisdiction, Papua New Guinea.

74–224028

Library of Congress 74 [2]

Subject-to-Name References

As in the case of personal headings, the heading established for a corporate body is used in both descriptive and subject cataloging. The same types of *see* references are provided. In addition, when a corporate name is used as a subject heading, one or more subject-to-name references are provided. These are *see also* references from topical headings usually subdivided by the subdivision —**Societies,** etc. to corporate headings related to the particular subject fields, e.g.,

Psychology—Societies, etc.

see also

Canadian Psychological Association

The purpose of these references, also called Red-to-Black references, is to enable the user to proceed from his particular field of interest in a subject file to names of individual corporate bodies which are active or associated in some way with the same field.

These references are normally not included in the printed list (except in the case of pattern headings and a few others). However, the Library of Congress has decided to make them available to outside libraries by including them in the Automated Name Authority File.

Following are the guidelines* for preparing subject-to-name references:

1)   Prepare subject-to-name references in the case of the following kinds of corporate headings when used as subject headings: names of all individual societies, institutions, firms, and governmental agencies. They are not made for names of congresses or jurisdictions.**

2)   Consider the subject heading referred *from* in each case the generic concept. Depending on the nature of the body in question, references from several generic headings (subdivided by place whenever possible) may be required in order to bring out all aspects.

Exception: Institutions, such as schools, hospitals, museums, churches, airports, etc., often require an additional reference from the name of the city in question subdivided by the generic concept. An art museum in a city requires three references (*see* example below).

Normally, in the case of societies, firms, industries, and governmental agencies, only references from the heading [generic concept]—[place] to the name in question are required even when a city is involved. Therefore, additional references from the name of the jurisdiction subdivided by the subdivisions —**Learned institutions and societies**; —**Industry**; or —**Executive departments** need not be made. Use the latter form of reference only when there is no other way to identify the organization in question.

In connection with societies and institutions, further subdivide the heading [generic concept] or [generic concept]—[place] by —**Societies, etc.**, wherever it is possible to do so, e.g., **Shooting—Belgium—Societies, etc.** Do not use the subdivision in connection with governmental agencies, firms, or industries.

3)   When constructing the reference, subdivide the generic heading by place in all cases where it is possible to do so.

4)   When subdividing generic headings by place in the construction of a subject-to-name reference, subdivide only by the name of the region or country, as appropriate.

After subdividing the generic heading, do not further subdivide by a locality within the country even if it is possible to do so. Do not subdivide directly to a particular locality within the country.

Exception: If appropriate in the case of Canada, Great Britain, the Soviet Union, and the United States, subdivide by the name of the pertinent province, constituent country, or state without further subdivision for all corporate bodies except firms. In the latter case, use only the name of the country, i.e., Canada, Great Britain, Russia, and United States, without further subdivision.

Examples are shown on page 114.

---

*Cf. *Cataloging Service* 115:28-29 (Fall 1975).

**Note that similar references are made for sacred books, but not for personal names or individual works including anonymous classics.

Examples:

Societies, etc.

> **Deutsche Atlantische Gesellschaft**
> *xx*   Europe—Defenses—Societies, etc.

> **Association of Public Health Inspectors**
> *xx*   Public health—Great Britain—Societies, etc.

> **Ueno Dobutsuen**
> *xx*   Zoological gardens—Japan

> **International Kart Federation**
> *xx*   Karting—Societies, etc.

> **Otago Home Economics Association**
> *xx*   Home economics—New Zealand—Societies, etc.

Government agencies.

> **South Carolina. Water Resources Commission**
> *xx*   Water resources development—South Carolina

> **Manitoba Water Services Board**
> *xx*   Water-supply—Manitoba

> **Arizona. Advisory Commission on Arizona Environment**
> *xx*   Environmental protection—Arizona
> Environmental policy—Arizona

Firms, etc.

> **Great Atlantic and Pacific Tea Company**
> *xx*   Grocery trade—United States

> **Goodyear Tire and Rubber Company, Akron, Ohio**
> *xx*   Tire industry—United States
> Rubber industry and trade—United States

> **Bank of America**
> *xx*   Banks and banking—United States

Churches.

> **Dom, Fulda, Ger.**
> > *xx*   Cathedrals—Germany, West
> >   Fulda, Ger.—Churches
>
> **Église au Christ-Roi**
> > *xx*   Churches—Switzerland
> >   Fribourg—Churches

Libraries.

> **New York Academy of Medicine. Library**
> > *xx*   Medical libraries—New York (State)
> >   New York (City)—Libraries
>
> **Staatlich Buchereistelle, Köln**
> > *xx*   Cologne—Libraries
> >   Public libraries—Germany, West
>
> **Fairfax County Public Library**
> > *xx*   Libraries, County—Virginia
> >   Public libraries—Virginia

Art museums.

> **Von der Heydt -Museum**
> > *xx*   Art museums—Germany, West
> >   Wuppertal—Museums
>
> **Art Museum of South Texas**
> > *xx*   Corpus Christi, Tex.—Museums
> >   Art museums—Texas

Higher education institutions.

> **Thanjavur Medical College**
> > *xx*   Medical colleges—India
> >   Tanjore, India (City)—Schools

OTHER INDIVIDUAL ENTITIES BEARING A PROPER NAME

In addition to the proper names discussed above, there are certain other individual entities bearing proper names which also serve as subject headings. These are discussed below.

Historical Events

Historical events identified by specific names are entered under their names, usually accompanied by dates. They may appear as main headings or as period subdivisions, e.g.,

> World War, 1939-1945.
> King Philip's War, 1675-1676.
> United States—History—King William's War, 1689-1697.
> Waterloo, Battle of, 1815.
> Lewes, Eng., Battle of, 1264.
> Canadian Invasion, 1775-1776.
> Northwestern Conspiracy, 1864.
> Canadian Spy Trials, 1946.
> Pacific Coast Indians, Wars with, 1847-1865.
> Chrysler Corporation Slowdown Strike, 1939.*
> Anthracite Coal Strike, 1887-1888.*
> New York (City)—Garment Workers' Strike, 1912-1913.*
> Westmoreland Co., Pa.—Coal Strike, 1910-1911.*
> American Revolution Bicentennial, 1776-1976.
> American Revolution Bicentennial, 1776-1976—Pennsylvania—Philadelphia.
> Dewey Celebration, New York, Sept. 28-30, 1899.
> Louisiana Purchase.

Names of other events may also be used as headings, e.g.,

> Brighton Run (Antique car race)
> National Library Week.

Named Projects

The word "project" is defined in a generic sense to refer to all named undertakings or plans for action toward a desired goal, including "projects," "operations," "programs," "plans," etc. The Library of Congress usually adopts the form of the name found in the work cataloged or other sources. If there is a choice, the form in which the generic word appears first is used. In either case, the first letter of the generic word is capitalized. Examples of headings for named projects are:

---

*For instruction concerning the forms of headings for strikes, consult *Library of Congress Subject Headings*, 8th ed., p. 1748. (Note under the heading **Strikes and Lockouts**.)

Operation Neptune.
Project Neptune.
MARC Project.
Right to Read Program.
Pacific Ocean Biological Survey Program.
National Program for Acquisitions and Cataloging.

Animals

Subject headings are sometimes required for works about famous animals, e.g.,

Man o' War (Race horse)
xx Race horses

Secretariat (Race horse)
xx Race horses

Prizes, Awards, Scholarships, etc.

Nobel prizes
Alfred P. Sloan national scholarships
National achievement award
Geroĭ Sovetskogo Soĭuza
x Gold Star (Medal)

Music Festivals*

Aldeburgh, Eng. Festival of Music and the Arts
xx Music festivals—England

Carmel, Calif. Bach Festival
xx Music festivals—California

Salzburg. Festspiele
xx Music festivals—Austria

Internationales Heinrich-Schütz-Fest
xx Music festivals—Austria

Music Cataloging Bulletin 8:1 (April 1977).

Holidays, Festivals, etc.

Yom Kippur
Memorial Day
Thanksgiving Day
Ascension Day
Christmas
Fools, Feast of

Ethnic Groups, Nationalities, Tribes, etc.

North Africans
North Africans in Belgium, [etc.]
Saracens
Arabs
Italians
Italians in the United States   [for aliens]
Italian Americans   [for natives]
Japanese in San Francisco   [for aliens]
Japanese Americans—California—
    San Francisco   [for natives]
Indians of North America
Tannekwe (African tribe)
Korana (African people)*

Tribes of American Indians are enumerated in the printed list.

For ethnic American groups, current practice** is to establish individual headings as required in the form of [ethnic name] Americans, e.g., German Americans, Japanese Americans, etc. The existing generic headings of the type [ethnic group] in the United States will only be used to designate aliens living in the United States, students from abroad, newly arrived immigrants, etc., and for ethnic groups currently identified by composite names in the Library of Congress system, e.g., Russian Germans, French Canadians, etc. The headings [ethnic group] in [country] will continue to be used to designate modern nationalities in countries other than the United States, e.g., Germans in Brazil.

Religions, Philosophical Systems, etc.

Buddhism
Christianity
Confucianism
Islam
Neoplatonism

---

*Newly established headings take this form.
**Cataloging Service 114:8 (Summer 1975).

GEOGRAPHIC NAMES

Geographic names are used widely in subject headings. They may serve as the main heading or appear as part of a heading, as a subdivision, or as a qualifier, e.g.,

Jamaica—Description and travel
Paris in literature
Japanese in San Francisco
Building permits—Belgium
Manning Provincial Park, B.C.

Because of the various types and forms of geographic names, this is probably one of the most complicated areas in cataloging practice. To compound the difficulty, the policy of superimposition has resulted in the persistence of many geographic headings established earlier according to different rules or policies.

Because many geographic names appear also in author headings, as corporate entry for governments, as parts of corporate names, or as additional designations or qualifiers, headings for these geographic names are generally established according to the *Anglo-American Cataloging Rules*. At the Library of Congress, geographic headings which are or may be used as author headings are established by the Descriptive Cataloging Division. Geographic names, such as natural features, which do not serve as author headings, are established by the Subject Cataloging Division, following the practice and policies of the U.S. Board on Geographic Names.

Following is a discussion of the general aspects of geographic headings and types of geographic names used in subject headings.

Language

Naturally, for places in English-speaking regions, names in the English language are used. For foreign places, on the other hand, a choice often has to be made between English names and vernacular names. According to *Anglo-American Cataloging Rules*, the English form of the name of a place is chosen if there is one in general use. This is in general agreement with Haykin's comments:

> The language of the heading is fundamentally an aspect of usage and should respond to it. Of the several forms of a place name found in works of reference or monographs, that one is to be preferred which is found in English-language works, representing, therefore, the usage in English-speaking countries . . . smaller, remote, or little-known geographic entities are likely to possess names only in the vernacular, or, to lack English forms. No choice remains in this case but to use the vernacular form and, in the instance where the vernacular employs a non-Roman alphabet, the transliterated form which is most often found in English-language publications.[3]

Based on these policies, the following forms are used in cataloging entries:

South America
>   *not* Sudamerica *or* America del Sur

Spain
>   *not* España

Bavaria
>   *not* Bayern

Vienna
>   *not* Wien

Rhine River
>   *not* Rhein

The vernacular form is chosen where there is no English form in general use or when the vernacular form is widely accepted in English language works, e.g.,

Mont Blanc

Occasionally, inconsistency occurs because of varying practices and policies at different times of the development of subject headings, e.g.,

Bavarian Forest
>   [Vernacular form: Bayrischer Wald]

Wienerwald
>   [English form not used: Vienna Woods]

Entry Element[4]

When a geographic name contains more than one word, there is again the problem of the choice of entry element. With few exceptions, names of political jurisdictions generally appear in their natural word order, without inversion, even for foreign names beginning with an article, e.g.,

La Rochelle, France

La Paz, Bolivia

One notable exception was the heading **Africa, South** which used to represent both the region and the country. Now the heading **South Africa** is used for the country and its government, and **Africa, Southern** for the geographic area.

The inverted form is used when the name of a natural feature begins with a generic term, followed by a specific term. The specific term is used as the entry word, e.g.,

Dover, Strait of

Michigan, Lake

In a small number of cases, when the generic term in a foreign language has no generic significance for the English-speaking users and when the vernacular form is well known, the direct form is retained, e.g.,

Costa del Sol
rather than Sol, Costa del

Mont Blanc
rather than Blanc, Mont

Geographic names containing adjectives indicating directions or parts are generally inverted, e.g.,

Africa, East	**Asia, Southeastern**
Africa, Central	**Asia, Western**
Africa, French Equatorial	**Alps, Eastern**
Africa, North	**California, Southern**
Africa, Southern	**Tennessee, East**
	Saxony, Lower

For a given place, when the inverted form is used in a main heading, the same form is used when the same place appears as a subdivision under another heading, e.g.,

Austria, Upper—Description and travel
Geology—Austria, Upper

However, the direct form is used when the geographic name forms part of a phrase, e.g.,

Asia, Southeastern—Description and travel
British in Southeastern Asia

Qualifiers

A qualifier is frequently added to a geographic name in order to identify it more clearly or to distinguish places with the same name. Haykin[5] discusses three types of qualifiers: generic, geographic, and political.

Generic qualifiers. The names of many natural features contain generic terms as an integral part, e.g.,

Ohio River
Rocky Mountains

If the generic term is not part of the name, but is required to distinguish between headings with the same name, a generic qualifier is added in parentheses, e.g.,

Golden Gate (Strait)

In a few cases of vernacular names established according to previous practice, an English generic term was added to the name, even though the generic term was redundant because the name already contained a generic term in the vernacular, e.g.,

Thian Shan Mountains
["Shan" means mountains in Chinese]

According to current practice, the generic term in the foreign language is replaced by its English equivalent, e.g.,

Yangtze River

Geographic qualifiers. The use of geographic qualifiers refers to the practice of adding to a local place name the name of a larger geographic entity in which the local place is located. According to the *Anglo-American Cataloging Rules*, geographic qualifiers are to be added to all local place names. However, because of the policy of superimposition, many local place headings established earlier according to different rules and practices continue to be used. Therefore, an understanding of both the earlier and current practices is necessary in order to comprehend the geographic headings being used on Library of Congress cataloging entries. A description of previous practice is given in Appendix G.

Current practice.* The provisions of the *Anglo-American Cataloging Rules* concerning geographic qualifiers are applicable to geographic headings which serve as author and subject headings as well as headings used in subject entries only, including the following categories:

Geographical regions and areas
Geographical features
Structures and buildings (except railroads)
Archaeological sites, ancient cities, etc.
Recreational areas, parks, reserves, monuments, etc.
Forests, moors, etc.
Trails

1) General rule: Assign the name of the country, colony, or dependent territory as the qualifier, using abbreviations (see Appendix H) where applicable, e.g.,

Cuanza River watershed, Angola
Porewa Valley, N. Z.
Brisbane Water, Australia
Buenos Aires metropolitan area, Argentine Republic

2) Exceptional countries: If the entity is in Canada, Great Britain, Malaysia, the Soviet Union, the United States, or Yugoslavia, assign, instead of the name of the country, the name of the appropriate first-order political subdivision, e.g.,

Black Dog Village site, Tex.
Wye Plantation, Md.
Tyasmin River, Ukraine
Andover-Redbridge Canal, Eng.
Buje region, Croatia

3) An entity located in more than one jurisdiction: Add the appropriate names, if not more than two, separated by "and," e.g.,

Lake Tahoe region, Calif. and Nev.

If more than two jurisdictions are involved, omit the qualifier, e.g.,

Mississippi Valley

**Cf. *Cataloging Service* 122:14-16 (Summer 1977).*

Frequently, for rivers, it may be necessary to distinguish between two rivers of the same name, each located in several jurisdictions. In such cases, add the names of the initial and final jurisdictions, separated by a hyphen, in the same order that the river flows, e.g.,

Red River, Tex.-La.

4) Narrower qualification: Add an additional qualifier when it is necessary to distinguish between two entities bearing the same name located in the same jurisdiction, e.g.,

Dyrham Park, Eng. (Avon)

5) Islands: If the entity is located on an island, add the name of the island or island group when either of these names is predominantly used to identify the entity, e.g.,

Belice River, Sicily

Normally, when the island is in close proximity to the land mass of the larger jurisdiction—e.g., Long Island, N.Y.—or the larger jurisdiction consists of islands— e.g., Japan, the Philippine Islands—the name of the country is used as the qualifier.

6) Cities: When the entity is located in a city, alternative provisions often prevail (see pages ix-xii of the introduction to *Library of Congress Subject Headings*, eighth edition). If the entity is to be entered under its own name—the normal situation for geographical features and quarters of cities—assign the name of the city as the qualifier, e.g.,

Buen Consejo, San Juan, P. R.

If the name of the city has been established without a qualifier, do not add the qualifier when adding the name of the city as a qualifier to the name of an entity within the city, e.g.,

Cedar Lake, Minneapolis
[*not* Cedar Lake, Minneapolis, Minn.]

The qualifier **(City)** in such headings as **New York (City)** is not retained when the name of the city is used as a qualifier,* e.g.,

Harlem River, New York
[*not* Harlem River, New York (City)]

It should be noted that in indirect geographic subdivision, the geographic qualifier is omitted when it is identical with the name of the larger geographic entity which already appears as the broader subdivision, e.g.,

---

*However, for sections within Mexico City, the form **[name of city section], Mexico City** is used.

San Diego, Calif.
Music—California—San Diego

Manning Provincial Park, B. C.
Hiking—British Columbia—Manning Provincial Park

Political or jurisdictional qualifiers. When two or more places belonging to different types of jurisdictions bear the same name, a qualifier indicating the type of jurisdiction is added in parentheses. In this case, the provisions in the *Anglo-American Cataloging Rules* are followed. The political qualifier is added after the geographic qualifier, if any. In older headings, political qualifiers were occasionally used with headings for cities, e.g., **Rome (City)**; **New York (City)**. In newly-established headings for cities which now always contain geographic qualifiers, the political qualifiers are not used.

The political qualifier is usually an English term, if available. The vernacular term is used when there is no equivalent term in English.

San Luis Potosí, Mexico (Intendencia)
San Luis Potosí, Mexico (State)

San Marino (Republic)
San Marino, Calif.

Naples
[heading for the city established earlier without geographic qualifier]
Naples (Kingdom)

Posen
Posen (Archdiocese)
Posen (Province)

References

See references are made from variant names or forms of names for geographic headings, e.g.,

IJssel River*
  x   Issel River
        Yssel River

---

*This heading is used for IJssel River which rises in Germany and flows through Netherlands into IJssel Lake. For IJssel River as a branch of the Rhine River in the province of South Holland, the heading **Hollandsche IJssel River** is used.

See also references from a generic heading to the specific geographic name are made for certain categories of headings, e.g.,

IJssel River
    xx   Rivers—Netherlands
              Rivers—Germany

Burdekin River, Australia
    xx   Rivers—Australia

The introduction to the eighth edition of *Library of Congress Subject Headings* includes a section on "Standard Reference Patterns for Nonprint* Headings," many of which are geographic headings.

    In addition, explanatory references, sometimes called history cards or information cards, are made for geographic headings which have undergone changes, with a note pertaining to different uses, if any, of the headings in descriptive and subject cataloging. Examples of information cards for geographic headings which have undergone changes begin on page 126.

---

*Note that nonprint geographic headings have been reduced recently to two categories only, regions of cities and metropolitan areas. Newly established headings not belonging to either of these categories will appear in the printed list. However, no effort is being made to print previously established headings except for reasons of revised forms or references.

Information Cards for Geographic Headings
Which Have Undergone Changes

Texas (Province)

In 1824 the Mexican Province of Texas was united with the Mexican Province of Coahuila to form the State of Coahuila and Texas. In 1835 a rival provisional government of Texas was established. In 1836 the State of Coahuila and Texas was divided; the Mexican portion continued under the name Coahuila and the remainder became the Republic of Texas. In 1845 this became a state of the United States.

Works by these jurisdictions are found under the following headings according to the name used at the time of publication:

Texas (Province)
Coahuila and Texas (State)
Texas (Provisional government)
Texas (Republic)
Texas.

(Continued on next card)
76

Texas (Province) (Card 2)

SUBJECT ENTRY: Works about this jurisdiction are normally entered under Texas. However, works on historical, political or cultural aspects of this jurisdiction for the 1824-1836 period are entered under Coahuila and Texas (State).

Library of Congress 76

Information Cards for Geographic Headings
Which Have Undergone Changes (cont'd)

Molise, Italy.

    In 1860 Molise (created in 1806 as a province of the Kingdom of Naples)
became Campobasso, a province of the Kingdom of Italy. In 1963 the
province was declared a region with the name Molise. The administration
of the region, however, did not become effective until 1970. In the interim
the area in question continued as the province of Campobasso. In 1970 the
region of Molise was effectively instituted superseding the provincial
administration; the region is divided into two provinces, one of which continues the name Campobasso and the other is named Isernia.

    Works by these jurisdictions are found under the following headings
according to the name used at the time of publication:

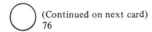

(Continued on next card)
76

Molise, Italy. (Card 2)

    Molise, Italy.
    Campobasso, Italy (Province)
    Isernia, Italy (Province)

    SUBJECT ENTRY: Works on this region as a whole are entered under
Molise, Italy. Works limited in subject coverage to one of the constituent
provinces created in 1970 are entered under Campobasso, Italy (Province)
and/or Isernia, Italy (Province). Works limited in subject coverage to the
pre-1970 period are entered only under Molise, Italy.

Library of Congress   76

Information Cards for Geographic Headings
Which Have Undergone Changes (cont'd)

Germany (Territory under Allied occupation, 1945-1955)

Headings for Germany until the end of World War II are found under

Germany.

Headings for the government of the Territory under Allied occupation which existed 1945-55 are found under

Germany (Territory under Allied occupation, 1945-1955)
Germany (Territory under Allied occupation, 1945-1955. British Zone)
Germany (Territory under Allied occupation, 1945-1955. French Zone)

(Continued on next card)
76

Germany (Territory under Allied occupation, 1945-1955)
(Card 2)

Germany (Territory under Allied occupation, 1945-1955. Russian Zone)
Germany (Territory under Allied occupation, 1945-1955. U. S. Zone)

Headings for the Deutsche Demokratische Republik are found under

Germany (Democratic Republic, 1949-   )

Headings for the Bundesrepublik are found under

Germany (Federal Republic, 1949-   )

(Continued on next card)
76

(Card 3 of this example is shown at the top of page 129.)

Information Cards for Geographic Headings
Which Have Undergone Changes (cont'd)

Germany (Territory under Allied occupation, 1945-1955)
(Card 3)

     SUBJECT ENTRY: Works about the pre-war country of Germany, the post-war zones of occupation collectively, or the region of the Democratic and Federal Republics together since 1949, are entered under Germany. Works about the eastern part of Germany before 1949, and/or the Democratic Republic are entered under Germany, East. Works about the western part of Germany before 1949, and/or the Federal Republic are entered under Germany, West.

Library of Congress   76

Types of Geographic Names

Geographic names used as subject headings fall into the following categories.

Jurisdictions. These include countries, principalities, colonies, territories, states, provinces, counties, cities, archdioceses, and dioceses. Forms of the headings conform to those used in descriptive cataloging as author or added entries. Qualifiers are added when required, e.g.,

> **Rostov on the Don, Russia**
> **Klundert, Netherlands**
>
> **Himeji, Japan (Fief)**
> **Nagano, Japan (Prefecture)**
> **Hildesheim (Diocese)**
> **Hohenlohe (Principality)**
>
> **Krakow (Archidiocese)**
> **Krakow (Grand Duchy)**
> **Krakow (Republic)**
> **Krakow (Voivodeship)**

Archaeological sites and ancient cities.* These were previously nonprint headings. Beginning in 1976, newly established headings in this category are printed in *Library of Congress Subject Headings*. Cities which went out of existence before the creation of modern states (ca.1500 A.D.) seldom produced official publications of their own and therefore are not likely to appear as author headings. However, they are required as subject headings for works about them. The general guidelines for establishing these headings are:

1) Use the form of the name most commonly applied to the city in standard encyclopedias, gazetteers, etc. The form of the name adopted is normally the ancient form, e.g., **Larsa**, not "Tall Sankarah."

2) Establish the name as an archaeological site, qualifying it with the name of the current larger jurisdiction (or island) in which the site is located, e.g.,

> **Taanach, Jordan**

Do not add the word "site" to the name if the site in question once existed as a city in its own right, and the name adopted represents the name of that city.

3) The ancient name of a city is not used as a heading if a modern city with a different name is now situated directly on the ancient site, and the ancient city developed into the modern city without major interruptions. In such a case, apply the general rule for a jurisdiction with name change, and use the modern name instead, e.g.,

> **Vienna**
>   *x*   Vindobona

If, however, the site has not been continuously or recurrently occupied until modern times, the modern name is ignored. In many instances, a modern village has developed accidently near an ancient site. Unless there is proof, it is assumed that there is no connection between the modern village and ancient site other than proximity and the ancient name is used for works dealing with the ancient city.

4) Make the following references:

> **[city name, modern country or island]**
>   *x*   **[alternate name(s), modern country or island]**
>   *xx*   **Cities and towns, Ruined, extinct, etc.–[modern country]**
>   **[modern country]–Antiquities**
>   **[special locality in country, if appropriate]–Antiquities**
>   **Excavations (Archaeology)–[modern country]**
>   **[people, empire, period, etc., if appropriate]**

5) For an archaeological site, establish the heading on the basis of the work cataloged and the decision of the Board on Geographic Names. Add the word "site," if the name is not that of an ancient city, and a geographic qualifier, e.g.,

> **Bowen site, Ind.**
> **San Antonio site, Mexico**
> **Blackwater Locality no. 1 site, N. M.**
> **Gours-aux-Lions site, France**

---

*Cf. *Cataloging Service* 118:11-12 (Summer 1976).

If the site is a cave site and the cave has been named, use the name of the cave as the site name, e.g.,

> **Saint Germain la Rivière Cave, France**
> **En Medio Shelter, N. M.**

Make the following references:

> [site name with geographic qualifier]
>   *x*   [alternate names with qualifier, if any]
>   *xx*   [modern country] –Antiquities
>   Excavations (Archaeology)–[modern country]
>   [people, empire, period, etc., if appropriate]
>   Caves–[modern country]   [add if a cave site]

Non-jurisdictional regions and natural features. These include continents, regions, metropolitan areas, regions of cities, city districts and sections,* islands, lakes, rivers, oceans, mountains, valleys, basins, forests, oases, deserts, caves, estuaries, moors, heaths, ocean currents, and many others. For foreign names, the transliterated forms used by the U.S. Board on Geographic Names are followed. A *see* reference from a variant form of the name based on the Library of Congress transliteration system is made. Examples of subject headings for non-jurisdictional regions and natural features are:

> **Africa, North**
> **Asia**
> **Atlantic Ocean**
> **Atlantic States**
> **North Atlantic region**
> **Balearic Islands**
> **Bali (Islands)**
> **Balkan Peninsula**
> **Alps**
> **Himalaya Mountains**
> **Himalaya region**
> **San Dieguito River watershed**
> **Amazon River**
> **Amazon Valley**
> **Buffalo, Mount, Australia**
> **Michigan, Lake**
> **Constance, Lake of**

---

*Note that headings for city districts and sections, e.g., **Georgetown, D.C.,** cannot be subdivided topically, nor are they used as geographic subdivisions.

Areas associated with cities.* There are four headings which the various areas associated with an individual city may be designated, for example:

> Boston
> Boston–Suburbs and environs
> Boston metropolitan area
> Boston region

In terms of territory, these four headings may be defined as follows:

[city name]: the territory over which the city exercises its control.

[city]–Suburbs and environs: any lands or regions associated with a particular city, including the neighboring residential areas lying outside the city, as well as smaller satellite jurisdictions; the term does not include the city itself.

[city] metropolitan area: a quasi-official name for a well defined area consisting of the city itself and those densely populated territories immediately surrounding the city which are socially and economically integrated with it.

[city] region: the city itself and its surrounding territory, the exact size of which is indefinite and may vary according to each individual work being cataloged.

Individual Parks, Reserves, etc.**

At the Library of Congress, names of individual parks, reserves, etc., to be used as subject headings on cataloging records are established by subject catalogers, unless the entity in question is organized and operated as a corporate body capable of authorship, in which case the name is established by a descriptive cataloger. The following statement presents guidelines to subject catalogers for establishing and assigning these names.

Types of named entities under consideration.

> Public and private parks of all kinds
> Nature conservation areas, natural areas, natural history reservations, nature reserves
> Wild areas, wilderness areas, roadless areas
> Forests, forest reserves and preserves
> Seashores, marine parks and reserves, scenic river areas
> Wildlife refuges, bird reservations and sanctuaries, game ranges and preserves, wildlife management areas
> Monuments, historic sites
> Trails

---

*Cataloging Service 122:16 (Summer 1977).

**Cataloging Service 111:5-8 (Fall 1974).

Form of the heading. Unless the entity in question is located within a city, the heading is entered under the name of the entity, qualified by the name of a larger geographic area, in accordance with the provisions of the *Anglo-American Cataloging Rules.*

> **Big Horn Canyon National Recreation Area, Mont. and Wyo.**
> **Cape Hatteras National Seashore, N. C.**
> **Deutsch-Luxemburgischer Naturpark, Ger.**
> **Patapsco State Park, Md.**

Headings for individual parks in cities take the form [city] –Parks–[name of park], e.g.,

> **New York (City)–Parks–Central Park.**

References (nonmunicipal entities). When establishing the heading, the following references are made:

1) Provide *see* references from variant forms of the name and if appropriate an inverted reference from the distinctive term.

> **Parc régional de Brière, France.**
> x Parc naturel régional de Brière, France
>   Brière, Parc régional de, France

2) Provide a *see also* reference from the generic heading subdivided by the name of the country (or Province, State, etc., in the case of Canada, Great Britain, the Soviet Union, or the United States). If the entity in question also is nationally owned and administered, and if it is located in Canada, Great Britain, the Soviet Union, or the United States, provide in addition a *see also* reference from this generic heading subdivided by the name of the country.

> **Groton State Forest, Vt.**
> xx Forest reserves–Vermont

> **Big Horn Canyon National Recreation Area, Mont. and Wyo.**
> xx Recreation areas–Montana
>   Recreation areas–United States
>   Recreation areas–Wyoming

3) In the case of any entity established at the national level, including national forest reserves, natural areas, wild and scenic rivers, wildlife refuges, historic sites, etc., as well as national parks, assign, in addition to the references specified in paragraphs 1) and 2) above, a *see also* reference from **National parks and reserves** subdivided by the name of the country, e.g., **National parks and reserves–United States.**

> **Cumberland Island National Seashore, Ga.**
> xx National parks and reserves–United States

4) If the entity in question is located in a larger park or reserve system, provide a *see also* reference from the name of the larger system.

> **Eleven Point Wild and Scenic River, Mo.**
> *xx*   Mark Twain National Forest, Mo.

5) Provide additional *see also* references from topical headings, if required by the peculiarities of the park, reserve, monument, etc., in question.

> **Hohokam Pima National Monument, Ariz.**
> *xx*   Arizona—Antiquities
> Hohokam culture

6) The model illustrating the above:

> **[name of entity, name of larger jurisdiction]**
> *x*   [variant name]
> [inverted name]
> *xx*   [generic heading—country or Province, State, etc., of Canada, Great Britain, the Soviet Union, or the United States]
> [generic heading—country] (If a *national* park, etc., and if located in Canada, Great Britain, the Soviet Union, or the United States)
> National parks and reserves—[country] (If a *national* park, reserve, area, etc.)
> [larger park name]
> [special topic]

7) The examples below illustrate the entire display of references specified above. (The form of the headings used may vary from currently existing LC headings.)

> **Adirondack Park, N.Y.**
> *xx*   Parks—New York (State)

> **Cumberland Island National Seashore, Ga.**
> *xx*   National parks and reserves—United States
> Parks—Georgia

> **Big Horn Canyon National Recreation Area, Mont. and Wyo.**
> *xx*   National parks and reserves—United States
> Recreation areas—Montana
> Recreation areas—United States
> Recreation areas—Wyoming

> **Groton State Forest, Vt.**
> *xx*   Forest reserves—Vermont

(List continues on page 135.)

Tule Elk National Wildlife Refuge, Calif.
    xx   National parks and reserves—United States
           Wildlife refuges—California
           Wildlife refuges—United States

Mount Hood National Forest, Or.
    xx   National parks and reserves—United States
           Forest reserves—Oregon
           Forest reserves—United States

Eleven Point Wild and Scenic River, Mo.
    xx   Eleven Point River
           Mark Twain National Forest, Mo.
           National parks and reserves—United States
           Wild and scenic rivers—Missouri
           Wild and scenic rivers—United States

Parc régional de Brière, France
    x   Brière, Parc régional de, France
       Parc naturel régional de Brière, France
    xx   National parks and reserves—France
           Parks—France

Hohokam Pima National Monument, Ariz.
    xx   Arizona—Antiquities
           Hohokam culture
           National parks and reserves—United States
           Parks—Arizona

References (municipal parks).
1) Provide a *see* reference from the name in direct order, qualified by the name of the city.

New York (City)—Parks—Central Park
    x   Central Park, New York

2) Provide *see* references from variant forms of the name, from [**city**. **park**] and, if appropriate, an inverted reference from the distinctive term.

Paris—Parks—Bois de Boulogne
    x   Boulogne, Bois de, Paris
       Paris. Bois de Boulogne

3) Provide a *see also* reference from the generic heading **Parks** subdivided by the name of the country (or Province, State, etc., in the case of Canada, Great Britain, the Soviet Union, or the United States).

New York (City)—Parks—Central Park
    xx   Parks—New York (State)

4) The model illustrating the above:

[name of city] –Parks–[name of park]
    x   [variant name]
         [inverted name]
         [name of park, city]
         [name of city. name of park]
    xx   Parks–[country or Province, State, etc., of Canada,
          Great Britain, the Soviet Union, or the United States]

Local subdivision. When the heading for a national park, reserve, etc., occurs as a local subdivision under a subject, it receives the same treatment as any geographic area. If the printed list of subject headings provides that the subject heading in question is subdivided indirectly and the park, etc., is situated wholly within one country (or wholly within one Province, State, etc., in the case of Canada, Great Britain, the Soviet Union, or the United States), indirect subdivision is used, e.g.,

Geology–Alberta–Banff National Park.

If the entity in question is situated within two or more countries (or two or more Provinces, States, etc., in the case of Canada, Great Britain, the Soviet Union, or the United States), then direct treatment is required, e.g.,

Geology–Great Smoky Mountains National Park.

When the heading for a park, reserve, etc. (including a national park, reserve, etc.), is used as a local subdivision under a subject heading, the heading for the park is always assigned to the work in question as a second subject (without topical subdivision).

    1.   **Botany–California–Yosemite National Park.**
    2.   **Yosemite National Park, Calif.**

Structures within the boundaries of parks, monuments, etc.
1) Administrative buildings: Names of specific buildings which are built to function mainly as service or administrative buildings in the operation of the park, etc., including headquarters buildings, club houses, lodges, etc., are established as subdivisions under the name of the park.

Yosemite National Park, Calif.–Rangers' Club

2) Incidental historic structures: Important historic buildings which happen to be situated in a park, monument, etc., but are not the prime reason for the park's existence, are established in their own right under the name of the structure. An example is the Garthright House, Va., which is located in the Richmond National Battlefield Park, Va. A *see also* reference from the park to the structure is made.
3) Principal historic structure: When a structure in a national historic site, monument, etc., is the only significant feature of that site, the question arises as to

whether to establish the name of the park, site, etc., or the name of the structure itself. If the heading for the structure, feature, etc., already exists in the catalog at the time the park is elevated to national historic status, the existing heading is retained and a *see* reference is made from the park name. If the name of the structure does not exist in the catalog at the time the park is given official status, the name for the latter is established with a *see* reference to it from the name of the structure. Both names should not be in use in the catalog at the same time. For example, the heading **Fort Davis, Tex.** was in use in the catalog before the historic site officially came into being. The *see* reference "Fort Davis National Historic Site, Tex." *see* **Fort Davis, Tex.** was made. On the other hand, since no heading for the Longfellow Home existed in the catalog at the time the Longfellow National Historic Site was established, the reference "Cambridge, Mass. Longfellow Home" *see* **Longfellow National Historic Site, Mass.** was made.

Other Man-Made Structures Bearing Proper Names

These include buildings, physical plants, roads, tunnels, bridges, aqueducts, and other structures. Examples of this type of heading are:

Croton Aqueduct

Camino Real
    x   Golden Road

Callao. Castillo Real Felipe
    x   San Felipe del Callao (Castle)

Naples. San Gregorio Armeno (Convent)

Bologna. San Domenico (Dominican monastery)

California. State Prison, San Quentin

Mountluc, France (Prison)

Mont Blanc Tunnel

Didyma, Asia Minor. Didymaeum
    x   Apollo Temple, Didyma, Asia Minor

Bridges within a city are entered as subdivisions under names of cities subdivided by —**Bridges**, e.g.,

San Francisco—Bridges—Golden Gate Bridge

When a physical plant owned or managed by a corporate body is the subject of a book, the name of the plant instead of that of the body is used as the subject heading,[6] e.g.,

New York (State) Commissioners of Fire Island State Park
[for works on the history, organization, and activities of
the Commissioners]

Fire Island State Park, N. Y.
[for works about the park itself]

This is particularly common in the case of railroads, e.g.,

Penn Central Company
[corporate heading for works about the firm]

Penn Central Railroad
[heading for works about the railroad itself]

History cards are provided which explain subject cataloging practice.

References:

Penn Central Railroad
    x   Penn Central Company
          [in the form of *For subject entries see . . .*]
          Penn Central Holding Company
          Penn Central Transportation Company
    xx   Railroads—United States

Information Card

Penn Central Company.

    The Pennsylvania Railroad Company was incorporated in 1846.
In Feb. 1968 it merged with the New York Central Railroad Company
(established in 1914) to form the Pennsylvania New York Central
Transportation Company. In May 1968 the name was changed to
Penn Central Company. A reorganization in Oct. 1969 divested the
Penn Central Company of all non-railroad holdings, changed its name
to Penn Central Transportation Company, and created the Penn Central Holding Company to oversee the railroad and other non-railroad
subsidiaries.

(Continued on next card)

74-211004

74 [2]

(Card 2 of this example is on page 139.)

Information Card (cont'd)

Penn Central Company. (Card 2)

Works by these bodies are found under the name used at the time of publication.

SUBJECT ENTRY: Works about these railroads are entered under the name or names of the railroad lines in existence during the latest period for which subject coverage is given. The names of the corporate bodies given above may not coincide with the names of the lines. Normally, the name of the line is the same as the corporate name without the word "company."

74–211004

Library of Congress   74 ₍2₎

REFERENCES

[1] David Judson Haykin, *Subject Headings: A Practical Guide* (Washington: Government Printing Office, 1951), p. 41.

[2] Charles A. Cutter, *Rules for a Dictionary Catalog* (4th ed. rewritten; Washington: Government Printing Office, 1904), p. 69.

[3] Haykin, p. 46.

[4] Haykin, pp. 48-49.

[5] Haykin, pp. 49-53.

[6] Haykin, pp. 40-41.

CHAPTER 7

SUBJECT HEADINGS CONTROL
AND MAINTENANCE

ESTABLISHING NEW HEADINGS

As a mechanism for vocabulary control, the Library of Congress has a policy that each new heading added to the list must be "established editorially." This means that a subject cataloger may propose any new heading that seems to be needed in cataloging a work. Before being added to the list the new heading must be approved at the weekly editorial meeting which is attended by the Chief and the Assistant Chief of the Subject Cataloging Division, the Principal Subject Cataloger, Assistants to the Principal Cataloger, and the Editor of subject headings. The editorial group usually considers such matters as terminology of the new heading, how well it fits into the list, whether it is compatible with similar headings or patterns in existence, and the cross references. The lack of specific rules is compensated to a large degree by the expertise of the subject catalogers at the Library of Congress and the knowledge and familiarity with the system on the part of the editorial group.

New headings being proposed and examined at the editorial meeting are generally of these four types: a heading representing a new object or concept, a combination (coordination) of existing headings, new subdivisions under existing headings, and cross references. Headings proposed for revision and updating are handled in the same way—they must be formally established in their new form.

As a means of subject headings control, the Library of Congress maintains an authority record for each heading. A subject authority record contains information regarding the following aspects of the subject represented:

1) the exact form of an approved subject heading,

2) the authorities consulted in determining the choice of the heading,

3) the references from related subject headings and from synonyms or alternative forms of the heading.

Following is an example of a Library of Congress subject authority card.

Treaty-making power (<u>Direct</u>)

<u>See</u> ref. from	<u>See also</u> ref. from
Treaty power	Constitutional law Executive power Legislative power Treaties

Verso of authority card:

Authorities:

   o Black's law dict. 4th ed.
   v Columbia University. Libraries. Law
      Library. Subject headings. (Treaty power)
   o Encyc. Amer. 1964 vol. 10, p. 625
   v Mikell, William Ephraim. The extent of
      the treaty-making power of the President
      and the Senate. University of Pennsyl-
      vania Law Review vol. 57, p. 435
   v Weaver, Samuel P. Constitutional law, p. 178

Work cataloged: Morley, Felix. Treaty law and
                 the Constitution. 1953.

Symbols used:
    o   not found in authority cited
    v   term found in authority cited is exactly identical in form with the
           proposed heading.
           If form found differs from form used, form found is enclosed in
           parentheses following the citation.

In general, *Webster's Third New International Dictionary* is used as the subject cataloger's main authority for usage. For subjects in specialized fields, subject reference works often have to be consulted.

See also references from the heading being established *to* a less comprehensive (i.e., narrower) or otherwise related subject or to an author heading are prepared, but not traced on the authority card, e.g.,

```
        Taxation

            see also

    Income tax
```

```
        Industrial procurement

          sa Priorities, Industrial
             Purchasing agents
             Purchasing departments
             Small orders
```

When a new heading being established contains as part of the heading an existing heading which consists of an obsolete form, the policy* is to retain the obsolete term in the new heading if the obsolete portion of the new heading appears in initial position. The reason for retaining the obsolete term is to avoid confusion and to keep the original heading and the new heading together in the alphabetical file.

Examples:

Original Heading	New Heading Based on the Old
Moving-pictures	**Moving-picture sequels**
Folk-lore	**Folk-lore and history**

However, if the obsolete portion of the heading does not appear in the initial position, the current or preferred form is used, e.g.,

Original Heading	New Heading Based on the Old
Moving-pictures	**Violence in motion pictures**
Folk-lore	**Law (in religion, folklore, etc.)**

REVISING AND UPDATING HEADINGS

In order to ensure the integrity of the catalog, a great deal of maintenance work is required. In view of the two major objectives of the catalog, each entry stands by itself as an individual entity, while it also stands as a part of a larger whole in relation to other entries. Two things are required. The entry must be compatible to similar or related entries and cross references must be provided to link related entries.

One major function in maintaining a logical structure of the subject catalog is the reconciliation of conflicts resulting from changes of headings. The rationale and the necessity for changing headings have been discussed earlier. Each change of heading affects not only the actual entries in the catalog under the old heading but also all the cross references that involve that heading. The magnitude of work involved is enormous. This is the reason that "the Library of Congress is and has been conservative in making changes, since it involves altering reference structures surrounding a given heading as well as accommodating the change in both the card catalogs and the machine-readable data base."** Nevertheless, a certain amount of change is inevitable.

---

*Cataloging Service 123:12 (Fall 1977).
**Cataloging Service 119:22 (Fall 1976).

Changes in subject headings generally fall into the following categories:

1) Simple one-to-one changes for the purpose of updating terminology or spelling, e.g.,

Corpulence	to **Obesity**
Aeroplanes	to **Airplanes**
Day nurseries	to **Day care centers**

2) Changes in conventional names of countries, e.g.,

Ceylon	to **Sri Lanka**
Czechoslovak Republic	to **Czechoslovakia**

3) Changes in the form or entry element, e.g.,

Africa, South	to **South Africa**

4) Changes in both form and terminology, e.g.,

Hygiene, Public	to **Public health**
Insurance, Social	to **Social security**

5) Changes resulting from splitting a compound heading or a heading containing two or more concepts into separate headings, e.g.,

Negroes	to **Afro-Americans**
	Blacks
English [etc.] ballads	to **Ballads, English—Texts**
	Folk-songs, English—Texts
	Songs, English—Texts

In effecting a change in the card catalog, one of the following procedures is followed, depending on the nature of the change and the extent of existing files:

All existing entries bearing the obsolete heading are revised to carry the new heading. All cross references related to the obsolete heading are also revised. In addition, a *see* reference is made from the obsolete heading to the new heading. This is the ideal way of making the changes, but a very costly one. It requires staff, time and maneuverability and space for relocating the sometimes large files of cards.

When the change which affects subdivisions of a heading is so slight that the obsolete and the new subdivisions file in the same location in the catalog, cards bearing the obsolete heading are not altered but are interfiled with those bearing the new heading. Visible guide cards are inserted to explain the interfiling (see Figure 1).

Split files, i.e., maintaining cards under both old and new headings, are used by the Library of Congress when a large existing file is involved and when obsolete and updated headings are dissimilar, or when the old heading is replaced by two or more new headings. Explanatory references are provided to connect the old and the new headings, e.g.,

SOCIAL SECURITY. This heading used beginning June 1975.*
See INSURANCE, SOCIAL for earlier materials.

INSURANCE, SOCIAL. This heading discontinued June 1975.
See SOCIAL SECURITY for later materials.

A longer explanation is given when the old heading is replaced by two or more new ones, e.g.,

NEGROES. This heading discontinued February 1976.
See AFRO-AMERICANS for later materials on the permanent residents of the United States. See BLACKS for later materials on persons outside the United States.

AFRO-AMERICANS. This heading used beginning February 1976.
See NEGROES for earlier materials.

BLACKS. This heading used beginning February 1976.
See NEGROES for earlier materials.

Figure 1 illustrates the use of elevated cards at the Library of Congress to indicate how the original and revised headings are filed.

Figure 1**

---

*The Library of Congress uses the date of cataloging for the cut-off. However, any library adopting the split files technique is free to choose any date (e.g., imprint date) that seems more appropriate to its catalog.

***Cataloging Service* 119: 25 (Fall 1976).

CHAPTER 8

FUTURE PROSPECTS

INTRODUCTION

It appears that the future of *Library of Congress Subject Headings* could take one of three alternative courses:

1) It could continue on the present course until it either runs aground or, by some stroke of luck, runs clear of obstacles and remains a usable, if not entirely logical, system;

2) It could be abandoned completely in favor of another system; or

3) Based on the current framework, an attempt could be made to render the system a more logical and consistent one through more rigorously defined rules and by incorporating recent theories and developments in the field of subject analysis.

In the course of three-quarters of a century since the Library of Congress list appeared and was adopted by most libraries in this country, it has received its share of criticism. In spite of dissatisfactions and the repeated cry for some action, the system has been proceeding on its own course. It is entirely conceivable and possible that this could go on for some time.

The second course is the most drastic one, but it is not totally inconceivable. Suggestions have been made to abandon the system and look for replacements. PRECIS has been suggested as a possibility. This system is logically constructed and has taken in the advantages of many recent theories developed in connection with classification research and subject analysis. The system was developed for automated operations, and could be a great improvement if adopted for the computerized catalog at the Library of Congress. The ideal time for such a change would have been at the inception of the MARC data base. It would then have formed a clear separation between the automated catalog and the manual catalog. However, as it happened, there is a considerable span of time when the card catalog and the MARC data base of the Library of Congress overlap. To adopt the PRECIS system now would create the problem of integration of PRECIS entries into files of records based on the Library of Congress subject headings. If and when it is decided that this is the course that should be taken, experiments should first be carried out to determine its adaptability to catalogs of different types and sizes of libraries, its cost-effectiveness, and its retrieval effectiveness in terms of different kinds of uses and different types of users of the subject catalog.

Another alternative, if Library of Congress subject headings system were to be abandoned, would be to develop a new system *de novo* which will take advantage of modern theory of subject analysis. The cost of such an undertaking will be high or even prohibitive. However, it will have the advantage of having a system developed and applied by the same agency. This coordination has been characteristic of the systems maintained and used at the Library of Congress. It is true of the Library of Congress Classification, the Library of Congress subject headings system, and, in recent years, the Anglo-American cataloging code and the Dewey Decimal Classification.

In the contemplation of the future of *Library of Congress Subject Headings*, one must also bear in mind the usefulness of the system to the many libraries in the country that rely on the Library of Congress for cataloging data. Whatever system adopted by the Library of Congress will unquestionably become the national standard. Many, if not most of the libraries, have no immediate prospect of closing their card catalogs and changing over to computerized catalogs. For these libraries, the need exists for a subject cataloging system which works economically in a manually-operated catalog. It may be a painful but necessary realization that the demands of the Library of Congress's own catalogs and those of other libraries may not be totally compatible. If the consideration were simply that of the Library's own catalogs, the solution would be relatively simple. But if the Library of Congress is to continue to function or to assume greater responsibilities as a national library or bibliographic center, the needs of other libraries must also be weighed in any decisions concerning the future of the subject catalog.

The third course, that of revamping and overhauling the present system, incorporating modern theory of subject analysis, may prove to be viable and probably the most practicable.

In a review of the Library of Congress subject headings system, Angell favors such a course:

> The most reasonable path . . . is considered to be the improvement of the list in its present terms. . . . This course provides the obvious advantages of orderly evolution. It also recognizes the fact that, during the course of its seven decades of growth, the list and the catalogs in which it is embodied have been of substantial service in the library community.[1]

The need of a code has been felt by many for a long time, but very little in terms of concrete achievements has been accomplished. Indeed, if this course is chosen, much work will need to be undertaken. The basic principles must be restated and current practices reconsidered. In the deliberation, the form of the catalog, i.e., computerized catalog or manually-operated catalog such as the card catalog, should be a major consideration. It is quite certain that the Library of Congress will close its card catalogs in the near future and that many large research libraries will follow. However, the fate of the card catalog in smaller, general libraries, which constitute the majority of libraries in this country, is uncertain. If the Library of Congress subject headings system is to continue to serve libraries across the country, the needs of all types of libraries and different forms of the catalog must be a primary consideration in any revamping effort. Following are some areas that warrant close scrutiny.

FUNCTIONS OF THE SUBJECT CATALOG

As discussed earlier, many of the problems in subject cataloging are caused by the fact that the functions of the subject catalog have never been precisely defined. Before one considers the basic principles of the system, some basic questions of function must be answered: What is it that the subject catalog is intended, or expected, to do? What is its true function? These questions must be considered also in view of other available tools for subject retrieval. Duplication of efforts of other readily available tools places a costly but not altogether necessary demand and burden on subject cataloging operations.

Many opinions with regard to the function of the subject catalog have been expressed, but no consensus has been reached. Frarey's comment in 1960 still rings true: "Present subject cataloging theory and practice is based primarily upon tradition and assumption and does not reflect any clear understanding of function or purpose."[2] Such understanding is necessary before we can know "why improvement should be made, for what purposes, and by what means."[3]

THE USER AND USAGE

In order to answer the foregoing questions adequately, a knowledge of who uses the subject catalog and for what purposes is necessary. Frarey's summary of user studies provides an excellent picture of the state-of-the-art up to the early 1950s.[4] Since then, there has been relatively little accomplished in this area. Many of the earlier studies suffered from inadequate or unsophisticated methodology, as Lilley has pointed out.[5] At the present, more sophisticated methodology is available for library use studies. For one thing, as Richmond has pointed out, the computerized catalog itself can serve as an excellent tool for catalog and user studies.[6]

Cutter's basic policy for cataloging is the "convenience of the public." If this policy is to continue to operate, one important requisite will be to define the "public" and to determine its "convenience." So far, it is mostly intuition and assumption on the part of the cataloger as to what a user may or may not need from the subject catalog. It is more projection than actual knowledge.

Another difficult area is "usage." Haykin recognizes this:

> One of the most serious weaknesses of the headings now found in our catalogs is that the terms chosen are not derived from precise knowledge of the approach used by many readers of different backgrounds.[7]

A knowledge of the users and their needs will be most helpful. However, it may be extremely difficult to adhere strictly to the policy of the "convenience of the public," because of the diversity of users and their purposes in using the catalog and the difficulty in delineating an "average" or "typical" user. A possible approach could be a strict reliance on consistency and regularity. Consistency and regularity (i.e., predictability) might then produce a new level of convenience. At least a logical and consistent system can be learned, while a system catering to conflicting demands of different groups may serve very few satisfactorily. This is the viewpoint expressed by Prevost:

No existing general list of subject headings, in its entirety, is a logically thought-out product. All are full of the inconsistencies and conflicting ideas concurrent on just growing. This does not mean that no rules have been made and followed; rather, it means that the rules are inconclusive and, particularly, that they themselves were not disciplined and co-ordinated prior to application, nor was there any intention to make them inflexible.[8]

The user's familiarity with a system of subject analysis enhances retrieval effectiveness. A recent user study conducted by Bates indicates that a user's familiarity with the principles and forms of subject headings improves significantly the chances of matching the user's search terms with those used in the subject headings system.[9] A logically and consistently constructed system is easier to learn and master than one given to irregularities and exceptions to rules.

SPECIFICITY AND PRE-COORDINATION

As discussed in an earlier chapter, specificity is the underlying principle of the alphabetical subject catalog. However, the concept of specificity has not been clearly defined. These questions warrant close attention: How specific is specific? Does specificity mean co-extensivity? The different ways of achieving specificity must be recognized before determining the degree and extent of precision required in each case.

If, as in the PRECIS system, it is found desirable to always attempt co-extensivity between the heading and the document, the system then must allow a greater degree of pre-coordination through synthesis of elements and aspects of subjects. This approach is more in line with modern theory of subject analysis—the concept of faceting and synthesis by allowing more flexible and freer combination of the elements in a heading. There are signs that the Library of Congress system, in recent editions, is moving gradually in that direction. One of the most palpable signs is the use of free-floating subdivisions, pattern headings, and subdivisions under names of places. The use of period and geographic subdivisions is still restricted, but there is no reason why this cannot be changed. One area which is moving rapidly in this direction is subject headings for music. The combination of media of performance according to established citation formulae allows a great degree of synthesis.

Under the current conditions, a move towards free synthesis without a corresponding development of rigorously-defined citation formulae can create chaos. Citation formula(e) governing how and in what order different concepts and elements can be put together to form a heading must be established. This requires an understanding of facet analysis. Facet analysis is the division of a subject into its component parts (facets). Each array of facets consists of parts based on the same characteristic, e.g., language facet, space facet, or time facet. Perhaps the technique developed for the PRECIS system[10] in terms of role operators may be adapted to the Library of Congress subject headings system. Other theories concerning facet analysis and citation order have been developed by the following:[11]

Kaiser: Concrete—Process

Coates: Thing—Material—Action

Ranganathan: PMEST

Vickery: Thing—Part—Constituent—Property—Measure—Patient—
Process/Action/Operation—Agent

Related to the principle of specific entry is the question of direct entry. The problem of direct versus classed entry and inverted entry must be resolved. If it is decided that a certain amount of classed entry and inverted entry is desirable or even inevitable in an alphabetical subject catalog, there should be guidelines as to the kinds and extent of such entries to be allowed in the system.

With regard to criteria for inverting headings, for instance, Angell offers this suggestion:

> A possible test for avoiding unacceptable inversions might be to ask the question: If the second term were used without the first, would the result be accurate, even if imprecise? If the answer is No, the inversion is unacceptable. This gives us ALIMENTARY CANAL without difficulty, and also many phrases beginning with the proper adjective, e.g., BROWNIAN MOVEMENT. Using this question as a test would furnish a ready means of determining whether or not the modifying adjective or noun has removed the generic character of the substantive. If it has, we do not want to invert. If it has not, we may still prefer the inversion.[12]

UNIFORM HEADING

The principle of uniform heading has served very useful purposes, particularly in terms of economy and of bringing works on the same subject together. It reduces the number of entries in a catalog, thereby minimizing congestion and costs. On the other hand, it has also presented problems by limiting access points and by requiring costly changes when updating terminology. Recently, the principle has been gradually relaxed. Examples are the use of "split files" and duplicate or multiple entries. This relaxation is, perhaps, inevitable in many cases. At the present, either a strict adherence or a total abandonment of the principle of uniform heading does not seem to be feasible, as long as *Library of Congress Subject Headings* is still serving as a tool for manual input and retrieval. Some general guidelines are perhaps needed to determine when and to what extent the principle is to be relaxed.

In the consideration of the principle of uniform heading, economy will, as always, play an important role. Nevertheless, economy should not be limited to the cost of the catalogers' time or the library's budget only. The users' time and effort should also be taken into consideration. The use of "split files," for example, is economical for the catalogers, but for the users, it means an extra step in the process of retrieval. The Library of Congress has adopted the rule of "literary warrant." The size of the file generally determines whether total revision of existing entries or the "split files" will be employed. Another factor which may be used as a criterion could be subject matter. In scientific and technological fields, for example, it is not crucial to have new and old materials on the same subject together, because the majority of users in these fields consult recent materials only. "Split files" will affect relatively few users. In humanities and social sciences, on the other hand, retrospective materials are often of equal or even greater value than current literature. In these fields, then, it is more important to keep new and old materials on the same subject together, so "split files" should probably be used more sparingly.

The above discussion assumes that the Library of Congress subject headings system is to continue to serve the manually-operated catalog. In a computerized catalog, the considerations are quite different. Congestion is not likely to be a problem and updating terminology should not require the same amount of effort and time as in a manually-operated catalog. Furthermore, the access points are not limited by the linear (one access point per entry) approach.

In summary, the degree to which the principle of uniform heading is to be maintained, if at all, will to a large extent depend on the forms of catalog the system is to continue to serve.

TERMINOLOGY

In recent years, this is the aspect that has received the severest criticism. Most of the criticism is directed at the obsolescence of many of the terms used in the system. The Library of Congress has responded more readily in the last year or two to the demands for updating terminology. "Split files" is a technique developed for coping with such changes without incurring prohibitive costs.

In addition to the currency of terminology, another aspect is how well the terms used in the subject headings system match the terms most likely consulted by users. One possible solution to this problem is to rely more on the documents being cataloged to generate terms used in the headings. The approach of the PRECIS system is an example of document-generated terminology. Each string of entry is generated from and tailor-made for the document in hand. However, this approach requires a tight control over synonymous terms. The PRECIS system has not been in operation long enough to have accumulated the problems of obsolescent terms as the Library of Congress system has over the years. Nevertheless, attempts should be made to render the system more receptive to terminology which is current and compatible with the literature and other tools of subject analysis. Because the principle of uniform heading places certain restrictions on the free use of current terminology, the two problems should be considered together.

With regard to updating terminology, the problem again assumes a different magnitude in a manually-operated catalog than in an automated catalog. It has been demonstrated that in a computerized system, changing a heading is a single operation if the name or subject authority file is linked to the bibliographic records. With this kind of capability, costs will no longer be such a prohibiting factor in updating terminology as in the past.

FORMS OF HEADINGS

In the Library of Congress subject headings system, phrase headings, headings with qualifiers, and headings with subdivisions have been used for similar functions. A time facet is expressed usually by means of a period subdivision, but sometimes by an adjectival phrase. The space facet, usually represented by a geographic subdivision, can also appear in the form of a [topic] in [place] phrase. The qualifier is most frequently used for distinguishing between homographs, but has also been used in place of a subject subdivision or an inverted adjectival heading (e.g., **Infants (Newborn))**. Syntagmatic relationships are expressed by relational words such as "and," "in," or "as," and sometimes expressed in the form of subdivisions.

It may be helpful to tighten up the use of the different forms of headings for specific purposes. One possibility is to use phrase headings to express compound subjects implying relationships and to use subdivisions to express facets or aspects of a main subject. Guidelines recently established by the Library of Congress which require the use of the subdivided form for geographic aspect in newly formed headings represent a step towards this direction.

One area that should be given some thought is the possibility of adopting a more structured language. Both Cutter and Haykin favor natural language, preferring phrases to headings with subdivisions. Haykin indicates that the subdivided form is resorted to "when no invariable, commonly used and accepted phrase is available with which to express the intended limitation of a subject."[13] PRECIS, on the other hand, is a structured language. The context is preserved, but not necessarily the natural word order. Linking words are usually removed. One primary reason for using natural language is no doubt the "convenience of the public," but a structured language ensures consistency and avoids many of the difficulties involved in the determination of usage and users' habits.

With regard to subdivisions, since a heading may be subdivided by more than one characteristic or facet, and therefore may contain several subdivisions in a string, a consistent citation order will help to preserve the context of the string as well as to ensure consistency. This is particularly important if a greater degree of synthesis suggested earlier is to be allowed. The role operators developed for the PRECIS system are a device for ensuring consistency in the order of elements in a string. Perhaps something similar could be developed for the Library of Congress subject headings system.

One difficulty may be how to distinguish between a compound subject and a single concept. One need not go to the extreme of Kaiser's approach in breaking up "bibliography" into "Books—Description" or Prevost's suggestion of expressing "international relations" in terms of "Nations—Inter-relations." It may be possible to consider adopting something similar to the definition of and method for identifying a "concept" developed for the PRECIS system: "A concept is that part of a subject which fits the definition of a single role operator."[14]

CROSS REFERENCES

There seems to be little question that *see* references connecting synonymous terms are absolutely necessary. The use of upward *see* references from narrow terms not used as headings to broader terms will be affected by the decision concerning precision. Fewer references of this type will be necessary if a larger number of narrow headings are introduced.

With regard to *see also* references, at least two areas must be considered. First, the structure of cross references should be reconsidered. What Cutter calls the syndetic device in the alphabetical subject catalog has great potential. Carried to perfection, it superimposes a classified structure on the alphabetical subject catalog and thereby provides it with the best of both worlds. An ideal structure of this type should be as tightly and logically constructed as a classification system. The mechanism for providing *see also* references from broad to narrow and between related terms is already in the Library of Congress system, except that the current approach seems to be to create cross references on a heading by heading basis, rather than fitting a concept into a classified structure and then determining its relationship to existing headings.

In a study of the syndetic structure of the Library of Congress subject headings system, Sinkankas finds the syndetic structure "to be incomplete; not all subject headings in LC were connected to the structure by any sort of syndetic device."[15] It would require a great effort to ensure that the hierarchy is complete and that there is no missing link or element. One possibility is to link this part of subject headings construction to a classification scheme in order to ensure that references are made from subjects to their subordinate elements and between coordinate subjects. Furthermore, these references, as Lancaster suggests, by cutting across formal hierarchical structures, frequently provide "associations that would not normally be indicated explicitly in a classified schedule,"[16] particularly one based on division by discipline. In this sense, the syndetic device has the potential of combining the advantages of the classificatory structure and the relative index of a classification scheme.

The desirability voiced by many writers concerning upward *see also* references should also be reconsidered. Here, of course, the economic factor also plays an important role. Will the gain justify the cost?

Secondly, the maintenance of references in catalogs of local libraries and their use should be studied. There is very little, if any, data on these aspects of the catalog. In an age when fast cataloging and on-line cataloging are emphasized, and greater reliance is placed on the clerical staff for cataloging work, one rather suspects that, in many libraries, the cross reference structure has fallen by the wayside. The increasing practice of Library of Congress of assigning duplicate entries, i.e., both a general and a specific entry to the same work [see Chapter 10], betrays a suspicion that perhaps many users of Library of Congress cataloging data are not keeping up with the cross references.

Cross references may be used to alleviate some of the problems associated with inverted headings. For example, when the noun in an adjective-noun heading is the generic term and the adjective is the specifying term, a *see also* reference from the generic term to the heading will make a *see* reference from the inverted form unnecessary, e.g.,

Nuclear chemistry
 xx Chemistry
  [*instead of* *x* Chemistry, Nuclear]

In this way, the need for inverted form is considerably reduced.

Before making *see also* references for the catalog of a particular collection, it is generally considered desirable to ensure that there are materials listed under both headings being connected. An alternate procedure would be to make all *see also* references whether or not the library holds any materials on the topic referred *from*. In this way, the *see also* references function as *see* references until such time as materials on the topic referred from are acquired. By such a method the user can be directed to a narrower or coordinate topic, even when the library does not hold materials on the broader topic. Alternate sources can then be located when the most obvious subject is not represented in the catalog.

TOWARDS A CODE FOR SUBJECT HEADINGS

There has never been an official code for the *Library of Congress Subject Headings.* Neither Cutter's rules, which were the only codification of subject headings in a dictionary catalog, nor the Vatican code, has been adopted officially. Haykin's *Guide*, though not a code, has come closest to being regarded as one, and he himself came close to forming such a code, but unfortunately did not complete the task. No really serious effort or attempt has been made since the 1950s, although there is a continuous cry for the need. Perhaps it is because of the tremendous amount of effort and time such a task will entail. Even the forming of the *Anglo-American Cataloging Rules*, which builds upon foundation already laid and represents a culmination of a long process of evolution, requires extremely strenuous and sustained efforts.

However, if and when the profession decides it is finally time to pursue such a task, several unofficial, individual attempts, in addition to those by Cutter, the Vatican Library, and Haykin, may be helpful. These include Prevost's proposal,[17] Metcalfe's "Tentative Code of Rules for Alphabetico-Specific Entry,"[18] of 1959, and Olding's "brief code"[19] of 1961. Each of these has something to offer and should not be ignored.

REFERENCES

[1] Richard S. Angell, "Library of Congress Subject Headings—Review and Forecast," *Subject Retrieval in the Seventies: New Directions: Proceedings of an International Symposium* (edited by Hans (Hanan) Wellisch and Thomas D. Wilson; Westport, Conn.: Greenwood Publishing Company, 1972), p. 161.

[2] Carlyle J. Frarey, *Subject Headings* (The State of the Library Art, vol. 1, part 2; New Brunswick, N.J.: Graduate School of Library Science, Rutgers-The State University, 1960), p. 63.

[3] Ibid., p. 67.

[4] Carlyle J. Frarey, "Studies of Use of the Subject Catalog: Summary and Evaluation," *Subject Analysis of Library Materials* (edited by Maurice F. Tauber; New York: School of Library Service, Columbia University, 1953), pp. 147-65.

[5] Oliver L. Lilley, "Evaluation of the Subject Catalog: Criticisms and a Proposal," *American Documentation* 5:41-60 (April 1954).

[6] Phyllis A. Richmond, "Research Possibilities in the Machine-Readable Catalog: Use of the Catalog to Study Itself," *Journal of Academic Librarianship* 2:224-29 (November 1976).

[7] David Judson Haykin, *Subject Headings: A Practical Guide* (Washington: Government Printing Office, 1951), p. 4.

[8] Marie Louise Prevost, "An Approach to Theory and Method in the Library of Congress Subject Headings," *Library Quarterly* 16:141 (April 1946).

[9] Marcia J. Bates, "Factors Affecting Subject Catalog Search Success," *Journal of the American Society for Information Science* 28:164 (May 1977).

[10] Derek Austin and Jeremy A. Digger, "PRECIS: The Preserved Context Index System," *Library Resources & Technical Services* 21:22 (Winter 1977).

[11] C. D. Needham, *Organizing Knowledge in Libraries: An Introduction to Information Retrieval* (2nd rev. ed.; London: A. Deutsch, 1971), p. 249.

[12] Angell, p. 154.

[13] Haykin, p. 27.

[14] Austin and Digger, p. 21.

[15] George M. Sinkankas, *A Study in the Syndetic Structure of the Library of Congress List of Subject Headings* (Pittsburgh: University of Pittsburgh Graduate School of Library and Information Sciences, 1972), p. 59.

[16] F. W. Lancaster, *Vocabulary Control for Information Retrieval* (Washington: Information Resources Press, 1972), p. 16.

[17] Prevost, pp. 140-51.

[18] John Metcalfe, *Subject Classifying and Indexing of Libraries and Literature* (New York: Scarecrow, 1959), pp. 263-92.

[19] R. K. Olding, "Form of Alphabetico-Specific Subject Headings, and a Brief Code," *Australian Library Journal* 10:127-37 (July 1961).

PART II

APPLICATION

PART II

APPLICATION

INTRODUCTION

Part I of this book contains a discussion of the principles, form, and structure of subject headings, all of which are preliminary to the ultimate purpose of subject headings, i.e., the application of subject headings to library materials. Part II deals with this practical aspect. The discussions that follow are based largely on information published in *Cataloging Service*, consultation with the staff of the Subject Cataloging Division of Library of Congress, and examination of Library of Congress cataloging entries.

Some of the factors contributing to effective subject cataloging are the cataloger's understanding of the nature and structure of subject headings, proper interpretation of the work being cataloged, and his or her ability to coordinate the heading(s) with the work. However, it is extremely difficult to codify the assignment of subject headings in cataloging specific works. For one thing, people read books differently. Frequently, different people reading the same book may acquire different ideas about the book. Sometimes, even the same person reading the same book at different times has different interpretations of the content. Subjective elements inevitably play a role in subject cataloging.

Still another factor which complicates the goal of uniform or consistent subject cataloging is the different degree of analysis and representation. This varies from *summarization* with the aim to express the overall subject content of a document, i.e., to assign a heading co-extensive with what is regarded as *the* subject, to *exhaustive* indexing, or *depth* indexing, which attempts to enumerate all significant concepts or aspects and, frequently, component parts, of a document. The following examples (pages 160-61) show the extremes of these approaches.

In the example shown in Figure 1, the subject heading brings out the overall subject, science. The individual disciplines covered by the schedule are not enumerated. In the example shown in Figure 2 (see page 161), on the other hand, separate headings are assigned to bring out the individual disciplines, e.g., Archaeology, Diplomatics, etc., instead of using the more comprehensive heading of **Classification—Books—Auxiliary sciences of history**.

The difference lies in the depth of analysis in each case. In the majority of Library of Congress cataloging records, the *summarization* approach, i.e., assigning subject headings which summarize the total contents of a work, is used. The example shown in Figure 2 is rather atypical of Library of Congress practice. In libraries where the *summarization* approach is felt to be insufficient, and a more in-depth analysis is desired, additional headings taken either from the printed list

Figure 1

United States.   Library of Congress.   Subject Cataloging Division.
    Classification. Class Q: science.   6th ed.   Washington, Library of Congress; [for sale by the Card Division] 1973.
    vii p., 282 l., 283-415 p.   27 cm. $9.00

    Kept up to date by the Division's L.C. classification—additions and changes, and by an irregular cumulative publication issued by Gale Research Company, entitled Library of Congress classification schedules: a cumulation of additions and changes, Class Q.
    First ed. published in 1905 by the Classification Division.
    Includes index.

(Continued on next card)

72-10222
MARC

72[r76]rev2

United States.   Library of Congress.   Subject Cataloging Division.   Classification ... 1973.   (Card 2)

    1. Classification Books—Science.   2. Classification, Library of Congress. I. Gale Research Company.   II. United States.   Library of Congress.   Classification Division.   Classification. Class Q: science.

Z696.U5Q   1973   025.4'6'5   72-10222
ISBN 0-8444-0075-0   MARC
―― ―――― Copy 3.   Z663.78.C5Q   1975

Library of Congress   72[r76]rev2

or from the work itself may be assigned to bring out individual topics or aspects of the work. Pauline Atherton's Subject Access Project (SAP) developed at Syracuse University is an experiment in augmentation of MARC records by adding subject access points based on words and phrases found within the index and/or table of contents of the work being analyzed.

Figure 2

United States. Library of Congress. Subject Cataloging Division.

Classification. Class C, Auxiliary sciences of history / Subject Cataloging Division, Processing Department, Library of Congress. – 3d ed. – Washington : The Library, 1975
vi, 126 leaves ; 26 cm.
First published in 1915 by the Classification Division.
Includes index.
ISBN 0-8444-0053-X
1. Classification–Books–Archaeology. 2. Classification–Books–Diplomatics. 3. Classification–Books–Archives. 4. Classification–Books–Chronology. 5. Classification–Books–Numismatics. 6. Classification–Books–Heraldry. 7. Classification–Books–Genealogy. 8. Classification–Books–Biography. 9. Classification–Books–Inscriptions. I. United States. Library of Congress. Classification Division. Classification. Class C, Auxiliary sciences of history. II. Title: Auxiliary sciences of history.

Z696.U5C 1975   025.4'6'9   75-619090
——— ———Copy 3.   Z663.78.C5C 1975   MARC

CHAPTER 9

GENERAL GUIDELINES

GENERAL CONSIDERATIONS

In an attempt to achieve some degree of uniformity and consistency in subject cataloging, several general aspects should be considered first.

Number of Headings

While it is difficult, and perhaps not practical, to regulate the number of subject headings to be assigned to each work, economy has been a general guide. For a work dealing with a single topic or concept, the ideal is to assign one heading. However, in most instances, this is not the case. Works dealing with complex subjects usually require more than one heading. Even works dealing with a single subject often require more than one heading.

General vs. Specific

The principle of specific entry requires that a work be assigned the most specific heading which represents exactly the contents of the work. In Cutter's words, assign the heading **Cats** to a work about cats. The question is, whether a more general heading, such as **Domestic animals** should also be assigned, since works about cats are likely to be of interest to users seeking information about domestic animals. On the whole, a general heading and a specific one comprehended within it, e.g., **Mathematics** and **Algebra**, are not assigned to the same body of material. A work about book classification is assigned the heading **Classification—Books**, but not **Library science** as well. However, this policy has been relaxed to some extent in recent years. In some situations, a general heading, sometimes called a generic heading, is assigned in addition to a specific heading to a work on the specific subject. One such policy was begun recently with regard to individual biographies [see Chapter 10].

Analytical Entries

On the other hand, there is the corresponding question of whether a more specific heading than the one which represents the total content of the work should be assigned in addition to the proper heading, e.g., assigning the headings **Cats** and

Siamese cat to a work about cats. The second heading represents a part of the work, and therefore constitutes an analytical entry. Following is an example of assigning a heading (the asterisked heading in the example below) which represents a part of the content of the work:

Title: *Small Gardens Are More Fun*
    *1.   **Landscape gardening.**
     2.   **Gardening.**

In some libraries, the first of the two headings is considered to be unnecessary, because there is a *see also* reference from **Gardening** to **Landscape gardening.**

The subject headings in the example shown in Figure 2 (see page 161) are, in fact, analytical entries, in that each heading represents a part of the book.

Policies concerning analytical entries or entries for partial contents vary from library to library and often depend on the individual case in hand. Subjects of local interest, for example, are often brought out by means of analytical entries. The emphasis on, and space occupied by, the specific topic is also a determining factor.

Duplicate Entries

Exceptions are made to the principle of uniform heading in many instances, particularly in cases where two constituent elements in a heading are of equal significance and it is felt desirable to provide access points to both. In these cases, specific instructions are given in the printed list, e.g.,

    1.   **United States—Relations (military) with Europe.**
    2.   **Europe—Relations (military) with United States.**

SPECIAL CONSIDERATIONS

Allowing different interpretations and approaches to subject cataloging among individual catalogers, the Library of Congress Subject Cataloging Division has certain guidelines concerning assigning appropriate subject headings, in an attempt to achieve the greatest possible degree of uniformity and consistency. Following is a summary and discussion of the guidelines.

Works on a Single Topic

The one heading which represents exactly the contents is assigned to such a work, e.g.,

Title: *Collective Bargaining Reconsidered: The Stamp Memorial Lecture*
    1.   **Collective bargaining—Addresses, essays, lectures.**

Title: *The Geomorphology of the Gippsland Lakes*
1.   Geomorphology—Australia—Gippsland Lakes.

Title: *The World Within the Tide Pool*
1.   Tide pool ecology.

Title: *Les adverbes en chinois moderne*
1.   Chinese language—Adverb.

Title: *The Craft of Making Wine*
1.   Wine and wine making—Amateurs' manuals.

Occasionally, when the most specific heading fitting the work does not exist and it is considered impractical to establish a new heading, the next broader heading is used, e.g.,

Title: *Essays on European Literature*
1.   Literature—Addresses, essays, lectures.

It is assumed that a work on a single topic will normally cover a certain range of subtopics. However, if the work in hand on a single topic also discusses in its range of subtopics a subtopic not normally found in such works, a heading for the special subtopic is assigned in addition to the heading for the main topic, providing the discussion of the special subtopic represents at least twenty percent of the paging of the text, e.g.,

Title: *Forest Types of Pakistan*
1.   Forest ecology—Pakistan.
2.   Forests and forestry—Pakistan.

Title: *Forest Survey Report in Manubar Area (Sangkulirang)*
1.   Forests and forestry—Indonesia—Kalimantan Timur.
2.   Timber—Indonesia—Kalimantan Timur.

Title: *Notes on Planning and Managing Agricultural Operations in West Godavari*
1.   Rice—India—West Godavari.
2.   Agriculture—India—West Godavari—Statistics.

Multi-Topical Works

For a work on more than one topic treated separately, a heading for each topic is assigned, e.g.,

Title: *Bibliography on Snow, Ice and Frozen Ground with Abstracts*
1.   Snow—Bibliography.
2.   Ice—Bibliography.
3.   Frozen ground—Bibliography.

If the various topics treated in the work are generically related (i.e., they are subsumed under the same common generic heading), the following guidelines prevail:

1) For a work treating *two* or *three* related topics, a generic heading, if available, which represents precisely these topics collectively (i.e., no other concepts are comprehended by the heading at the same time) is assigned instead of the two or three separate headings. For example:

Title: *The Distinctive Excellences of Greek and Latin*
1. Classical literature—Addresses, essays, lectures.
   [instead of separate headings for Greek literature and Latin literature]

If such a generic heading does not exist, Library of Congress catalogers are instructed to establish a new heading. If the generic heading includes in its scope not only the two or three topics in question, but others as well, a separate heading for each of the topics is assigned instead of the generic heading. For example, for a work about travels in Brazil, Ecuador, and Peru, three separate headings are used instead of the heading for South America. Further example:

Title: *Crofter-fishermen in Norway and Scotland*
1. Fishermen—Norway.
2. Fishermen—Scotland.

2) For a work treating *four* or *more* related topics, a single generic heading which represents all topics comprehensively is assigned, if one exists or can be established. If such a heading does not exist and cannot be established, separate headings for each topic are used, if there are no more than four. If there are more than four topics, either several very comprehensive headings, or a single heading for form only, e.g., **American essays**, is used.

For works treating several topics in relation to each other, the headings representing the relationships are assigned, e.g., **Fungi in agriculture**; **Radio and literature**; etc. If such headings do not exist, Library of Congress catalogers may establish new headings if the relationship is significant or use separate headings for each topic if the relationship is incidental or trivial.

Multi-Element Works

This type of works differs from multi-topical works in that they treat a single central topic considered from different aspects or containing various elements, e.g.,

Title: *Chemical Plant Management in the United States*
1. Chemical plants—United States—Management.

However, many works treat subjects which are much more complex and there are no pre-coordinated headings. In these cases, Library of Congress often uses two or more headings to bring out each concept individually. Examples:

Title: *Methods of Conducting a Wind Tunnel Investigation of Lift in Roll at Supersonic Speeds of Sweptback Wings*
1. Airplanes—Wings, Sweptback—Testing.
2. Lift (Aerodynamics)
3. Rolling (Aerodynamics)
4. Aerodynamics, Supersonic.
5. Wind tunnels.

Title: *A Method of Setting up the Eigenvalue Problem for the Linear, Shallow-Water Wave Equation for Irregular Bodies of Water with Variable Water Depth and Application to Bays and Harbors in Hawaii*
1. Ocean waves.
2. Wave equation.
3. Eigenvalues.
4. Oceanography—Data processing.
5. Bays—Hawaii.
6. Harbors—Hawaii.

If a work discusses a principle and then illustrates by providing the facts of an individual case in considerable detail, two headings are assigned, the first designating the principle and the second one bringing out the special case.

Viewpoint of Author or Publisher

The author's or publisher's viewpoint is often brought out by the subject heading, particularly concerning the intention regarding readership (juvenile or adult) and the approach (fact or fiction, etc.), e.g.,

Title: *Paraprofessions: Careers of the Future and the Present*
1. Vocational guidance—Juvenile literature.
2. Occupations—Juvenile literature.

Title: *The Shield Ring*
1. Great Britain—History—Norman period, 1066-1154—Juvenile fiction.

In the case of general textbooks intended for special groups of persons, in addition to the heading(s) for the topic(s), a heading indicating the special interest and/or application is assigned, e.g.,

[For a textbook of psychology for nurses]
1. Psychology.
2. Nursing—Psychological aspects.

Topics without Representation in the Subject Headings List

If the topic of the work being cataloged is not represented in the list and, because of various factors such as uncertain terminology, it is impossible to establish it as a valid subject heading, it is the practice of the Library of Congress to assign a more general heading or several related headings, whatever designates most accurately the topic of the work, in view of the various headings available. It is recognized that this is not a satisfactory approach and this procedure is followed only when a more precise or more specific heading is not available.

Title Cataloging

Because titles of works usually state in the words of the author or publisher the subject matter in the work, they are extremely important and often helpful in subject cataloging, in spite of the fact that in a few cases, they may be misleading. In scientific and technical fields, particularly, the term or expression used in the title is likely to be what the user consults. At the Library of Congress, the subject catalogers make use of titles which explicitly state the subject matters of the works in the following ways. The subject content of the work is described using the following methods.

By subject corresponding to the title. The subject heading assigned corresponds directly to the topic designated in the title. In those cases where a similar heading must be assigned instead of the topic occurring in the title because of the special scope or twist of the work, a second heading is assigned to correspond exactly to the topic of the title, e.g.,

> Title: *Computers and the Union*
> 1. **Electronic data processing and industrial relations.**
> 2. **Trade-unions—Great Britain—Data processing.**

By a *see* reference. In some cases, the term or expression used in the title may be made into a *see* reference to the heading actually assigned.

By title added entry. If no other means are available, the title added entry may be used to bring out the exact topic of the work. Lubetzky[1] has criticized this practice and it is recognized at the Library of Congress that this is not the most satisfactory approach, and it is used only as a last resort.

By partial title added entry.* Often the concept of a work can be represented by a word or phrase occurring in its title. In most instances a heading which corresponds to this concept exists or can be established and assigned to the work. Sometimes, however, for new concepts it is impossible or impracticable to establish the concept and a broader heading or headings which represent the concept only

---

Cataloging Service 121:16 (Spring 1977).

approximately must be assigned. Whenever this occurs, the concept can still be made retrievable in the catalog either by the title added entry, or, if the concept is not represented by the first words of the title proper, a partial title added entry. These added entries also allow the cataloger to retrieve the works when the concept can be established as a heading. This practice is discussed below:

1) A partial title added entry is used when the subject heading assigned does not accurately represent the concept of the work and the concept is named in the title proper but does not occur in the initial position. The added entry is not used, however, if the concept is represented by a *see* reference to the heading assigned.

2) The partial title added entry is not assigned unless all possibilities of establishing the concept as a subject heading have been exhausted.

3) The practice applies to titles in all languages. However, it is not followed if the concept has an acceptable subject heading equivalent when it is translated into English.

4) A partial title added entry is traced as "Title:" before any series added entries. Examples:

> Title: *Estimating Manual for Hydraulic Excavators*
> 1. **Excavation—Estimates—United States.**
> 2. **Excavating machinery.**
> I. Title.
> II. Title: Hydraulic excavators.

> Title: *Vom Güternahverkehr zum Regionalverkehr*
> 1. **Freight and freightage—Germany, West—Congresses.**
> I. Puf, Peter-Rüdiger.
> II. Münster. Universität. Institut für Verkehrswissenschaft.
> III. Title: Regionalverkehr.
> IV. Series: Münster. Universität. Institut für Verkehrswissenschaft. Beiträge ; Heft 80.

Author as Subject*

Previously, the Library of Congress had the policy of not assigning to a work a subject heading which matched exactly an author heading (main or added entry). This policy was discontinued in 1972 and current practice is to assign subject headings as required by the work regardless of whether they duplicate the main or added entries for the same work. This policy change affects the following types of works in particular: autobiographies, correspondence, corporate histories and reports, nontopical compilations of general laws, and artistic reproductions with commentary.**

Cataloging Service 106:4-5 (May 1973).

**For discussion and examples see following chapters on specific types of materials and special subject areas.

The discussion above concerns subject cataloging in general. In the Library of Congress subject headings system, several types of materials and special subject areas receive special or unique treatment. These are discussed in the following chapters.

REFERENCES

[1] Seymour Lubetzky, "Titles: Fifth Column of the Catalog," *Library Quarterly* 11:412-30 (1941).

CHAPTER 10

SUBJECT CATALOGING OF SPECIAL TYPES
OF MATERIALS

SERIALS

Subject headings chosen for serial publications, particularly periodicals and journals, are headings which attempt to cover the subject range of the entire publication and not parts or individual issues.

Serial publications on specific topics or places are assigned appropriate topical or geographical headings with form subdivisions which bring out the specific bibliographic forms. The most frequently used form subdivisions for serial publications are:

- –Abstracts–Periodicals
- –Collected works
- –Congresses
- –Directories
- –Indexes
- –Periodicals
- –Societies, etc.
- –Societies, periodicals, etc.
    [under personal name headings]
- –Yearbooks

For appropriate use of these subdivisions, consult the introduction to the eighth edition of *Library of Congress Subject Headings*.

The subdivision –**Periodicals**, in particular, is used widely with serial publications. It is used as a form subdivision under topical or geographical headings or subdivisions, for true serials issued indefinitely at regular intervals. However, it is not used under names of organizations or with publications which are issued regularly in revised form, e.g., *J. K. Lasser's Your Income Tax* (not regarded as a true serial). It may be used as a further subdivision after another form subdivision, e.g.,

Tuberculosis–Statistics–Periodicals

However, by tradition, the subdivision –**Periodicals** is not used under the following form subdivisions:

—Addresses, essays, lectures
—Amateurs' manuals
—Atlases
—Catalogs
—Catalogs and collections
—Collected works
—Congresses
—Directories
—Discography
—Film catalogs
—Gazetteers
—Guide-books
—Handbooks, manuals, etc.
—Juvenile films
—Juvenile literature

—Juvenile phonorecords
—Laboratory manuals
—Maps
—Observers' manuals
—Outlines, syllabi, etc.
—Phonotape catalogs
—Photo maps
—Registers
—Road maps
—Social registers
—Thematic catalogs
—Union lists
—Voting registers
—Yearbooks
—Zoning maps

The subdivision —**Periodicals** is also used with serials which appear annually but do not summarize the year. For serials which do summarize the year, the subdivision —**Yearbooks** is used.

In determining the appropriate subdivisions to be used, the cataloger should not be guided by the wording of the title alone. The actual form and nature of the publication are the basic criteria.

Following are examples of subject cataloging of serials reflecting current Library of Congress practice.

Abstracts

Title: *Current Physics Advance Abstracts: Atoms and Waves*
1.   Atoms—Abstracts—Periodicals.
2.   Matter—Properties—Abstracts—Periodicals.
3.   Physics—Abstracts—Periodicals.

Title: *Current Physics Advance Abstracts: Solid State*
1.   Solid state physics—Abstracts—Periodicals.

Title: *MLA Abstracts of Articles in Scholarly Journals*
(Modern Language Association of America)
1.   Philology—Abstracts—Periodicals.

Almanacs

Title: *Poor Joe's Pennsylvania Farm Almanack*
1.   Almanacs, American.

Title: *Riesengebirgs-Buchkalendar*
1.   Almanacs, German.
2.   Germans in the Krkonoše region, Czechoslovakia and Poland—Periodicals.

Bibliographies

Title: *Bibliographic Guide to Black Studies* (Schomburg Center for Research and Black Culture)
  1.   **Afro-Americans—Bibliography—Catalogs.**
  2.   **Blacks—Bibliography—Catalogs.**
  3.   **Schomburg Center for Research and Black Culture.**

Title: *Technical and Scientific Books in Print*
  1.   **Technology—Bibliography—Catalogs.**
  2.   **Science—Bibliography—Catalogs.**

Title: *The Psychological Reader's Guide*
  1.   **Psychology—Bibliography—Periodicals.**

Title: *Asian Developments: A Bibliography*
  1.   **Asia—Bibliography—Periodicals.**

Biographical Reference Works

Title: *Community Leaders of America.* annual
  1.   **United States—Biography.**

Title: *Who's Who in Finance*
  1.   **Capitalists and financiers—Great Britain—Registers.**

Book and Media Reviews

Title: *The Library Journal Book Review*
  1.   **Books—Reviews—Periodicals.**

Title: *Book Review Digest*
  1.   **Books—Reviews—Periodicals.**
  2.   **Bibliography—Periodicals.**

Title: *Litteris: An International Critical Review of the Humanities*
  1.   **Humanities—Bibliography—Periodicals.**
  2.   **Books—Reviews—Periodicals.**

Title: *Filmfacts*
  1.   **Moving-pictures—Reviews—Periodicals.**

Catalogs

Title: *"Austria" Netto-Katalog*
1.   **Postage-stamps—Europe—Catalogs.**

Title: *Catalogo nazionale Bolaffi della grafica*
1.   **Prints, Italian—Catalogs.**

Title: *Bale Catalogue of Israel*
1.   **Postage-stamps—Israel—Catalogs.**

Conferences, Congresses, Symposia, etc.

Topical headings with the subdivision —**Congresses** are used with this type of publication. When the collected papers of a congress are offered in a condensed form, the subdivision —**Congresses** alone is used, not —**Congresses—Abstracts.** The subdivision —**Addresses, essays, lectures** is used, instead of —**Congresses,** for one or several lectures, originally delivered on the occasion of an individual congress, but later published under separate cover, and no longer strictly identifiable with the original congress.

Title: *Summary Record of Proceedings* (annual Premiers' Conference)
1.   **Canada—Economic conditions—1945-   —Congresses.**
2.   **Canada—Politics and government—1945-   —Congresses.**

Title: *Proceedings. 1961/62-*   (Boston Colloquium for the Philosophy of Science)
1.   **Science—Philosophy—Congresses.**

Title: *Proceedings, Annual Meeting* (Western Dry Kiln Clubs)
1.   **Lumber—Drying—Congresses.**

Directories

Title: *Blackbook*
1.   **Afro-Americans as businessmen—Directories.**
2.   **Chicago metropolitan area—Commerce—Directories.**

Title: *The Physiotherapists Register*
1.   **Physical therapists—Great Britain—Directories.**

Title: *American Dental Directory*
1.   **Dentists—United States—Directories.**

Title: *Catalog of Speedways: United States and Canada*
1.   **Automobile racing—United States—Directories.**
2.   **Automobile racing—Canada—Directories.**

(Examples continue on page 174.)

Title: *Directory with Who's Who in Liberia*
   1.   **Liberia—Directories.**
   2.   **Liberia—Biography.**

Title: *Official Directory, Licensed Contractors of California*
   1.   **Contractors—California—Directories.**

Title: *Europ Production*
   1.   **Europe—Manufactures—Directories.**

Title: *Adressbuch der Stadt Neviges*
   1.   **Neviges, Ger.—Directories.**

Government Publications

Library of Congress practice seems to vary from title to title. No pattern is apparent.

Title: *Annual Report* (Honolulu. Liquor Commission)
   1.   **Liquor problem—Hawaii—Honolulu—Periodicals.**

Title: *Annual Report* (Natal Provincial Library Service and Museum Services)
   1.   **Libraries—South Africa—Natal—Periodicals.**
   2.   **Natal Provincial Library Service.**

Title: *Annual Report of Treasurer of the State of Colorado*
   1.   **Finance, Public—Colorado.**

Title: *Annual Report* (Philippines (Republic). Dept. of Social Welfare)
   1.   **Public welfare—Philippine Islands.**

Title: *Administration Report* (Assam. State Electricity Board)
   1.   **Electric utilities—Assam.**

Title: *Informe de labores* (Mexico. Secretaría de Obras Públicas)
   1.   **Mexico—Public works.**

Title: *Program Budget for the City of Washington, D. C.*
      (District of Columbia. Commissioner)
   1.   **Program budgeting—Washington, D. C.**
   2.   **Budget—Washington, D. C.**

Title: *Milwaukee Water Works* (Milwaukee. Superintendent of
Water Works)
    1.   **Milwaukee—Water-supply—Collected works.**

Title: *Air Carrier Operations in Canada* (Canada. Aviation
Statistics Centre). quarterly
    1.   **Aeronautics, Commercial—Canada—Statistics—Periodicals.**

Handbooks

Title: *Michigan Manual*
    1.   **Michigan—Politics and government, 1951-**   **—Handbooks,**
manuals, etc.

Indexes

The use of the subdivision —**Bibliography**—**Indexes** either under topical subjects or under names of individual corporate bodies is not authorized. For any bibliography which is indexed in sufficient detail as to be usable also as an index to the subject field, the subdivision —**Indexes** rather than —**Bibliography** is used.

For indexes to the publications of an individual corporate body, the subdivision —**Bibliography** (instead of —**Indexes**) without further subdivision under the name of the corporate body is used.

For indexes to collections of objects (paintings, films, postage stamps, farm machinery, etc.) a heading under the name of the object with the subdivision —**Catalogs** is assigned.

Title: *Quarterly Bibliography of Computers and Data Processing*
    1.   **Electronic data processing—Indexes—Periodicals.**
    2.   **Electronic digital computers—Indexes—Periodicals.**

Title: *Indian Geological Index*
    1.   **Geology—India—Indexes—Periodicals.**

Title: *Oceanic Abstracts with Indexes*
    1.   **Oceanography—Abstracts—Periodicals.**
    2.   **Marine biology—Abstracts—Periodicals.**
    3.   **Ocean engineering—Abstracts—Periodicals.**
    4.   **Oceanography—Indexes—Periodicals.**
    5.   **Marine biology—Indexes—Periodicals.**
    6.   **Ocean engineering—Indexes—Periodicals.**

Title: *Elenchus Bibliographicus Biblicus*
    1.   **Bible—Periodicals—Indexes.**

(Examples continue on page 176.)

Title: *Readers' Guide to Periodical Literature*
    1.   Periodicals—Indexes.

Title: *An Index to Book Reviews in the Humanities*
    1.   Books—Reviews—Indexes.
    2.   Humanities—Book reviews—Indexes.

Title: *Index to IEEE Periodicals*
    1.   Institute of Electrical and Electronics Engineers—
       Bibliography.

Irregular Serial Publications, Each Issue of Which Consists of Papers Written by Various Authors

A topical heading subdivided by —**Collected works** is assigned.

Title: *Microbiologia*
    1.   Microbiology—Collected works.

Lists of Dissertations and Theses (See discussion on page 182.)

Monographic Series

Title: *Smithsonian Contributions to Zoology*
    1.   Zoology—Collected works.

Title: *Studies in Pre-Columbian Art and Archaeology*
    1.   America—Antiquities—Collected works.
    2.   Indians—Antiquities—Collected works.
    3.   Indians—Art—Collected works.

Periodicals

Periodicals which cover very broad or general subjects are not assigned subject headings. Headings such as **American periodicals** are topical headings and not form headings. In other words, the heading **American periodicals** is assigned to a work about American periodicals, but not used with periodicals such as **Saturday Evening Post** or **Atlantic Monthly**.

Title: *The Smith*
    [no subject heading]

Title: *Dialogo*
    [no subject heading]

Title: *Yesterday*
1. United States—Social life and customs—Periodicals.
2. United States—History—Periodicals.

Title: *Colonial Annapolis*
1. Annapolis—Periodicals.

Title: *Music Canada*
1. Music, Popular (Songs, etc.)—Canada—Periodicals.

Title: *The Journal* (Academy of Parish Clergy)
1. Pastoral theology—Periodicals.

Title: *Hong Kong Law Journal*
1. Law—Periodicals—Hong Kong.

Title: *Umschau Jahrbuch*
1. Science—Periodicals.
2. Technology—Periodicals.

Society Publications

For detailed instruction, consult page lxv in the introduction to the eighth edition of *Library of Congress Subject Headings*. (See also discussion on pages 204-209 on works about corporate bodies.) Example:

Title: *Annual Report* (Academy of Time)
1. Horology—Periodicals.
2. Academy of Time.

Society Publications Devoted to One Person

Title: *The London Collector*
1. London, Jack, 1876-1916—Societies, periodicals, etc.

Statistics

Title: *Encuesta anual de restaurantes, hoteles y servicios*
(Instituto Nacional de Estadística (Ecuador)).
1. Service industries—Ecuador—Statistics—Periodicals.
2. Restaurants, lunch rooms, etc.—Ecuador—Statistics—Periodicals.
3. Hotels, taverns, etc.—Ecuador—Statistics—Periodicals.

(Examples continue on page 178.)

Title: *Scottish Abstract of Statistics*
1. Scotland—Statistics—Periodicals.

Title: *Encuesta anual de recursos y atenciones de salud*
1. Health facilities—Ecuador—Statistics—Periodicals.
2. Ecuador—Statistics, Medical—Periodicals.

Union Lists

Title: *Catálogo coletivo de periódicos do Estado de São Paulo*
1. Periodicals—Bibliography—Union lists.
2. Catalogs, Union—Brazil—São Paulo.

Title: *Union List of Serials in New Jersey*
1. Periodicals—Bibliography—Union lists.
2. Libraries—New Jersey.

Yearbooks

Title: *Jahrbuch der österreichischen Byzantinistik*
1. Byzantine studies—Yearbooks.

Title: *Year Book* (Freight Transport Association)
1. Transportation, Automotive—Great Britain—Freight—Yearbooks.

Title: *Current British Foreign Policy*
1. Great Britain—Foreign relations—1945-   —Yearbooks.

REFERENCE BOOKS

When the heading **Reference books** subdivided by a special topic is used, a second heading in the form of [topic]—**Bibliography** is always assigned in addition, e.g.,

1. Reference books—Chemistry.
2. Chemistry—Bibliography.*

---

*This represents a recent change in policy. Previously, only the first heading was assigned with a *see also* reference from the second heading.

Dictionaries

In addition to the instruction provided in the introduction to the eighth edition of the subject headings list, the following also pertains to treatment of dictionaries:

Alternative subdivisions. The subdivision —**Dictionaries** is the standard subdivision for the concept of dictionaries. However, many other subdivisions are in use which designate special categories of dictionaries, or dictionary-like materials. These are listed below. For definitions, see the introduction to the eighth edition (pages xix-lxviii).

—Abbreviations	—Glossaries, vocabularies, etc.
—Acronyms	—Language—Glossaries, etc.
—Concordances	—Language (New words, slang, etc.)
—Dictionaries, Juvenile	—Nomenclature
—Dictionaries and encyclopedias	—Registers
—Dictionaries, indexes, etc.	—Slang
—Directories	—Terminology
—Gazetteers	—Terms and phrases

Further subdivision by language. The subdivision —**Dictionaries** is further subdivided by language, e.g.,

Science—Dictionaries—German.

None of the subdivisions listed above except —**Dictionaries** receives this treatment.

The subject heading [subject]—**Dictionaries** is always further subdivided by language of the dictionary, except when the language is English, e.g.,

Science—Dictionaries.
not Science—Dictionaries—English.

Bilingual subject dictionary. For a subject dictionary which gives the terms of language A in terms of language B, two headings are used:

1. [subject]—Dictionaries—[language A]
2. [language A]—Dictionaries—[language B]

e.g.,

Title: *Norsk-engelsk Ordliste for Fiskarar*
1. **Fisheries—Dictionaries—Norwegian.**
2. **Norwegian language—Dictionaries—English.**

If language B is also given in terms of language A, two additional headings are assigned:

    3.   [subject]−Dictionaries−[language B]
    4.   [language B]−Dictionaries−[language A]
e.g.,

Title: *Dictionnaire jurisdique français-néerlandais*
    1.   Law−Dictionaries−French.
    2.   French language−Dictionaries−Dutch.
    3.   Law−Dictionaries−Dutch.
    4.   Dutch language−Dictionaries−French.

Polyglot subject dictionary. For a polyglot dictionary giving for three or more languages the equivalent terms in one language (i.e., language A, B, C, etc., into language Z), the following headings are assigned:

    1.   [subject]−Dictionaries−Polyglot.
    2.   Dictionaries, Polyglot.
e.g.,

Title: *Dictionnaire gastronomique: 6 langues*
    1.   Food−Dictionaries−Polyglot.
    2.   Dictionaries, Polyglot.

Biographical dictionaries. The subdivision −**Dictionaries** is not used in the case of biographical dictionaries. That is, a biographical heading is not further subdivided (e.g., [**class of persons, organization, place, etc.**]−**Biography**) by the subdivision −**Dictionaries**. For example:

Title: *Who's Who in America*
    1.   **United States−Biography.**
          [*not* United States−Biography−Dictionaries]

Bibliographies*

    A recent Library of Congress policy requires that whenever one of the following types of headings is assigned to a work, a duplicate entry will be made under [**topic**]−**Bibliography.**

        Bibliography−Bibliography−[topic]
        Bibliography−Best books−[topic]
        Reference books−[topic]

---

*Cf. *Cataloging Service* 118:10-11 (Summer 1976).

Examples:

1. Bibliography—Bibliography—Outdoor recreation.
2. Outdoor recreation—Bibliography.

1. Bibliography—Best books—Economics.
2. Economics—Bibliography.

1. Reference books—Chemistry.
2. Chemistry—Bibliography.

Imprints*

The form subdivision —Imprints under names of particular regions, countries, cities, etc., is used for lists of works published in a particular place without consideration as to the language in which they were published, e.g.,

United States—Imprints.

A phrase heading [language] imprints is used for a list of works published in a particular language. The heading may be subdivided to bring out the place of origin, e.g.,

English imprints—India.

As a general rule, only the heading [place]—Imprints is assigned in the case of a list of works published in a place where a single language is predominant. In other words, the heading English imprints—United States is not necessary for the first example listed above.

The phrase heading [language] imprints subdivided by place is always accompanied by a second heading [place]—imprints to designate the imprints of the place without regard to language, e.g.,

Title: *Books from Pakistan Published During the Decade of Reforms, 1958-1968*
1. English imprints—Pakistan.
2. Pakistan—Imprints.

For catalogs listing imprints existing at designated localities or available from specified sources, the subdivision —Catalogs is added to the headings discussed above, e.g., for a work listing a library's special collection of books published in India in English,

1. English imprints—India—Catalogs.
2. India—Imprints—Catalogs.

Note that in both headings, the place name (i.e., India) refers to place of origin.

---

*Cf. *Cataloging Service* 118:10-11 (Summer 1976).

The subdivision —**Bibliography** is not used to further subdivide the imprint phrase heading or the subdivision —**Imprints** because these headings already imply "list of publications."

Lists of Theses and Dissertations*

The following types of headings are used with lists of theses and dissertations:

1.   [topic]—**Bibliography.**
2.   [institution]—**Dissertations.**
3.   **Dissertations, Academic—[country]****—**Bibliography.**

Tracing 3 is assigned to all lists of theses and dissertations. If the list is limited to a specific subject, tracings 1 and 3 are used, e.g.,

Title: *Doctoral research on Russia and the Soviet Union, 1960-1975*
1.   **Russia—Bibliography.**
2.   **Dissertations, Academic—Bibliography.**

Title: *Doctoral dissertations in history*
1.   **History—Bibliography.**
2.   **Dissertations, Academic—United States—Bibliography.**

If the list is limited to an institution, tracings 2 and 3 are used, e.g.,

Title: *Master's theses accepted at Louisiana Polytechnic Institute*
1.   **Louisiana Polytechnic Institute, Ruston—Dissertations.**
2.   **Dissertations, Academic—United States—Bibliography.**

If the list is limited to a specific subject and a particular institution, all three are assigned, e.g.,

Title: *University of Idaho theses in language & literature*
1.   **Philology, Modern—Bibliography.**
2.   **Idaho. University—Dissertations.**
3.   **Dissertations, Academic—United States—Bibliography.**

Catalogs

The subdivision —**Catalogs** is used under topical headings for listings of merchandise, art objects, manufactures, publications, collectors' items, technical equipment, etc., which are available or are located at particular places or occur on

---

*Cf. *Cataloging Service* 123:13 (Fall 1977).

**The local subdivision is on the level of the country or larger geographic units even when a particular institution is involved.

a particular market, often systematically arranged with descriptive details, prices, etc., e.g.,

>   Automobiles–Catalogs.
>   Manuscripts–Catalogs.
>   Art objects–Catalogs.
>   Food service–Equipment and supplies–Catalogs.

Whenever applicable, an additional subject entry is made under the name of the society or institution from which the objects listed are available or at which they are located. This heading is not further subdivided by –Catalogs.

>   1.   [name of objects] –Catalogs.
>   2.   [name of individual society or institution]

If the catalogs represent a named collection or a part thereof, an additional heading under the name of the collection (without the subdivisions –Catalogs) is assigned, e.g.,

>   1.   Stone implements–Africa–Catalogs.
>   2.   [name of owner] –Archaeological collections.

Exceptions and/or special situations.
1) Exhibitions.* For catalogs of exhibitions, the subdivision –**Exhibitions** instead of –**Catalogs** is used under the name of the objects. Because of the temporary nature of the display, an additional subject entry is not made under the name of the institution where the exhibition was held (unless the items on display are a permanent part of the institution's collection, in which case the secondary entry is made), e.g.,

>   Title: *Paper in Prints* [exhibition held at the National Gallery of
>   Art, May 1-July 4, 1977]
>   1.   **Paper–Exhibitions.**
>   2.   **Prints–Exhibitions.**

>   Title: Los Angeles Art Association. *Loan Exhibition of International
>   Art, October 15 to December 15, 1937.*
>   1.   **Art–Exhibitions.**

2) Natural objects and musical items. The subdivision –**Catalogs and collections** instead of –**Catalogs** is used, e.g.,

>   Title: *Directory of Coleoptera Collections*
>   1.   **Beetles–Catalogs and collections.**

>   Title: *Univers du pianoforte*
>   1.   **Pianos–Catalogs and collections.**

---

*For further discussion of art exhibitions, see Chapter 11.

3) Library catalogs on specific subjects. Two headings are assigned as follows:

    1.   [subject]—Bibliography—Catalogs.
    2.   [name of institution]

Example:

    1.   **Engineering—Bibliography—Catalogs.**
    2.   **Centro Argentino de Ingenieros, Buenos Aires. Biblioteca.**

Tracing 1 becomes the following if the catalog is limited to periodicals:

    1.   [subject]—Periodicals—Bibliography—Catalogs.

e.g.,

Title: New York (City). Engineering Societies Library.
    Periodicals Currently Received as of September 30, 1971.
    1.   **Technology—Periodicals—Bibliography—Catalogs.**
    2.   **New York (City). Engineering Societies Library.**

In the case of union catalogs, the following is used:

    [subject]—Bibliography—Union lists.

e.g.,

Title: *A Catalogue of Pamphlets on Economic Subjects Published*
    between 1750 and 1900 and Now Housed in Irish Libraries
    1.   **Economics—Bibliography—Union lists.**
    2.   **Libraries—Ireland.**

For union catalogs of periodicals, the following is used:

    [subject]—Periodicals—Bibliography—Union lists.

e.g.,

Title: *Utenlandske Periodika i Norge: Biologi*
    1.   **Biology—Periodicals—Bibliography—Union lists.**

4) Catalogs of audiovisual materials. Tracing 1 takes the following form for catalogs of AV materials (all forms treated collectively) on a particular subject:

    1.   [subject]—Audio-visual aids—Catalogs.

or

    1.   [subject]—Study and teaching—Audio-visual aids—Catalogs.

For works which list only one form of audio-visual aids, e.g., films, the subdivision appropriate for that form is used:

    [subject]—Discography.
    [subject]—Film catalogs.
    [subject]—Phonotape catalogs.
    [subject]—Video tape catalogs.

Example:

Title: *Instructional Aids in Industrial Education*
    1.   **Industrial arts—Study and teaching—Audio-visual aids—Catalogs.**
    2.   **Technology—Film catalogs.**

5) Publishers' catalogs. The following headings are assigned to a catalog of books issued by an individual publishing house:

    1.   **[name of publishing house]**
    2.   **Catalogs, Publishers'—[country]**
    3.   **[country]—Imprints—Catalogs.**

If the catalog is limited to a special topic, an additional heading is assigned:

    4.   **[topic]—Bibliography—Catalogs.**

CHILDREN'S MATERIALS

In 1965, the Library of Congress initiated the Annotated Card Program for children's materials. The purpose of the program was to provide more appropriate and in-depth subject cataloging of juvenile titles through more liberal application of subject headings and through the use of headings more appropriate to juvenile users. In some cases, existing Library of Congress subject headings must be reinterpreted or modified in order to achieve these purposes. In other cases, new headings have to be created. As a result, a list of over three hundred headings which represent exceptions to the master Library of Congress list has been compiled. This list was first issued as a separate publication entitled *Subject Headings for Children's Literature*. Beginning with the eighth edition of *Library of Congress Subject Headings*, this list has been published both as a part of the master list and as a separate publication and is kept up to date by means of additions published in the front of each issue of *Supplement to LC Subject Headings*.

The term "annotated card" came from the practice of providing a summary of the content of the work in a note. In subject cataloging, two sets of headings are assigned: the regular headings and headings for children's literature. The juvenile headings which may or may not differ from the regular headings are enclosed in brackets on Library of Congress cataloging records, e.g.,

Title: *Machines*
    1.   **Machinery—Juvenile liteature. [1. Machinery]**

Title: *Tom Brown's Schooldays*
    [1. School stories. 2. England—Fiction]

Title: *China*
    1.   **China—History.**
    [1. China—History]

(Examples continue on page 186.)

Title: *Rainbows, Clouds, and Foggy Dew*
    1.   Meteorology—Juvenile literature.
    [1.   Weather]

Title: *Bike-ways (101 things to do with a bike)*
    1.   Cycling—Juvenile literature.
    [1.   Bicycles and bicycling]

Title: *Grandma Didn't Wave Back*
    [1.   Grandmothers—Fiction.
    2.   Old age—Fiction]

Title: *Anna (Anna Khlebnikova de Poltoratzky, 1770-1840)*
    1.   Khlebnikova de Poltoratzky, Anna, 1770-1840—Juvenile fiction.
    [1.   Russia—Fiction.
    2.   Family life—Russia—Fiction]

For fiction, in particular, the use of topical headings subdivided by the subdivision —**Fiction** is more liberal on annotated cards than on regular cataloging records.

For treatment of nonbook materials for children, see discussion following.

NONBOOK MATERIALS

Subject cataloging of nonbook materials, like descriptive cataloging, is still in the process of development. A subcommittee of the American Library Association is currently engaged in the task of drafting proposed guidelines for subject cataloging of nonbook materials.

In current Library of Congress practice, the same types and forms of headings are assigned to works on the same subject whether they are in book form or not. Medium designators are not used as form subdivisions, except in the case of —**Juvenile films** and —**Juvenile phonorecords**. These are free-floating subdivisions used with headings assigned to juvenile films and sound recordings.* Following are examples of subject cataloging of nonbook materials:

Seeing the Soviet Union: Industry and Commerce. [Filmstrip]
    1.   **Russia—Economic conditions—1965-**

Self-Fulfillment: Becoming the Person You Want to Be. [Slide set]
    1.   **Self-realization.**

Shaping News for the Consumer. [Motion picture]
    1.   **Television broadcasting of news.**
    2.   **Journalism.**

The Art of Selling. [Transparencies]
    1.   **Selling.**

---

*Exception: The subdivision —**Juvenile phonorecords** is not used with music headings. For examples of subject cataloging of musical sound recordings, see Chapter 11.

The Art of China. Part 1: The Art of Realism. [Filmstrip]
    1.   Art, Chinese.
    2.   Realism in art—China.

Lee and Grant at Appomattox. [Sound recording]
    1.   **Appomattox Campaign, 1865—Drama.**

Machines Change Clothing. [Filmstrip]
    1.   Clothing trade—Juvenile films.
    [1.   Clothing trade]

Folk Tales and Legends from Great Britain. [Sound recording]
    1.   Tales, English—Juvenile phonorecords.
    [1.   Folklore—Great Britain]

The main difference between subject cataloging of book form materials and nonbook materials is probably in the more liberal use of subject headings for the latter, partly because nonbook materials cannot be browsed by users and therefore greater reliance is placed on the subject catalog to bring out the subject content of the materials. Analytical, or partial content, subject entries are used more frequently with nonbook materials.

For films particularly, Library of Congress catalogers follow certain guidelines which are summarized below.

Films*

Fiction films. Nontopical films, such as feature films, are not assigned form headings such as **Comedy films; Horror films; Western films.** Nor are entries provided under headings for special formats, e.g., telefeatures, motion picture features, trailers, short features; or for special techniques, e.g., animated, silent.

Topical headings subdivided by the subdivision —**Drama** are assigned to those individual films in this category which are on particular identifiable subjects in the same manner that dramas in book form are treated, e.g., **Baseball--Drama; World War, 1939-1945—Drama; Merlin—Drama.** It should be noted that the form subdivision —**Drama** is used only in connection with fiction films, with the connotation of "dramatization of"; it does not apply to topical films such as documentary films in order to bring out the medium.

Topical films. At least one subject heading is assigned to each topical film. With the exception of juvenile films, form subdivision is not added to the heading to indicate that the piece in hand is a film.

In general, the rules governing the assignment of subject headings to books also apply to films. However, because of the virtual impossibility of browsing through the film collection, users rely heavily on the subject catalog for the retrieval of films on a given topic, the Library of Congress often provides fuller information

---

*For the definition of a film, see Appendix A.

concerning the subject content of the films. The special treatments accorded films are described below:

1) *All* important topics mentioned in the summary statement on the cataloging record receive a subject entry. In particular, if one specific topic is especially emphasized in the summary in order to illustrate a more general concept, both the specific topic and the general concept are assigned subject headings.

Examples:

Film on the highlights of Colombia, with much footage on coffee production.
1. **Colombia—Description and travel.**
2. **Coffee—Colombia.**

Film on the industries of India, with emphasis on the steel industry.
1. **India—Industries.**
2. **Steel industry and trade—India.**

Film documenting the intellectual expansion in Medieval Germany, as illustrated by the Nuremberg chronicle.
1. **Schedel, Hartmann, 1440-1514. Liber cronicarum.**
2. **Germany—Intellectual life—History.**

2) If a geographic region and a special topic are described, subject entries under both the region and the topic are provided.

Examples:

Film on the oases of the Sahara.
1. **Oases.**
2. **Sahara—Description and travel.**

Film on the program in New York City to solve the drug abuse problem.
1. **Drug abuse—New York (City).**
2. **New York (City)—Social conditions.**

3) If a film uses a particular person as a representative of a particular profession in order to describe the profession, entries are made under both the name of the individual and the professional activity (such films will normally not be regarded as biographies).

Examples:

Film on a day in the life of the matador Jaime Bravo.
1. **Bravo, Jaime.**
2. **Bull-fighting.**

Film on how Paul Taylor, an exponent of modern dance, functions as a performer.
1. **Taylor, Paul, 1930-**
2. **Modern dance.**

4) Commercial for particular brands of products are assigned subject heading under the product (generic name). If the particular type of commercial is identified, e.g., TV commercial, an entry is also made for the type.

Examples:

Film for television which advertises American Airlines.
1. **American Airlines, Inc.**
2. **Television advertising.**

Film for television which advertises Bayer aspirin.
1. **Aspirin.**
2. **Television advertising.**

5) Experimental films normally require no additional heading beyond the one heading, **Experimental films.**

Example:

Experimental film which pictures a drunken teenage party, the participants of which show expressions of desire and frustration.
1. **Experimental films.**

Juvenile films. A juvenile film is defined as a film intended for persons through the age of fifteen. To any subject heading assigned to a juvenile film the subdivision —**Juvenile films** is added in the same manner as —**Juvenile literature,** etc., for book form materials, e.g.,

Astronomy—Juvenile films.

This subdivision is free-floating.

The subdivision —**Juvenile films** is used instead of the subdivision —**Drama** for juvenile fiction films on particular subjects, e.g.,

Adult film:	**Washington, George, Pres. U.S., 1732-1799—Drama.**
Juvenile film:	**Washington, George, Pres. U.S., 1732-1799—Juvenile films.**

In addition to the normal Library of Congress subject headings indicated above, all juvenile films, both topical and nontopical, are assigned bracketed children's literature subject headings in the same manner as for juvenile books, e.g.,

Shapes and Surfaces. [Filmstrip]
1. **Science—Study and teaching (Primary)—Juvenile films.**
2. **Individualized instruction—Juvenile films.**
3. **Form perception—Juvenile films.**
4. **Space perception—Juvenile films.**
[1. **Science.**
2. **Form perception.**
3. **Space perception.**
4. **Size and shape**]

Special juvenile films.

1) Folk tales. A subject entry is made, whenever possible, under names of individual heroes and figures around whom series of tales or legends have been told. Examples: Paul Bunyan, Steamboat Bill, Old Stormalong, etc. In addition, an entry is made for the form, even in the case of individual tales, e.g., **Tales, American— Juvenile films.**

2) Juvenile reading films. Subject entry is made not only under the topic of the film, if one exists, but also for the form. The normal heading for the latter entry is **Reading** (the subject headings **Readers** or **Primers** will not be used in connection with films).

Example:

Reading readiness film for primary grades on the subject of the rain.

    1.   **Rain and rainfall—Juvenile films.**
    2.   **Reading readiness—Juvenile films.**
    3.   **Reading (Primary)—Juvenile films.**

BIOGRAPHY*

Definition

For the purpose of cataloging, biography has been defined as the special genre of works consisting of life histories of individuals, including those written by the individuals themselves, i.e., autobiographies.

Individual biography refers to a work devoted solely to the life of a single individual. *Collective biography* refers to a work which consists of two or more life histories. A *complete biography* covers the entire life story of an individual, while a *partial biography* presents only certain details of the person's life.

A work is regarded as a *true* biography if it makes a serious attempt to present *personal* details of the life of an individual. A work on other topics but containing chance facts about an individual's life is not considered a true biography. In general, a work with less than 20 percent biographical details is not treated as true biography at the Library of Congress. In other words, many partial biographies are excluded. For example, a work which discusses a person's contributions to his profession (i.e., the books he authored, the works of art he created, his or her philosophy or theory, the movement he led, foreign policy, his scientific discovery, etc.), his dwelling places, the museums established in his honor, his art collections and other personal property, his contemporaries, the times in which he lived, and similar externals, without presenting personal facts of his life and lending them importance in the work is not regarded as a true biography.

Personal details include early years, education, marriage, personal habits and personality, career, travels, personal experiences and tragedies, last years and death, etc.

---

*Cf. *Cataloging Service* 106:4-5 (May 1973); 115:26-27 (Fall 1975); 117:12 (Spring 1976); 119:19-22 (Fall 1976); 123:12-13 (Fall 1977). Most of the examples used in this discussion represent recent policy changes which are often not reflected on entries for previously cataloged works.

Subdivisions Which Designate Biography

The subdivisions listed below are used by the Library of Congress to designate biography. These are used with main headings denoting class of persons, disciplines, organizations, ethnic groups, places, and events. Subdivisions used under names of individuals are listed in Appendix D. For special meanings and uses of the listed subdivisions, consult the introduction (pages xviii-lxxii) to the eighth edition of the Library of Congress subject headings list. All subdivisions listed below are free-floating.

SUBDIVISIONS WHICH DESIGNATE BIOGRAPHY						
Subdivisions	Class of Persons	Disci-plines	Organi-zations	Ethnic Groups	Place	Events, wars
Anecdotes						X
Anecdotes, facetiae, satire, etc.	X	X				
Bio-bibliography		X				
Biography (1)	X	X	X	X	X	X
Biography--Anecdotes, facetiae, satire, etc.					X	
Biography--Portraits					X	
Correspondence (2)	X					
Genealogy	X			X	X	
Iconography	X					
Interviews	X	X		X		
Personal narratives (3)						X
Portraits	X			X		X

1) —**Biography.** This subdivision is used as the generic subdivision for the concept of biography, designating not only individual and collective biography, but also autobiography, personal reminiscences and personal narratives. It is used under the pertinent class of persons rather than the corresponding field or discipline, if a choice is possible.

This subdivision is a free-floater under names of special diseases for works classed in medicine for biographical accounts of particular diseases, but is never used under the heading for the patients of specific diseases, e.g., **Cancer—Biography,** not "Cancer patients—Biography."

The subdivision —**Biography** is not to be further subdivided by —**Dictionaries.**

2) —**Correspondence.** The subdivision —**Correspondence, reminiscences, etc.,** formerly used under classes of professional persons, is now obsolete. Instead, one or both of the following is used:

[class of persons]—**Biography**
[class of persons]—**Correspondence**

The subdivision −**Biography** is used, in addition to its other meanings, for personal reminiscences by a member of a particular profession. The subdivision −**Correspondence** is used as a form subdivision under classes of persons for the collected letters of a member or members of a particular class of persons.

3) −**Personal narratives.** This subdivision, previously also used under headings for class of persons, is now used only under names of events and wars, as a form subdivision for autobiographical accounts of experiences in connection with these events or wars.

Collective Biography*

General collective biography. The form heading **Biography** is assigned to a work containing biographies of persons not limited to a particular period, place, or a specific field or discipline, e.g.,

Title: *The Vital Spark: 101 Outstanding Lives*
1. Biography.

For general collective biography in special forms, use the appropriate form headings, e.g., **Anecdotes; Autobiographies; Diaries; Interviews; Letters; Obituaries; Portraits**, etc.

Title: *Heitere Muse: Anekdoten aus Kultur u. Geschichte*
1. Anecdotes.

Title: *Confessions and Self-Portraits: 4600 Years of Autobiography*
1. Autobiographies.

Title: *A Treasury of the World's Great Diaries*
1. Diaries.

The main heading **Biography** is subdivided by period if the biographees belong to a specific period, e.g.,

Title: *Men in the News: Personality Sketches from the New York Times*
1. Biography−20th century.

Collective biography of a group of persons not associated with a particular field or discipline. If a collective biography does not pertain to a special field or discipline but involves an organization, ethnic or national group, place, event, or war, the appropriate heading indicating the special aspect with the subdivision −**Biography** or a more specific subdivision is assigned, e.g.,

---

*The treatment described in this section applies to collective biographies containing four or more life histories. For a collective biography containing two or three life histories, see discussion of individual biography.

Shoshone County Nursing Home—Biography
Afro-Americans—Genealogy
Jews—Biography
British in India—Biography
New York (City)—Biography—Portraits
European War, 1914-1918—Anecdotes

If the work focuses on a particular historical period of a specific place, two headings are assigned: a heading for the period with subdivision —**Biography**, and a heading for the place with subdivision —**Biography**, e.g.,

Title: *Founders of Colonial Virginia*
1. Virginia—History—Colonial period, ca. 1600-1775—Biography.
2. Virginia—Biography.

In some cases, several headings are assigned in order to cover all aspects of the work, e.g.,

Title: *To Be Somebody: Portraits of Nineteen Beautiful Detroiters*
1. Afro-Americans—Michigan—Detroit—Biography.
2. Detroit—Biography.

Title: *Blacks Who Served with the Army in Vietnam*
1. Afro-Americans—Washington, D.C.—Biography.
2. Washington, D.C.—Biography.
3. United States. Army—Biography.
4. Vietnamese Conflict, 1961-1975—Afro-Americans—Biography.
5. Vietnamese Conflict, 1961-1975—Biography.

For a collective biography of wives who have no special career of their own, the heading **Wives—Biography** or a heading denoting a special group of wives, e.g., **Army wives; Diplomats' wives; Non-commissioned officers' wives; Teachers' wives**, etc., is used. Note also headings for various classes of persons not limited to a field or discipline, such as **Men; Women; Children; Adolescent boys; Adolescent girls; Young men; Young women; Widows; Widowers**, etc.

Collective biography of persons belonging to a particular field or discipline. For this type of works, a heading in the form of [**class of persons**]—**Biography** is used, e.g.,

Title: *Men and Ideas in Economics: A Dictionary of World Economists, Past and Present*
1. Economists—Biography.*

Title: *El Niño que fue*
1. Authors, Chilean—Biography.
2. Children—Biography.

(Example continues on page 194.)

---

*Note that the subdivision —**Dictionaries** is not used as a further subdivision of —**Biography** for biographical dictionaries.

Title: *Superstars*
    1.   Athletes—Biography.

Many of these headings are further subdivided by place, e.g.,

> **Artists—California, Southern—Biography**
> **Painters—Italy—Biography**
> **Physicians—Massachusetts—Boston—Biography**

Previously, a distinction was made between a class-of-persons heading with a national qualifier, e.g., **Engineers, American** (designating nationality) and one with a geographic subdivision, e.g., **Engineers—United States** (designating location). Because, in practice, the distinction is not always clear and the file of titles under the geographic subdivision all too often represented contents identical with those in the file with the adjectival qualifier, the Library of Congress has decided recently to eliminate the headings with the adjectival qualifier indicating nationality and use the heading with geographic subdivision to designate either "currently in" or "originally from," except for headings related to *belles lettres*, because of the additional complication of language.

By naming the appropriate class of persons, the field or discipline discussed in the biography is designated. Therefore, no additional heading under the name of the field or discipline is necessary. However, if a term representing the special class of persons is not available, the heading for the corresponding discipline with the subdivision —**Biography** is used instead. For example, the heading **Art—Biography** encompasses every class of persons associated with the field of art, including artists, dealers, collectors, museum personnel, etc., e.g.,

Title: *International Who's Who in Art and Antiques*
    1.   **Art—Biography.**
    2.   **Artists—Biography.**

If appropriate for the work being cataloged, a more specific form subdivision is used instead of —**Biography**, e.g.,

> **Entertainers—Interviews**
> **Poets, English—Correspondence**
> **Afro-American artists—Portraits**

If a geographic subdivision is also used, the place is interposed between the class of persons and the biographical subdivision, e.g.,

> **Physicians—New York (State)—Biography**
> **Entertainers—California—San Francisco—Interviews**

For a collective biography of women associated with a particular field of discipline, at least two headings are assigned: [**class of persons**]—**Biography**, and [**feminine class of persons**]—**Biography**, e.g.,

Title: *Lives of America's Famous Lady Wrestlers*
    1.   **Wrestlers—United States—Biography.**
    2.   **Women wrestlers—United States—Biography.**

Title: *Famous American Actresses*
1.   Actors–United States–Biography.
2.   Actresses–United States–Biography.

If a biography of persons associated with a field or discipline also involves an organization, ethnic group, place, or event, both headings, one indicating the field and one indicating the other aspect, are assigned, e.g.,
   1)   Organization

Title: *Chemists in the Dept. of Agriculture*
1.   Chemists–United States–Biography.
2.   United States. Dept. of Agriculture–Biography.

   2)   Ethnic group

At least two headings are assigned: the class of persons, and the class of persons qualified by the ethnic group. However, the heading designating the ethnic group only is not used (i.e., **Afro-Americans–Ohio–Biography**), e.g.,

Title: *Black College Teachers in Ohio*
1.   College teachers–Ohio–Biography.
2.   Afro-American college teachers–Ohio–Biography.

   3)   Place

Normally, an additional heading under the name of the place (e.g., **Ohio–Biography**) is not required. However, if the work is of interest to genealogists or local historians or has local significance, an additional heading for the place is assigned. (Note: such headings are usually not assigned when the place in question corresponds to a country or larger region.)
Example:

Title: *The Lives of Early Abilene, Tex., Cowboys*
1.   Cowboys–Texas–Abilene–Biography.
2.   Frontier and pioneer life–Texas–Abilene.
3.   Abilene, Tex.–Biography.

   4)   Event or war

Title: *Lives of Entertainers Who Served in World War I*
1.   Entertainers–Biography.
2.   European War, 1914-1918–Biography.

Family histories.* For the history of a family, the following headings are assigned: a heading in the form of [surname] **family**, and a heading bringing out the place, e.g.,

1.   Smith family.
2.   Virginia–Genealogy.

The second subject entry is omitted in the case of **United States–Genealogy**.

---

*For treatment of genealogical materials in general, see Chapter 11.

If more than one family is named on the title page, each family is designated by a separate entry if there are no more than three. If more than three families are named, subject headings are assigned only for the most important three (normally the first three listed).

An additional subject entry under the name of the progenitor is made in the case of a family history if he is mentioned on the title page and his name already exists in the catalog as an author heading, e.g.,

1. **Jefferson family.**
2. **Jefferson, Thomas, Pres. U.S., 1743-1826.**

Previously established headings in a form such as **Smith family (William Smith, 1669-1743)** are no longer used.

Individual Biography

Personal name heading. The name of the biographee serves as the main heading for an individual biography. The form of the heading is the same as that used as main or added entries (see chapter on proper names above). In general, a work containing the lives of two or three persons treated either collectively or separately is assigned individual headings for each person, instead of being treated as a collective biography as discussed above.

Subdivisions under personal names. Appropriate subdivision(s) are added to the name heading if the biography deals with specific aspect(s) of the person's life. The subdivisions to be used with personal name headings are listed under model headings:

Category	*Model Heading*
Founders of religion	**Jesus Christ**
Literary authors	**Shakespeare**
Musicians	**Wagner**
Philosophers	**Thomas Aquinas, Saint**
Statesmen, politicians, etc.	**Lincoln**
	Napoleon
	Washington

For complete lists of subdivisions under these model headings, see Appendix D. Note that except with literary authors, the subdivision —**Biography** is not used under personal names.

When a person with multifaceted careers belongs in more than one category, the subdivisions appropriate to the category emphasized in the work being cataloged are used. For example, if the person is treated as a statesman in the work although he is known as a literary author as well, the corresponding subdivisions for statesmen are used. On the other hand, if another work deals with the same person as a literary author, the appropriate literary subdivisions are used. In cases where there is direct conflict between two patterns, the subdivisions belonging to the field in which the person is better known are used. For example, if a work discusses the ethics of a person who is better known as a philosopher, the literary subdivision —**Religion and ethics** is not used under his or her name, even for a work discussing the person as a literary author, since this subdivision conflicts directly with the pattern subdivision —**Ethics** used under philosophers. Therefore, although the heading for Aristotle may be subdivided by subdivisions for literary authors, the pattern subdivisions for philosophers are used in cases of conflict.

Additional headings for individual biographies.

1) Topical headings denoting a particular topic or field of activity.

When a biography emphasizes a particular topic or field of activity to which the person is related and the personal heading assigned to the work is subdivided by a topical subdivision, an additional heading under the name of the field is assigned in order to bring out the special topic or aspect. Examples:

[philosopher]—[specific discipline or topic]

An additional topic is made under the name of the field or a more specific topic (if the work is on a subtopic of the field), e.g.,

1. Thomas Aquinas, Saint, 1225?-1274—Ethics.
2. Ethics.

1. Kant, Immanuel, 1724-1804—Ethics.
2. Duty.

1. Hegel, Georg Wilhelm Friedrich, 1770-1831—Law.
2. Law—Philosophy.

[founder of a religion]—[. . .] interpretations

An additional entry is made under the specific religion, ethnic group, region, etc., with further subdivision if appropriate, e.g.,

1. Jesus Christ—Afro-American interpretations.
2. Afro-Americans—Religion.

[founder of a religion]—Attitude towards [specific topic]

An additional entry is made under the appropriate topic, e.g.,

1. Jesus Christ—Attitude towards Jewish dietary laws.
2. Jews—Dietary laws.

[statesman]—Relations with [specific group]

An additional entry is made under the specific group, e.g.,

1. Lincoln, Abraham, Pres. U.S., 1809-1865—Relations with Jews.
2. Jews in the United States.

[statesman] –Views on [specific topic]

An additional entry is made under the topic, e.g.,

1.   Lincoln, Abraham, Pres. U.S., 1809-1865–Views on slavery.
2.   Slavery in the United States.

2)   Biographical headings. In addition to the personal name heading of the biographee and any topical heading, the same biographical headings* with the same subdivisions assigned to collective biographies on the same topics are assigned to individual biographies:

(i) Biographical headings for persons associated with a field or discipline.

To a work of true biography of a person associated with a field or discipline, headings of the following type are assigned in addition to the personal name heading:

[class of persons] –[place] –[subdivision] **

Examples:

1.   [personal name]
2.   Physicians–New York (State)–Biography.

1.   [personal name]
2.   Entertainers–California–San Francisco–Biography.

For a person who is active in several fields, separate biographical headings are used to bring out only those careers described in the work in hand. No attempt is made to name every activity in which the person was engaged. It should rarely be necessary to assign more than two such headings.

If the work being cataloged focuses only on one career aspect, only the heading for that one aspect is assigned, e.g., for a work about Schweitzer's experiences as a medical missionary,

1.   Schweitzer, Albert, 1875-1965.
2.   Missionaries, Medical–Gabon–Biography.

Catalogers are advised not to make value judgments in the selection of the class of persons to which the biographee belongs. Headings which represent career,

---

*Additional biographical headings are not assigned to lives of legendary or fictitious persons.

The subdivision –Biography** represents the generic concept of biography, including autobiography, personal reminiscences, personal narratives, etc. If more appropriate for the work being cataloged, a more specific subdivision may be used, e.g., –**Anecdotes, facetiae, satire, etc.**; –**Correspondence**; –**Iconography**; –**Interviews**; –**Portraits**; etc., all being free-floating subdivisions.

profession, or special pursuit are selected. For example, Hitler is best described as a head of state, not a war criminal, dictator, National Socialist, etc.

Following are the guidelines for special treatment of certain classes of persons:

Founders of religion. A biographical heading is assigned in addition to the personal name heading and any other topical heading.

Christ	*use* **Christian biography**
Mohammed	*use* **Islam—Biography**
Buddha	*use* **Buddhists—Biography**

Literary authors. See discussion of literary works in Chapter 11.

Patients, handicapped, etc. When a biographical account of a person afflicted with a specific disease is classed as a medical work, the name of the disease with subdivision —**Biography** is assigned, e.g., **Cancer—Biography**. The heading for the corresponding class of persons, e.g., **Cancer patients** is not used.

For a person's story of a particular affliction, if the work is classed in social sciences, a heading of the type [**class of persons**]—**Biography** is assigned, e.g.,

Title: *Sun and Shadow*, by Rose Resnick
1. **Resnick, Rose.**
2. **Blind—Biography.**

Pet owners. Biographical headings are not assigned to personal accounts of life with a particular kind of pet, unless the owner is professionally involved with the animal, such as trainers, horsemen, keepers, etc.

Philosophers. Most of the pattern subdivisions used under names of philosophers as listed under **Thomas Aquinas, Saint** refer to their contributions in special fields as philosophers, e.g., —**Aesthetics**; —**Ethics**; etc. When headings of this type are assigned to a work, the biographical heading is omitted. It is used only with works in which true biographical facts are presented as an important aspect of the work.

Sports figures and athletes. For true biographical works about such persons, the sport in which the biographee is engaged is designated by assigning the heading for the class of persons, e.g., **Football players; Golfers; Swimmers;** etc., with the subdivision —**Biography** (or more specific subdivision, if appropriate), e.g.,

1. **King, Billie Jean.**
2. **Tennis players—United States—Biography.**

Headings denoting special classes of players of individual games are not used for individual biography, i.e., **Baseball players—Biography** is used, but not **Pitchers (Baseball)—Biography**.*

Statesmen or heads of state. When the work being cataloged presents personal facts concerning the life of a politician, statesman, or ruler, two headings are assigned: the personal name, and the biographical heading with the appropriate subdivision, e.g.,

> **Great Britain—Kings and rulers—Biography.**
> **Presidents—United States—Biography.**
> **Roman emperors—Biography.**

If, in addition to biographical details, the work also discusses political affairs in which the biographee participated during a period of the country's history, a heading for this special aspect is also assigned, i.e.,

> **[place]—History—[period subdivision]**
> **[place]—Politics and government—[period subdivision]**

Example:

Title: *Life and Times of D. Webster*
1. **Webster, Daniel, 1782-1852.**
2. **Statesmen—United States—Biography.**
3. **United States—Politics and government—19th century.**

For a work which describes the times in which a politician, statesman, etc., lived and that person's relationship to those times, but which contains no biographical details about the person, the biographical heading is omitted.

Name of ruler versus historical period. To works on the life and times of a ruler, three headings are assigned: personal name heading, biographical heading, and history heading, e.g.,

1. **Charles I, King of Great Britain, 1600-1649.**
2. **Great Britain—Kings and rulers—Biography.**
3. **Great Britain—History—Charles I, 1625-1649.**

To a personal biography of the ruler, the first two headings are assigned. To a work on the events of the reign, without biographical facts about the ruler, only the last type of heading is assigned.

---

*This policy is the opposite of that for *collective* biography, where specific categories of players, e.g., **Pitchers (Baseball)—Biography** are designated when possible and practical.

Travelers. Biographical headings are not assigned to personal accounts of travel, unless the journey described in the work is intimately associated with the career of the traveler, such as statesmen, animal collectors, musicians who travel, or unless the traveler is a literary author, e.g.,

Title: *Italian Journey, 1786-1788*, by Goethe
1. Goethe, Johann Wolfgang von, 1749-1832—Journeys—Italy.
2. Italy—Description and travel—1501-1800.
3. Authors, German—Biography.

Wives. Biographical accounts of wives who are active in a special field receive the normal biographical headings in their own right. However, to the accounts of a wife who has no special career of her own and the work relates her personal experiences in association with a famous man and his career, the following headings are assigned:

1. [name of husband]
2. [biographical heading for career of husband]
3. [name of wife]
4. Wives*—[place]—Biography.

Example:

Title: *General Custer's Libbie*
1. Custer, George Armstrong, 1839-1876.
2. Generals—United States—Biography.
3. United States. Army—Biography.
4. Custer, Elizabeth Bacon, 1842-1933.
5. Wives—United States—Biography.

Similar treatment is given to the biography of a woman associated with a famous man, e.g.,

Title: *Julie: The Royal Mistress*
1. St. Laurent, Julie de, 1760-1830.
2. Edward Augustus, Duke of Kent, 1767-1820.
3. Mistresses—Great Britain—Biography.
4. Great Britain—Princes and princesses—Biography.

(ii) Biographical headings for persons belonging to no particular field or discipline.

If the individual biography does not pertain to a special field or discipline, the subdivision —**Biography** or a more specific subdivision is used where appropriate under the name of the pertinent organization, ethnic group, place, event, or war,

---

*This practice is contrary to that for *collective* biography of wives, where headings for the specific classes of wives are assigned, e.g., **Statesmen's wives; Army wives,** etc.

bringing out any and all important associations by which the person could be identified, e.g.,

Title: *John Smith, Small Town Resident*
1.   [name of town]—Biography.
2.   Smith, John.

The period in which the biographee lived is ignored unless it is an important aspect of the work.

Special Types of Biographical Works

Autobiographies and autobiographical writings. The personal name heading is assigned to autobiographies even though it duplicates an author entry. This is a change of policy from earlier practice of not assigning to a work a subject heading which exactly matched an author entry, e.g.,

Title: *The Autobiography of Theodore Roosevelt*
1.   Roosevelt, Theodore, Pres. U.S., 1858-1919.
2.   Presidents—United States—Biography.

Title: *Trenta anys de teatre*, by Alberto Llanas
1.   Llanas, Alberto, 1847-1915—Biography.
2.   Dramatists, Catalan—Biography.

Other autobiographical writings such as memoirs, correspondence, diaries, are treated similarly, e.g.,

Title: *Correspondance de Napoléon Ier*
1.   Napoléon I, Emperor of the French, 1769-1821.
2.   France—Kings and rulers—Correspondence.

In the case of correspondence from one person to another, a subject entry is made not only under the name of the person writing the letters, but also under the name of the person to whom the letters are addressed.

Partial biography. A partial biography is treated like an individual biography. An additional topical heading to bring out the special field is assigned if it is more specific than the field implied in the biographical heading. In other words, the heading **Chemistry** is not used if **Chemists—Biography** is assigned. Examples (* indicates the topical heading):

Title: *The Personal Life of Patton During the Campaigns of WW II*
1.   Patton, George Smith, 1885-1945.
*2.   World War, 1939-1945—Campaigns—Western.
3.   Generals—United States—Biography.
4.   United States. Army—Biography.

Title: *Oppenheimer's Personal Efforts to Develop the Bomb*
    1.   Oppenheimer, J. Robert, 1904-1967.
   *2.   Atomic bomb—History.
    3.   Physicists—United States—Biography.

Note the treatment of comparable nonbiographical works:

Title: *The Campaigns of Patton in WW II*
    1.   World War, 1939-1945—Campaigns—Western.
    2.   Patton, George Smith, 1885-1945.

Title: *History of the Atomic Bomb Under Oppenheimer Leadership*
    1.   Atomic bomb—History.
    2.   Oppenheimer, J. Robert, 1904-1967.

Festschriften.* In addition to a topical heading or headings covering the subject matter of the festschrift as a whole (usually with the subdivision —**Addresses, essays, lectures**), a subject entry is made for the honoree regardless of whether the festschrift contains information actually devoted to the honoree.** The biographical heading is not assigned unless at least 20 percent of the text is devoted to true biographical details concerning the honoree, excluding discussions about the honoree's contributions to the field.
Example:

Title: *Miscellanea Anglo-Americana: Festschrift für Helmut Viebrock*
    1.   English literature—History and criticism—Addresses, essays, lectures.
    2.   American literature—History and criticism—Addresses, essays, lectures.
    3.   Viebrock, Helmut, 1912-

Art reproductions with commentary. When collections of paintings, drawings, engravings, etc., are accompanied by commentary, a subject entry under the name of the artist is made regardless of the author entry. However, the biographical heading (indicating the class of persons) is not assigned unless the accompanying text presents substantial information about the artist's personal life (at least 20 percent of the text). If the text is limited to a discussion of the artist's works and artistic ability, the biographical heading is omitted.

---

*Cf. *Cataloging Service* 124:21 (Winter 1978).
The personal name heading is subdivided by the form subdivision —Addresses, essays, lectures** if the work contains information about the honoree.

WORKS ABOUT CORPORATE BODIES*

The treatment of works about corporate bodies is similar in many ways to that of biography.

Corporate Bodies Discussed Collectively

For a work about a specific type of corporate body, the generic term is assigned as the heading, e.g., **Libraries; Trade and professional associations; Trade-unions, Catholic**; etc.

Many of the headings for corporate bodies are subdivided by place, e.g.,

> Libraries—Finland
> Libraries—Alaska
> Psychiatric hospitals—Massachusetts—Boston

However, in many, though not all, cases, when a city is involved, the heading is inverted, e.g.,

> Boston—Libraries

A large number of the over two hundred free-floating subdivisions used under names of cities pertain to particular types of structures or institutions of a city discussed collectively. These are listed below for ready reference:

City Subdivisions Pertaining to
Institutions, Structures, etc.

—Almshouses	—Fortifications, military installa-
—Armories	tions, etc.
—Auditoriums, convention facilities, etc.	—Fountains
—Bars, saloons, etc.	—Gates
—Bridges	—Hospitals
—Buildings	—Hotels, motels, etc.
—Canals	—Laboratories
—Castles	—Libraries
—Cemeteries	—Markets
—Charities	—Monasteries
—Churches	—Monuments
—Clubs	—Morgues
—Convents	—Mosques
—Correctional institutions	—Museums
—Courtyards	—Nightclubs, dance halls, etc.
—Docks, wharves, etc.	—Office buildings
—Dwellings	—Palaces

(List continues on next page.)

---

*Cf. *Cataloging Service* 88: 7-9 (January 1970); 106:4 (May 1973).

City Subdivisions Pertaining to
Institutions, Structures, etc. (cont'd)

—Playgrounds	—Stables
—Plazas	—Statues
—Public buildings	—Stores, shopping centers, etc.
—Recreational facilities	—Streets
—Restaurants	—Synagogues
—Schools	—Temples
—Sepulchral monuments	—Theaters
—Shrines	—Tombs
—Slaughter-houses	—Towers
—Sports facilities	—Walls

When one of these subdivisions is used under the name of a city, the resulting subject heading in the form of [city]—[topic] is regarded as a generic heading as far as that topic and city are concerned. A recent Library of Congress policy requires that this type of heading be assigned whenever the work in hand deals with the topic and city in question, regardless of what other heading or headings may be assigned to the same work. In other words, if the heading required for the work is of the [topic]—[city] type, a generic heading consisting of the name of the city with one of the subdivisions listed above is also assigned, even though the subdivision in this case may be a more comprehensive term than the first heading assigned, e.g.,

1. Psychiatric hospitals—Massachusetts—Boston.
2. Boston—Hospitals.

1. Boarding schools—Massachusetts—Boston.
2. Boston—Schools.

1. Art museums—Massachusetts—Boston.
2. Boston—Museums.

1. War memorials—France—Paris.
2. Paris—Monuments.

1. Girls—Societies and clubs—Massachusetts—Boston.
2. Boston—Clubs.

The topic represented in the [city]—[topic] headings normally states the topic in question at its broadest possible level, whereas special aspects of that topic are brought out by [topic]—[city] headings. In this manner the catalog offers a two-level approach to the city and topic. In those cases where the two types of headings are at the same level, e.g., [city]—Churches versus Churches—[country]—[city], only the [city]—[topic] heading is assigned.

However, an exception is made in cases where such headings represent *see also* references to specific names, including names of structures, institutions, etc. In such instances, both references are made even when they contain topics at the same level, e.g.,

[city]. [name of dwelling]
    xx   [city]–Dwellings
          Dwellings–[country, Province, etc.]

Works about Individual Corporate Bodies

The name of the corporate body is assigned as the subject heading for a work about an individual corporate body, even if the subject entry duplicates the main entry or an added entry, as in the case of corporate reports and some corporate histories. Examples:

Title: *A Report on the Growth of the Executive Office of the President, 1955-1973.*
   1.   United States. Executive Office of the President.

Title: Louisiana State University Library. *Annual Report.*
   1.   Louisiana State University, Baton Rouge. Library.

At the Library of Congress, the form of the corporate heading is established by descriptive catalogers (see chapter on proper names).

For a festschrift in honor of a corporate body, in addition to the topical headings (usually with the subdivision –**Addresses, essays, lectures**) assigned, a subject entry is also made under the name of the honoree.

Name Changes in Corporate Bodies

When a corporate body changes its name, the present policy in accordance with the *Anglo-American Cataloging Rules* is to provide for all names of a corporate body in the catalog linked by explanatory references.* The subject cataloger is then faced with the problem of selecting one of the various names for use as the subject heading for the work in hand. The current policy of the Library of Congress is described below. It should be noted that two different policies are in use, one for corporate bodies in general, and one specifically for political jurisdictions. Also, special rules are applied in each case, depending on the nature of the change involved, e.g., linear changes, mergers, separations, or combinations.

Corporate bodies (other than jurisdictions).
1)   Linear name changes. That is, a body which has undergone successive name changes. This is the most commonly-occurring kind of name change.

If separate headings have been established for the different names of a corporate body, the subject heading for a work about the corporate body is the name used during the latest period covered by the work.

---

*For forms of headings and references, see Chapter 6.

Example: (All headings treated according to the *Anglo-American Cataloging Rules.*)

National Association of Physical Plant Administrators of Universities and Colleges.

The Association of Superintendents of Buildings and Grounds of Universities and Colleges was established in 1914. Its name was changed in 1948 to Association of Physical Plant Administrators of Universities and Colleges, and in 1954 to National Association of Physical Plant Administrators of Universities and Colleges.
Works by this body are found under the name used at the time of publication.

Subject entry: Works about this body are entered under the name used during the latest period covered.

Earlier names are not assigned as additional subject entries even though the work in hand may also discuss the earlier history of the body when known by the earlier names.

If the latest name covered by the work is not used as a heading but is represented by a *see* reference, the heading referred to is used as subject heading.

Example: (Earlier names treated according to the *A.L.A. Cataloging Rules*)

Vanderbilt University, *Nashville. Divinity School*

The Biblical Dept. was established in 1875. Its name was changed in 1916 to School of Religion; and in 1956 to Divinity School.
Works by this body published before the change of name in 1956 are found under

Vanderbilt University, *Nashville. School of Religion*

Works published after the change of name in 1956 are found under

Vanderbilt University, *Nashville. Divinity School*

Subject entry: Works about this body are entered under its latest name, Vanderbilt University, Nashville, Divinity School, unless subject coverage is limited to the pre-1956 period in which case entry is made under: Vanderbilt University, Nashville. School of Religion.

Thus, a work about the Biblical Department of Vanderbilt University would be entered under **Vanderbilt University, Nashville. School of Religion** because a reference has been made from the Biblical Department to the School of Religion.

It should be noted that in the case of corporate bodies with linear name changes, descriptive cataloging and subject cataloging follow different policies. In descriptive cataloging, a work by a particular body which has undergone a name change is entered under the name used at the time of publication, without regard to the question of coverage. In subject cataloging, subject coverage is the criterion.

2)   Mergers. In cases of mergers, i.e., when two or more bodies join to form a new body, subject entry is made under the name of the new organization resulting from the merger, unless subject coverage is limited to the pre-merger period; in that case subject entry is made under the name of one or more of the original bodies, as required.

3)   Separations. When a corporate body has split into two or more bodies, a work dealing with the original body and the bodies resulting from the split is entered only under the names of the bodies resulting from the split. A work limited to the period after the split is entered under as many of the names of the resulting bodies as required. When the subject coverage of a work is limited to the pre-separation period, subject entry is made under the name of the original body.

Political jurisdictions.

1)   Linear name changes. The subject heading assigned is the latest name regardless of the period covered by any work in hand, as long as the territorial identity remains essentially unchanged.

For-subject-entry-see references are made from all earlier names established as jurisdictional names but not used as subject headings, e.g.,

> Congo (Democratic Republic)
> For subject entries see Zaire.

2)   Mergers or separations. If the territorial identity mentioned above changes, it will normally be because a merger or separation has taken place.

In such instances, subject entry is made under only the later name or names, except when the work in hand is limited to historical, political, or cultural matters pertaining to the earlier jurisdiction or jurisdictions in existence before the separation or merger. In the latter case the earlier name or names is used as required.

The expression "historical, political, or cultural matters" noted above represents a means of selecting for subject heading purposes the appropriate name of a jurisdiction which has undergone territorial changes, when the work in hand deals only with the period before the change. According to the formula, although the current name is the preferred name, the name before the change may also be used under certain circumstances, depending upon the actual topic of the work. It is assumed that the physical environment associated with the territory in question is little affected by political changes, and readers would normally search the catalog under the latest form of the name for works dealing with it or subject fields which study it, regardless of the period in question. Therefore, the latest form of the name is used for works on the sciences, medicine, agriculture, etc. On the other hand, the cultural or intellectual world is much affected by political changes, and readers would normally search the catalog under the earlier name for works involving these topics. Therefore, the earlier form of the name is used for works on history, society, intellectual life, etc. In other words, with regard to Life and Physical Sciences, the latest name is used; for Humanities, Law and Social Sciences, the earlier name is used. In summary, in contrast to linear changes, the earlier names of political jurisdictions are still used, but are reserved for "historical" situations.

Scope notes explaining these principles are placed in the catalog in each instance of a change of this type. Example (using Papua New Guinea which resulted from the merger of New Guinea (Ter.) and Papua in 1945):

PAPUA NEW GUINEA

Here are entered works on Papua New Guinea for all periods and subjects with the exception that works limited in subject coverage to the historical, political or cultural aspects of Papua New Guinea for the pre-1945 period are entered under PAPUA and/or NEW GUINEA (TER.).

PAPUA

Here are entered works limited in subject coverage to the historical, political or cultural aspects of Papua for the pre-1945 period. All works covering the same area for which these limitations do not apply are entered under the name of the present jurisdiction, PAPUA NEW GUINEA.

NEW GUINEA (TER.)

Here are entered works limited in subject coverage to the historical, political or cultural aspects of New Guinea (Ter.) for the pre-1945 period. All works covering the same area for which these limitations do not apply are entered under the name of the present jurisdiction, PAPUA NEW GUINEA.

WORKS ABOUT INDIVIDUAL WORKS*

For a work which is a criticism of, or commentary on, another work, a subject entry is made under the uniform heading for the work commented on, even if it duplicates an author-title added entry.

---

*Cf. *Cataloging Service* 116:5-6 (Winter 1976).

For works about the Bible, see separate discussion on the Bible and other sacred scriptures in Chapter 11.

Works about Individual Nonliterary Works

For a commentary on a work by a personal or corporate author, the following headings are assigned:

1) a subject heading consisting of the author's name followed by the uniform title of the work commented on,

2) the same topical headings which have been assigned to the original work, regardless of whether the commentary itself contains the actual text of the original work, e.g.,

Title: *Marx's Capital*, by Helmut Reichelt
1. Marx, Karl, 1818-1883. Das Kapital.
2. Capital.
3. Economics.

Title: *Familienplanung und Empfängnisverhütung*, by J. M. Reuss
1. Birth control—Religious aspects—Catholic Church.
2. Catholic Church. Pope, 1963-   (Paulus VI) Humanae vitae.

Note that the title used in the subject entry is the uniform title and not necessarily the title as it appears in the commentary. The reason for using the uniform title is to group together all commentaries about a particular work regardless of variant titles or titles in other languages under which the work has appeared.

Works about Individual Literary Works

An author-title subject entry is made, e.g.,

Title: *Notes on The Tempest*, by David Hirst
1. Shakespeare, William, 1564-1616. Tempest.

Title: *The Two Faces of Hermes: A Study of Thomas Mann's Novel,*
"The Magic Mountain," by R. D. Miller
1. Mann, Thomas, 1875-1955. Der Zauberberg.

If appropriate, the following subdivisions may be used with author-title subject entry:

[author. title]
—Bibliography
—Concordances
—Exhibitions
—Illustrations
—Juvenile films
—Juvenile phonorecords
—Sources

If another literary author subdivision is applicable, a second heading under the name of the author with the appropriate subdivision is assigned in addition to the author-title entry, for example,

Title: *Law Versus Equity in the Merchant of Venice*
1.   Shakespeare, William, 1564-1616.   Merchant of Venice.
2.   Shakespeare, William, 1564-1616—Knowledge—Law.

In the case of a work discussing an individual literary work with regard to a particular theme, a topical heading is assigned in addition to the author-title subject entry, e.g.,

1.   Heller, Joseph.   Catch-22, a dramatization.
2.   World War, 1939-1945—Literature and the war.

1.   Mitchell, Margaret, 1900-1949.   Gone with the wind.
2.   United States—History—Civil War, 1861-1865—Literature and the war.

Works about Works Entered under Title

The subject heading used is in the form of the uniform title, e.g.,

Anglo-American cataloging rules

Saturday review

Women's wear daily

Arabian nights

Beowulf

Chanson de Roland

For works about the Bible, see Chapter 11.

Works about Individual Legends and Romances

To a work discussing a single legend or romance, or a specific version of it, two headings are assigned: the catalog entry for the specific legend or romance, i.e., the uniform title or the author-title entry, and the form heading subdivided by —**History and criticism** or other appropriate subdivision, e.g.,

Title: *Le pelerinage de Charlemagne: sources et paralleles,* by Francis James Carmody
1.   Charlemagne.   **Voyage à Jerusalem et à Constantinople.**
2.   Charlemagne, 742-814—Romances—History and criticism.

Title: *Le haut livre du Graal, Perlesvaus*
1.   **Perlesvaus.**
2.   Grail—Legends—History and criticism.

Commentator versus Author

Texts of individual works by one author are often published together with commentary, interpretations, or exegesis relating to it by another person. If such a text is entered under the author of the original work, it is treated as another edition and no subject entry is made for the original work, e.g.,

> Title: *A Casebook on Gerontian*, edited by E. San Juan
> (includes a number of critical articles on Gerontian), main
> entry under Eliot, Thomas Stearns
> [no subject entry]

If the main entry is under the commentator, an author-title subject entry is made for the work discussed, even if it duplicates an author-title *added* entry (in this case an analytic entry for the portion of the original work included), e.g.,

> Title: *Lord Byron's Childe Harold's Pilgrimage to Portugal*,
> by D. G. Dalgado
> 1. Byron, George Gordon Noël Byron, Baron, 1788-1824.
>   Childe Harold's pilgrimage.
> 2. Byron, George Gordon Noël Byron, Baron, 1788-1824—Criticism
>   and interpretation.
> I. Byron, George Gordon Noël Byron, Baron, 1788-1824.
>   Childe Harold's pilgrimage. Selections. 1974.

EDITIONS OF WORKS*

It is the policy of the Library of Congress to assign to each new edition (the term edition includes issue, reprint, and translations, but not adaptations) of a work previously cataloged the same subject headings as those assigned to the original edition, provided that the contents of the new edition do not vary significantly from the original. However, in some cases, revised headings are assigned to the new edition when the subject cataloging of the earlier edition of the work is found to be deficient or represents obsolete practices. In such cases, the entries for the previously cataloged edition on the Library of Congress cataloging entry, as well as on the MARC record, are updated in accordance with the decision for the new edition.

---

*Cf. *Cataloging Service* 112:14-15 (Winter 1975).

CHAPTER 11

SUBJECT AREAS REQUIRING SPECIAL TREATMENT

LITERATURE

Types of Headings

For works in the field of literature (*belles lettres*), the following types of headings are available.

Literary form headings.
1) Headings representing literary forms or genres, e.g.,

> **Drama**
> **Poetry**
> **Fiction**
> **Romances**
> **Satire**

2) Headings indicating language or nationality, e.g.,

> **American literature**
> **Japanese literature**
> **French literature**
> **Hindu literature**

English literature is the pattern heading for subdivisions.

In cases where the language and the nationality of a specific body of literature are not represented by the same term, or when the body of literature within a region or country is written in a non-indigenous language, there are two ways of designating the content, one stressing the language and one stressing the nationality or place:*

> **French literature—American authors**
> **American literature (French)**

---

*Cf. *Cataloging Service* 117:13-14 (Spring 1976).

The Library of Congress makes extensive use of both techniques. In many cases, both techniques are applied for a single literature, resulting in a double subject entry. The Subject Cataloging Division is gradually reviewing this practice to determine which of the two techniques to use in each case. The reassessment is not yet complete. As new decisions are made, they will be announced in *Cataloging Service.*

A recent change in policy affects the treatment of literature of developing countries, especially those countries, such as former colonies, where a body of literature exists in an imposed, non-indigenous language. The current policy stresses the literature as a regional or national literature and designates the language by a qualifier, e.g.,

Papua New Guinea literature (English)
Algerian literature (French)
Indic literature (English)
Egyptian literature, Modern (French)

A *see* reference is always made from the alternative form, and all earlier instances of duplicate entry are being cancelled, e.g.,

Nigerian literature (English)
  x English literature–Nigerian authors

The literature of Arabic speaking countries represents an exception to these provisions. The Arabic literature of a particular country is brought out by local subdivision under the heading **Arabic literature**, e.g.,

Arabic literature–Algeria [Egypt, Jordan, etc.]

A *see* reference is made from the alternative form, e.g.,

Arabic literature–Algeria
  x Algerian literature (Arabic)

The writings of authors belonging to particular nonlinguistic subgroups within a country (e.g., Jewish authors, Catholic authors, Women authors) are designated by means of a subdivision under the pertinent literature, e.g.,

South African literature (English)–Women authors

Literature written in indigenous languages of a country is represented by the literature heading without qualifiers, e.g.,

Urdu literature

When the use of indigenous languages by subgroups extends to neighboring countries or areas, this is brought out by local subdivision, e.g.,

Urdu literature–South India

3)   Combination of language/nationality and form:

> **American poetry**
> **English drama (Comedy)**
> **Epic poetry, Italian**
> **Fantastic fiction, American**
> **French drama**
>
> **African drama (English)**
>
> **Ghanaian poetry (English)**

Many of the literature headings are subdivided by periods as appear in the printed list. The headings **English poetry**; **English drama**; etc., serve as patterns for other subdivisions.

Topical headings representing themes, characters or features in literary works. Patterns:

> [topic] in literature
> [personal name] in fiction, drama, poetry, etc.
> [topic or name*] —Drama
> [topic or name*] —Fiction
> [topic or name*] —Literary collections
> [topic or name*] —Poetry**

Examples:

> **Politics in literature**
> **Characters and characteristics in literature**
> **Shakespeare, William, 1564-1616, in fiction, drama, poetry, etc.**
> **Lincoln, Abraham, Pres. U.S., 1809-1865, in fiction, drama, poetry, etc.**
> **Lincoln, Abraham, Pres. U.S., 1809-1865—Drama**
> **Slavery in the United States—Fiction**
> **World War, 1939-1945—Literary collections**
> **Bangladesh—History—Poetry**

---

*Includes geographic, personal, or corporate names, except names of literary authors. For distinctions among, and appropriate uses of, these headings, see following discussion on works of and about literature.

In the case of a geographic heading, a duplicate entry in the form of **Poetry of places— [place] is also assigned, e.g.,

Title: *Poesie napoletane*
1. **Poetry of places—Italy—Naples**
2. **Naples—Social life and customs—Poetry.**

Other topical headings, e.g.,

> Criticism, Textual
> Literary forgeries and mystifications
> Literary research
> Literature and medicine
> Literature and society
> Religion and literature

Headings combining form and topic, e.g.,

> Christmas plays
> College and school drama
> Detective and mystery stories, English
> Western stories

In literature there are two categories of works requiring different treatment: literary works (or specimens) and works *about* literature. Their treatment is described below.

Literary Works*

Collections of two or more independent works by different authors.

1)   Literary form headings. Literary form headings are assigned to collections of two or more independent works by different authors, e.g.,

Title: *Poems by the Fireside: A Treasury of Family Favorites*
1.   American poetry.
2.   English poetry.

Title: *Novelle per tutte le stagioni: antologia*
1.   Short stories, Italian.

Title: *Caribbean Voices: An Anthology of West Indian Poetry*
1.   West Indian poetry (English)

Title: *Anthologie de romances*
1.   Romances, Spanish.

Title: *Poetry of the Seventies: An Anthology of Contemporary Verse*
1.   English poetry—20th century.

Title: *"Und dennoch müssen wir leben . . . ": Eine Welt-Anthologie*
        d. Daseinsbejahung
1.   Poetry, Modern—20th century.

---

*Cf. *Cataloging Service* 107:5 (December 1973); 114:7 (Summer 1975).

Note that the free-floating subdivision —**Collected works** is not used with literary form headings. The subdivision —**Collections** and the qualifiers (**Collections**) and (**Selections, Extracts, etc.**) represent previous practice and are no longer used. Headings such as **American poetry (Collections)** and **French literature (Selections, Extracts, etc.)** are now obsolete.

2) Topical headings. If the collection is centered on a theme, a person, a place, or an event, a topical heading subdivided by either the subdivision —**Literary collections** when the works in the collection are written in two or more literary forms, or one of the major literary forms (—**Drama**; —**Fiction**; or —**Poetry**)*, is assigned in addition to the literary form heading(s). The form subdivisions —**Drama**, —**Fiction**, and —**Poetry** are used under an identifiable topic to a collection of literary works on that topic. However, vague and rather general topics such as love, fate, mankind, religion, industriousness, are generally avoided. Examples:

Title: *Le madri*
1. Mothers—Literary collections.
2. Italian literature—20th century.

Title: *Greek Poets on Poetry*
1. Greek poetry.
2. Poetry—Poetry.
3. Greek poetry—Translations into English.
4. English poetry—Translations from Greek.

Title: *Eight Plays for Hand Puppets about George Washington*
1. Puppets and puppet plays.
2. Washington, George, Pres. U.S., 1732-1799—Drama.**

Title: *Golf Story Omnibus*
1. Short stories, American.
2. Golf—Fiction.

Title: *Deu odes a Barcelona*
1. Poetry of places—Spain—Barcelona.
2. Barcelona—Description—Poetry.
3. Catalan poetry—19th-20th centuries.

When a phrase heading which combines both form and topical aspects into one heading (e.g., **Detective and mystery stories, American; Science fiction, American; Sea stories; Christmas plays; Ghost plays; Political plays**) is available, this heading is used to bring out both aspects. See examples on page 218.

---

*The subdivision —**Stories** has been discontinued. However, there still exists a few phrase headings which are used in connection with certain kinds of stories, e.g., **Sea stories; Detective and mystery stories.**

For literary anthologies *about* an individual literary author, the phrase heading [name of author**] **in fiction, drama, poetry, etc.** is used regardless of the literary form(s).

Title: *A Saddlebag of Tales: A Collection of Stories*, by members of
     Western Writers of America
    1.   **Western stories.** [1. The West—Fiction. 2. Short stories]

Title: *Teenage Space Adventures*
    1.   **Science fiction.**

If a second heading is assigned for a very specific topic, the phrase heading combining a more general topic with the literary form is not used. Instead, a literary form heading is used, e.g.,

    1.   **American drama**
         [*instead of* Christian drama]
    2.   **Trinity—Drama.**

In the case of fiction about animals, only one heading is assigned, in the form of either **Animals, Legends and stories of** for animal stories in general or [**name of animal**, e.g., **Dogs**]—**Legends and stories** for stories about a particular animal.

Works by individual authors*—Collected works.**

    1)   Literary form headings. In general, literary form headings are not assigned to collected works by an individual author. In other words, the heading **English drama—Early modern and Elizabethan, 1500-1600** is not used with the complete plays of Shakespeare. However, there are two exceptions to this general rule. The literary form heading is assigned if it combines form and topic in one heading, such as **Western stories; Detective and mystery plays**; e.g.,

Title: *The Sacketts: Beginnings of a Dynasty*, by Louis L'Amour
    1.   **Western stories.**

The form heading is also assigned if the form is highly specific, such as **Allegories; Fables; Fairy tales; Radio stories; Amateur theatricals; Carnival plays; Children's plays; College and school drama; Didactic drama; Radio plays**; etc., e.g.,

Title: *Fables and Allegories for Young and Old*, by the author of The Story
     of the Bible [i.e., Charles Foster]
    1.   **Fables.**
    2.   **Allegories.**

Headings of the following types are *not* considered to be "highly specific": **American fiction; Short stories; Tales; English drama; English drama (Comedy); Comedy; Farce; Melodrama; One-act plays; Tragedy; Tragicomedy.**

---

    *Works by joint authors such as *The Maid's Tragedy* by Beaumont and Fletcher are treated in the same manner as works by individual authors.
    **Cf. *Cataloging Service* 114:7-8 (Summer 1975).

2) Topical headings. If the works in the collection are centered on an identifiable topic or based on the life of an individual or an event, a topical heading with an appropriate literary form subdivision (—**Fiction***; —**Drama***; —**Poetry***; or —**Literary collections**) is assigned. A phrase heading combining the form and topic is used if it is available. Vague and rather general topics such as love, fate, mankind, religion, industriousness are generally avoided.

Examples:

Title: *Neue Harfenklänge für Israel: jüdische Poesien,* by Julius Sturm
    1.   **Jews—Poetry.**

Title: *Paraboles et paraphrases évangéliques,* by R. Sineux
    1.   **Bible. N.T. Gospels—History of Biblical events—Poetry.**

Title: *Somebody Loves You,* by Helen Steiner Rice
    1.   **Christian poetry, American.**

Works by individual authors—Individual works.
1) Literary form headings. Literary form headings are *not* assigned to individual works of literature.
2) Topical headings. For individual works in the form of poetry or drama, a topical heading (except for very general vague topics such as love, mankind, fate, religion, etc.) with the subdivision —**Poetry** or —**Drama** is assigned, e.g.,

Title: *Lawrence Bloomfield in Ireland: A Modern Poem,* by
        William Allingham
    1.   **Ireland—Social life and customs—Poetry.**

Title: *The Anniversaries,* by John Donne
    1.   **Drury, Elizabeth, d. 1610—Poetry.**

Title: *King Richard the Third,* by William Shakespeare
    1.   **Richard III, King of England, 1452-1485—Drama.**

Title: *Two Strikes: A Baseball Comedy in Two Acts*
    1.   **Baseball—Drama.**

For an imaginary work based on a literary author's life, the phrase heading **[author's name] in fiction, drama, poetry, etc.** is used. A heading such as "Shakespeare, William, 1564-1616—Poetry" is not used because it may be interpreted to mean a work about Shakespeare's poetry.

---

*The subdivisions —**Juvenile fiction;** —**Juvenile drama;** and —**Juvenile poetry** are used for juvenile works of *belles lettres.* Note also specific juvenile headings such as **Children's stories; Nursery rhymes;** etc.

Example:

Title: *The Laurel Bough*, by S. E. Silliman
1. **Marlowe, Christopher, 1564-1593, in fiction, drama, poetry, etc.**

For individual works of fiction, topical headings are only assigned to biographical fiction, historical fiction, and animal stories:

(i) Biographical fiction

Title: *The Reluctant Queen*, by M. C. Haycraft
1. **Mary, Queen, consort of Louis XII, King of France, 1496-1533–Fiction.**

Title: *Joseph the Provider*, by Thomas Mann
1. **Joseph, the patriarch–Fiction.**

Title: *Mermaid Tavern: Kit Marlowe's Story*, by George William Cronym
1. **Marlowe, Christopher, 1564-1593, in fiction, drama, poetry, etc.**

(ii) Historical fiction

   The term "historical" fiction is used broadly at the Library of Congress to include fiction about any named entity, such as movement, corporate body (except jurisdictions), camp, park, structure, geographical feature (except regions), ethnic groups (except those groups who are representative of Western culture), and specific events and periods in history. The topical heading is *not* assigned when the event or period is merely the backdrop to the actual story. It is assigned only when the event or period is the principal focus of the work.

Examples:

Title: *Homestead of the Free: The Kansas Story*, by A. L. Fisher
1. **Kansas–History–1854-1861–Fiction.**

Title: *Southward Lies the Fortress: (The Siege of Singapore)*, by T. S. Lim
1. **Singapore–Siege, 1942–Fiction.**

(iii) Animal stories

   For a fictional work about a particular kind of animal, a heading in the form of **[kind of animal]–Legends and stories** is assigned, e.g.,

Title: *Spotty*
1. **Dogs–Legends and stories.**

Medieval legends and romances. The *texts* of European pre-1501 legends and romances and all non-European legends and romances require a topical heading consisting of the name of the historical or legendary person, object, etc., subdivided by **–Legends** or **–Romances**, e.g.,

Alexius, Saint—Legends
Faust—Legends
Grail—Legends
Charlemagne, 742-814—Romances
Arthurian romances
[an exception to the usual form which would be
Arthur, King—Romances]

These headings are assigned to all works containing texts of legends or romances regardless of whether the work in hand represents a complete cycle, or a single legend or romance, e.g.,

Title: *The High History of the Holy Graal*, by Perlesvaus
1.   Grail—Legends.

They are also used for modern versions of legends and romances of medieval origin (i.e., characters and plots remain essentially unaltered), e.g.,

Title: *Mulla's Donkey and Other Friends: Adaptations*, by Mehdi
Nakosteen
1.   Nasreddin Hoca—Legends.

In other words, the subdivisions —**Legends** and —**Romances** take precedence over the subdivisions —**Fiction**, —**Drama**, or —**Poetry** which would normally be used for works of this kind after 1501.

Example:
Title: *Idylls of the King*, by Tennyson
1.   Arthurian romances.
[not Arthur, King—Poetry]

Works about Literature

Works about literature, exclusive of those about individual authors' works, are assigned the appropriate headings which represent the subject content of the works, e.g.,

Title: *The Illusion: An Essay on Politics, Theatre, and the
Novel*, by David Caute
1.   Literature and society.
2.   Politics in literature.
3.   Communism and literature.

Title: *An Apologie for Poetrie*, by Sir Philip Sidney
1.   Poetry—Early works to 1800.

Title: *Geschichte der poetischen Theorie und Kritik von den
Diskursen der Maler bis auf Lessing*, by F. Braitmaier
1.   Poetry.
2.   Criticism—History.
3.   Aesthetics—History.
4.   Literature—Aesthetics.

If the work focuses on a particular literature or form, one or more literary form headings with the subdivision —**History and criticism** are assigned.

> Title: *Estonian Literature*
>   1.   Estonian literature—History and criticism.
>
> Title: *Tendencias de la novela española actual (1950-1970)*
>   1.   Spanish fiction—20th century—History and criticism.
>
> Title: *Fictional Technique in France, 1802-1927*
>   1.   French fiction—19th century—History and criticism.
>   2.   French fiction—20th century—History and criticism.
>
> Title: *Los orígenes de la novela*
>   1.   Classical fiction—History and criticism.

The subdivision —**History and criticism** may be further subdivided, e.g.,

> Title: *Western American Writing: Tradition and Promise*, by Jay Gurian
>   1.   American literature—The West—History and criticism—Addresses, essays, lectures.
>
> Title: *Einführung in die Bücherkunde zur deutschen Literatur-wissenschaft*
>   1.   German literature—History and criticism—Bibliography.

Topical subdivisions and period subdivisions under headings for literature are spelled out in the printed list. For national literatures, the headings **English literature; English drama; English fiction**; etc., serve as model headings for subdivisions (except period subdivisions which are not transferable).

Frequently, when the work deals with a minor form of a particular period but the literary form heading has no provision for period subdivisions, a second, broader heading with the appropriate period subdivision is also assigned, e.g.,

> Title: *Die Illusion der Wirklichkeit im Briefroman des achtzehnten Jahrhunderts*, by Hans Rudolf Picard
>   1.   Epistolary fiction—History and criticism.
>   2.   Fiction—18th century—History and criticism.

For discussions about particular themes with regard to a particular literature and/or form, paired headings are assigned: literary form heading(s) (with the subdivision —**History and criticism**) and topical heading(s) (usually in combination with the phrase ... **in literature**, a free-floating form, i.e., any existing heading may be used with the phrase ... **in literature** to form a heading), e.g.,

> Title: *Italy in English Literature, 1755-1815*, by Roderick Marshall
>   1.   Literature, Comparative—English and Italian.
>   2.   Literature, Comparative—Italian and English.
>   3.   English literature—History and criticism.
>   4.   Italy in literature.

Title: *Drama und dramatischer Raum im Expressionismus*, by
 K.-J. Göbel
1. German drama—20th century—History and criticism.
2. Expressionism.

For discussions of the theme of wars in literature, the headings assigned are in the form of [name of war]—Literature and the war, e.g.,

Title: *Heroes' Twilight: A Study of the Literature of the Great War*
1. European War, 1914-1918—Literature and the war.
2. English literature—20th century—History and criticism.

Where form and topic are combined into one heading, this heading is used with the subdivision —History and criticism, e.g., Detective and mystery stories, American—History and criticism; Religious drama—History and criticism.

For a work discussing the portrayal of a person (all categories of persons, including literary authors) in literature, a heading in the form of [name of person] in fiction, drama, poetry, etc. is assigned in addition to literary form headings, e.g.,

Title: *Images of a Queen, Mary Stuart in Sixteenth Century Literature*,
 by J. E. Phillips
1. Mary Stuart, Queen of the Scots, 1542-1587, in fiction, drama, poetry, etc.
2. Literature, Modern—15th and 16th centuries—History and criticism.

The history and criticism of medieval legends and romances,* (and indexes, concordances, etc., to them) require a topical heading subdivided by —History and criticism; —Dictionaries; —Indexes or other appropriate subdivisions, e.g.,

Title: *The Grail from Celtic Myth to Christian Symbol*
1. Grail—Legends—History and criticism.

Title: *An Index of Proper Names in French Arthurian Verse Romances*
1. Arthurian romances—Indexes.

Works about Individual Authors*

Works about individual authors are assigned headings in the form of the name of the author with appropriate subdivisions. The heading, **Shakespeare, William, 1564-1616**, serves as the model heading for subdivisions. This is the reason why a number of subdivisions not appropriate for Shakespeare are listed under his name, e.g.,

Shakespeare, William, 1564-1616—Biography—Exile

---

*For works about an individual legend or romance or about an individual literary work, see discussion on "Works about Individual Works" in Chapter 10.

These subdivisions are listed because they are usable under certain other literary authors. For an updated list of subdivisions under literary authors, see Appendix D.

These subdivisions may be used with any literary authors when appropriate, e.g.,

> Title: *The Children of Charles Dickens*, by F. R. Donovan
> 1. **Dickens, Charles, 1812-1870—Characters—Children.**

> Title: *Dickens Studies*
> 1. **Dickens, Charles, 1812-1870—Societies, periodicals, etc.**

For a work of criticism and/or interpretation of an author's works (for criticism and interpretation of an individual work, see discussion on "Works about Individual Works" in Chapter 10), a heading in the form of the name of the author with the subdivision **—Criticism and interpretation** or another more specific subdivision is assigned, e.g.,

> Title: *The Dark Glass: Vision and Technique in the Poetry of Dante Gabriel Rossetti,* by R. R. Howard
> 1. **Rossetti, Dante Gabriel, 1828-1882—Criticism and interpretation.**

> Title: *Reminiscencias griegas y latinas en las obras del Libertador*, by Mario Briceño Perozo
> 1. **Bolívar, Simón, 1783-1830—Knowledge—Classical literature.**

If the work contains biographical information as well as criticism of the author's literary efforts, two headings are assigned: the name of the author without subdivision, and a biographical heading,* e.g.,

> 1. **Keats, John, 1795-1821.**
> 2. **Poets, English—19th century—Biography.**

To a true biography of a literary author, two headings are assigned: the name of the author subdivided by **—Biography,** and the biographical heading, e.g.,

> 1. **Keats, John, 1795-1821—Biography.**
> 2. **Poets, English—19th century—Biography.**

In the case of partial biography or biography in special form, assign the two required headings specified above with appropriate subdivisions, e.g.,

> 1. **Keats, John, 1795-1821—Relationship with women.**
> 2. **Poets, English—19th century—Biography.**

To ensure consistency in treatment, the Library of Congress uses as a general guideline, 20 percent and 80 percent for the distinction between biography and criticism, which is diagrammed as follows:

---

*Cf. *Cataloging Service* 119:20-21 (Fall 1976).

Work with Biography-Criticism Mix

Assign: 1. [author] – Criticism and interpretation	Assign: 1. [author] 2. [class of authors] –Biography	Assign: 1. [author] – Biography 2. [class of authors] – Biography

| 20% | 80% | 100% |

Increasing % biography

BIBLE AND OTHER SACRED SCRIPTURES*

Biblical Texts

Subject headings are *not* assigned to Biblical texts *except* in the following cases:

1) Paraphrases of Biblical texts. Because paraphrases of Biblical texts are entered under the name of the paraphraser according to the *Anglo-American Cataloging Rules*, form headings are assigned as follows:

Bible–Paraphrases
[used for texts of paraphrases in two or more languages]

Bible–Paraphrases, English [French, German, etc.]
[used for texts of paraphrases in a particular language]

Paraphrases of parts of the Bible follow the same pattern, e.g.,

Bible. O.T. Psalms–Paraphrases, English

2) Harmonies. The same pattern is followed:

Bible. N.T. Gospels–Harmonies, English

3) Translations of a version. Because in descriptive cataloging, the translation of a version of a Biblical text is entered under the uniform title containing the name of the translator but ignoring the version from which the translation is made, a form heading is assigned to bring out the version. For example, an English translation of the Targum Onḳelos made by Etheridge and published in 1968 was entered under the uniform title, **Bible. O.T. Pentateuch. English. Etheridge. 1968.** The following subject entry is made:

---

*Cf. *Cataloging Service* 83:11-12 (September 1968); 88:6 (January 1970); 116:6 (Winter 1976).

> 1. Bible. O.T. Pentateuch. Aramaic. Targum Onḳelos—
> Translations into English.

Works about the Bible

Works about the Bible or its parts receive subject headings in the form of the uniform title used in descriptive cataloging (omitting designations for the language, version, and date), with the appropriate subdivisions, e.g.,

> Title: *Our Religious Heritage*, by G. P. Fowler
> 1. Bible—Introductions.

> Title: *Les aventures de Dieu*, by François Cavanna
> 1. Bible. O.T. Genesis—Cartoons, satire, etc.

> Title: *Commentary on Romans*, by W. S. Plumer
> 1. Bible. N.T. Romans—Commentaries.

> Title: *Lass deine Augen offen sein: Bildmeditationen z. Vaterunser*
> 1. Lord's prayer—Meditations.

However, if the work is about a particular version or translation of the Bible, it is specifically designated, e.g.,

> Bible—Versions
> Bible. N.T. English—Versions—Rheims
> Bible. English—Versions—Coverdale

Works about *paraphrases* of the Bible or its parts are assigned headings such as

> Bible—Paraphrases—History and criticism
> Bible—Paraphrases, English—History and criticism
> [for works about English paraphrases]
> Bible. O.T. Psalms—Paraphrases, English—History and criticism

Apocryphal Books

The headings **Apocryphal books; Apocryphal books (New Testament);** and **Apocryphal books (Old Testament)** are used with appropriate subdivisions as subject headings for works dealing collectively with apocryphal books. Subdivisions follow the pattern established under the Bible, e.g.,

Apocryphal books—Introductions

Apocryphal books (New Testament)—Commentaries

Apocryphal books (New Testament)—Theology

Apocryphal books (Old Testament)—Criticism, interpretation, etc.

Hymn of the soul—Criticism, interpretation, etc.

Other Sacred Scriptures

The heading **Bible** serves as the pattern of subdivisions for other sacred scriptures, e.g.,

Vedas. R̥gveda—Criticism, interpretation, etc.

Koran—Commentaries

MUSIC

In the field of music, works generally fall into two categories: works about music (including criticism and instruction and study) and musical works. Similar to the works in the field of literature, the works about the subject and its specimens are treated differently in subject cataloging.

Since the publication of the eighth edition of *Library of Congress Subject Headings*, there have been extensive changes in music headings. The changes and additions are announced in *Music Cataloging Bulletin* of the Music Library Association and incorporated into the supplements to the printed list. Note that the section on "Music Headings" in the introduction to the eighth edition (p. vii) has been revised and printed in the supplement.

Works about Music

Works about music are assigned topical headings reflecting the subject content of the works.* The subdivision —**History and criticism** and the subdivision —**Instruction and study** are used with music headings instead of —**History** and —**Study and teaching**.

For works about individual composers and musicians, see discussion on biography in Chapter 10.

For a work about a particular musical composition, see discussion on works about individual works in Chapter 10.

---

*For a discussion of subject cataloging in general, see Chapter 9.

Examples of works about music:

Rubenstein, Raeanne. *Honkytonk Heroes: A Photo Album of Country Music.*
1.   Country musicians—United States—Pictorial works.
2.   Country music—United States—History and criticism.

Whitwell, David. *A New History of Wind Music*
1.   Wind instruments.

Woodwind Anthology: A Compendium of Articles from the Instrumentalist on the Woodwind Instruments
1.   Woodwind instruments—Instruction and study.

Liang, David Ming-Yueh. *The Chinese Ch'in: Its History and Music*
1.   Ch'in (Musical instrument)

Raynor, Henry. *A Social History of Music: From the Middle Ages to Beethoven*
1.   Music and society.
2.   Music—History and criticism.

Musical Works

For musical works, form headings (i.e., headings which describe what the works are rather than what the works are about) are assigned.

Instrumental music. For instrumental music, the following aspects are usually brought out by means of subject entries: musical forms, media of performance, and groupings (e.g., chamber music headings). These elements are used in headings separately or in combination.

Typical headings showing these aspects are:

1)   Musical forms

        Canons, fugues, etc.
        Concertos
        Overtures
        Sonatas
        Suites
        Symphonies

2)   Media of performance

        Glass-harmonica music
        Guitar music
        Hu ch'in music
        Oboe d'amore music
        Piano, oboe, trumpet, violin, double bass with string orchestra
        Violin and harpsichord music

3)   Chamber music
      Trios
      Quartets
      Quintets
      Sextets
      Septets
      Octets
      Nonets

String trios	[quartets, etc.]
Brass trios	[”]
Wind trios	[”]
Woodwind trios	[”]

4)   Combinations
      Canons, fugues, etc. (String quartet)
      String quartets (Violin, viola, violoncello, double bass)
      Suites (Viola with instrumental emsemble)
      Woodwind trios (Bassoon, clarinet, flute)

A recent major change in policy concerns headings with qualifiers specifying instruments. Previously, all such headings were enumerated in the printed list. Now, such headings are no longer printed when the main heading has a general scope note. This was made possible by the establishment of a citation formula (i.e., instruction for specifying the instruments according to a fixed order). In formulating a specific heading required by the work being cataloged, catalogers of music are advised to follow the instructions given in the revised introduction to the eighth edition of the printed list and to consult the notes given under main headings for each category.

The nonprint headings include the following categories:

1)   Headings for instrumental chamber music not entered under musical form:

      Trios
      Quartets
      Quintets
      [Etc.]

Brass trios	[quartets, etc.]
String trios	[”]
Wind trios	[”]
Woodwind trios	[”]

2)   Headings for musical forms which take qualifiers for instrumental medium:

      Canons, fugues, etc.
      Chaconnes
      Chorale preludes*
      Marches

(List continues on page 230.)

---

*Qualified if the medium is other than organ.

> Minuets
> Monologues with music
> Overtures*
> Passacaglias
> Polkas
> Polonaises
> Potpourris
> Rondos
> Sacred monologues with music
> Sonatas
> Suites
> Symphonic poems*
> Symphonies*
> Trio-sonatas
> Variations
> Waltzes

The citation order, or order of precedence, for specifying instruments has been established as follows:

1) keyboard instruments
2) wind instruments
3) plectral instruments
4) percussion and other instruments
5) bowed string instruments**
6) unspecified instruments
7) continuo

The instruments in each category are given in alphabetical order, with the exception of bowed string instruments which are given in score order, e.g., (i.e., violin, viola, violoncello, double bass).

Examples:

> Nonets (Bassoon, clarinet, flute, horn, oboe, violin, viola,
>   violoncello, double bass)

> Octets (Harpsichord, piano, clarinet, flute, oboe,
>   percussion, violin, violoncello)

> Quintets (Bassoon, cornet, trombone, violin, continuo)

In headings for duets, this citation order is not always followed. However, all headings for duets are enumerated in the printed list because of the requirement of *see* references from the alternative form. Catalogers should consult the printed list for duet headings.

---

*Qualified if the medium is other than orchestra.

**Note that the instruments are not specified for string quartets and string trios composed for standard instrumentation, i.e., violins (2), viola, and violoncello for string quartet and violin, viola, and violoncello for string trio.

When two or more of a particular instrument are needed for performance, the arabic number is now given after the name of the instrument and enclosed in parentheses, e.g.,

> **Violins (3), viola, violoncello with string orchestra**
>
> **Pianos (2), guitars (3), percussion with orchestra**
>
> **Wind quintets (Horn, trombones (2), trumpets (2))**
>
> **Concertos (Pianos (2), guitars (3), percussion)**
>
> **Piano music (Pianos (2), 6 hands)**
>
> **Sextets (Piano, violins (2), violas (2), violoncello)**
>
> **Quartets (Unspecified instruments (3), continuo)**

Examples of subject headings assigned to instrumental music:

Holst, Gustav. *Lyric Movement, for Viola and Small Orchestra*
  Reduction for viola and piano by Imogen Holst.
  1.   **Viola with chamber orchestra—Solo with piano.**

Mendelssohn-Bartholdy, Felix. *Spinning Song, Quartet for Woodwind Ensemble. Op. 67, no. 4.* Transcribed by Albert Chiaffarelli
  1.   **Woodwind quartets (Bassoon, clarinet, flute, oboe), Arranged.**

Stamitz, Karl. *Quartet, F Major, op. 19, no. 6, for Bassoon, Violin, Viola, and Cello*
  1.   **Quartets (Bassoon, violin, viola, violoncello)**

Krommer, Franz. *Harmonie, für 2 Oboen, 2 Clarinetten, 2 Horn, 2 Fagott und den grossen Fagott*
  1.   **Suites (Bassoons (3), clarinets (2), horns (2), oboes (2))**

Harrison, Lou. *Symphony on G*
  1.   **Symphonies—Scores.**

Beethoven, Ludwig van. *Grand Symphony, in C. Arr. for 2 Performers on the Pianoforte*
  1.   **Symphonies arranged for piano (4 hands)**

Beethoven, Ludwig van. *Beethoven Organ Works.* (Contains "Suite for a mechanical organ," Preludes, op. 39, and Fuge, D major, K.31)
  1.   **Organ music.**
  2.   **Canons, fugues, etc. (Organ)**
  3.   **Suites (Organ), Arranged.**

Vocal music. For vocal music, headings which bring out the forms, voice range, number of vocal parts, and accompanying medium* are used. Typical headings for vocal music are:

1) Secular vocal music

    Ballads**
    Cantatas, Secular (Equal voices)
    Chansons, Polyphonic
    Choruses, Secular (Men's voices) with percussion***
    Lieder, Polyphonic
    Madrigals (Music)**
    Operas
    Part-songs**
    Song cycles
    Songs**
        (Also headings for various kinds of songs, e.g., **Children's songs; War-songs**)
    Vocal trios, Unaccompanied

2) Sacred vocal music

    Cantatas, Sacred (Women's voices)
    Carols**
    Chants**
    Chorales
    Choruses, Sacred (Mixed voices) with band and organ***
    Hymns**
    Masses
    Motets
    Oratorios
    Part-songs, Sacred
    Psalms (Music)
    Requiems (Unison)
    Sacred songs (Medium voice) with harpsichord
    Vespers (Music)

Some of these headings when applied to specific works require a duplicate entry, e.g.,

    Susato, Tylman. *Le premier livre des chansons à deux ou à trois parties.*
    1.   **Part-songs, French.**
    2.   **Chansons, Polyphonic.**

Instructions for making duplicate entries are given in the printed list under the heading indicating the specific form, i.e., **Chansons, Polyphonic** in the case above.

---

*Medium not specified for larger vocal works, i.e., operas, oratorios, etc.

May be used with national or ethnic modifiers, e.g., **Ballads, American [English, French, etc.]; **Chants (Jewish)**.

***Library of Congress is dropping the number of parts in these headings. Headings such as **Choruses, Secular (Mixed voices, 5 pts.) with percussion instruments** have been replaced by headings of the type **Choruses, Secular (Mixed voices) with percussion**.

The revised introduction to the printed list (see *Supplement to LC Subject Headings, 1974-1976*) indicates that the following categories of headings for vocal music have also become nonprint headings:

> **Choruses; Choruses, Sacred;** and **Choruses, Secular,** qualified by number of vocal parts and accompanying medium
>
> **Songs** and **Sacred songs,** qualified by voice range and accompanying medium.

Examples of subject headings assigned to works of vocal music:

Koh, Bunya. *Four Seiban Songs for Voice and Piano*
1. **Songs (Medium voice) with piano.**

Melismata: Musicall Phansies, compiled by Thomas Ravenscroft
1. **Part-songs, English.**
2. **Madrigals (Music), English.**
3. **Glees, catches, rounds, etc.**

Schubert, Franz Peter. *Magnificat: for Four-Part Chorus of Mixed Voices with Piano acc.*
1. **Choruses, Sacred (Mixed voices) with orchestra—Vocal scores with piano.**
2. **Magnificat (Music)**

Hurd, Michael. *The Widow of Ephesus: Chamber Opera in One Act*
1. **Operas—Vocal scores with piano.**

Forster, John. *Pretzels: A Musical Revue*
1. **Musical revues, comedies, etc.—Librettos.**

Mendelssohn-Bartholdy, Felix. *Ach Gott, von Himmel sieh' darein: choral cantata: baritone solo, mixed choir and orchestra*
1. **Cantatas, Sacred—Scores.**
2. **Psalms (Music)—12th Psalm.**
3. **Psalms (Music)—103d Psalm.**

Subdivisions. General subdivisions for music headings are:

> **—Scores**
> **—Parts**
> **—Scores and parts**
> **—Solo(s) with piano**

Headings containing the first three subdivisions listed above are being removed from the printed list as nonprint headings. This is also true of headings in the form of [xxxx], **Arranged.** The subdivision **—Solo(s) with piano** is always printed under a heading since a reference is always needed, e.g.,

Concertos (Violin)—Solo with piano
    xx   Violin and piano music, Arranged

The subdivision **—To 1800** previously used for earlier music is no longer used by the Library of Congress.*

The heading **Operas** with its subdivisions serves as the pattern of subdivisions for any heading involving larger vocal works with orchestra.

Topical Headings with Subdivisions Indicating Music

These headings are used in addition to music headings discussed above, when appropriate, e.g.,

The American Bicentennial Song Book in Two Volumes: Twenty Decades of American Songs
1. American Revolution Bicentennial, 1776-1976—Songs and music.
2. Songs, American.

Fortner, Wolfgang. *Elisabeth Tudor: Szenen aus dem Leben der Regentinnen Elisabeth der Ersten von England unde Maria Stuart, Königin von Schottland. . .*
1. Operas—Vocal scores with piano.
2. Elizabeth, Queen of England, 1533-1603—Drama.
3. Mary Stuart, Queen of the Scots, 1542-1587—Drama.

Sing and Be Joyful: Chapel Songbook, compiled by Samuel Sobel
1. Jews—Hymns.
2. Hymns, Hebrew.

Sound Recordings

Sound recordings of music are treated in the same manner as other musical works. No special subdivisions are used to bring out the format.

Examples:

Music from the Synagogue. [Sound recording]
1. Symphonies (Organ)
2. Sacred songs (Medium voice) with organ.
3. Synagogue music.

---

*Cf. *Music Cataloging Bulletin* 8:2 (February 1977).

Music from the South. [Sound recording]
1. Folk music, American—Southern states.
2. Afro-American songs.
3. Spirituals (Songs)
4. Gospel music—United States.

Hotline. [Sound recording]
1. Rock music—United States.

If the recording contains more than one work, separate headings are assigned to bring out the individual works, e.g.,

Beethoven, Ludwig van. *Piano Concerto, no. 1, in C major, op. 15. Choral fantasia, op. 80.* [Sound recording]
1. Concertos (Piano)
2. Piano with orchestra.
3. Choruses (Mixed voices) with orchestra.

Mozart, Johann Chrysostom Wolfgang Amadeus. *Sämtliche Quintette mit Streichern. Complete Strings* [sic] *Quintets.* (contains eight quintets). [Sound recording]
1. String quintets (Violins (2), violas (2), violoncello)
2. Quintets (Horn, violin, violas (2), violoncello)
3. Canons, fugues, etc. (String quartet)
4. Quintets (Clarinet, violins (2), viola, violoncello)
5. Suites (Violins (2), viola, violoncello, double bass)

Hovhaness, Alan. *Avak, the Healer. Armenian Rhapsody no. 1 on Armenian Mountain Village Tunes. Prayer of Saint Gregory. Tzaikerk; Evening Song.* [Sound recording]
1. Solo cantatas, Secular (High voice)
2. String-orchestra music.
3. Trumpet with string orchestra.
4. Flute, kettledrums, violin with string orchestra.

Live. [Sound recording]
1. Blues (Songs, etc.)—United States.
2. Piano music (Boogie woogie)

Wagner, Richard. *Meistersinger, Act 1.* [Sound recording]
1. Operas—Excerpts.

Chopin, Fryderyk Franciszek. *Introduction and Polonaise Brillante, op. 3. Grand Duo Concertante* [sic] *on Themes from Meyerbeer's Robert le Diable.* [Sound recording]
1. Violoncello and piano music.
2. Sonatas (Violoncello and piano)

(Examples continue on page 236.)

Tournemire, Charles. *Seven Chorale-Poems for Organ on the Seven Words of Christ, op. 67.* [Sound recording]
    1.   **Organ music.**
    2.   **Jesus Christ—Seven last words—Songs and music.**

Pattern References*

The Library of Congress has established patterns of *see also* references for the following categories of music headings:

Pattern headings	*Categories*
Baritone music	Brass instruments (i.e., Baritone, Cornet, Euphonium, Horn, Trombone, Trumpet, and Tuba music)
Bassoon music	Woodwind instruments (i.e., Bassoon, Clarinet, English-horn, Flute, Oboe d'amore, Oboe, Piccolo, Recorder, and Saxophone music)
Guitar music	Plectral instruments (i.e., Guitar, Harp, Lute, and Mandolin music)
Glockenspiel music	Percussion instruments (i.e., Glockenspiel, Kettledrum, Marimba, Vibraphone, and Xylophone music)
Celesta music	Celesta, Harpsichord, and Organ music
Double-bass music	Double-bass, Viol, Viola de gamba, Viola d'amore, and Violone music
Band music	Band, Chamber-orchestra, Dance-orchestra, String-orchestra music, and String ensembles
Accordion ensembles	Accordion ensembles and Salon-orchestra music

References for music headings, other than those listed in the above categories, are listed individually under each heading.

Other Recent Changes**

Subject headings for pre-1800 keyboard works. Prior to 1975, the Library of Congress assigned subject headings containing the word "harpsichord" to all printed and recorded editions of works composed for the harpsichord before 1800,

---

*Cf. *Music Cataloging Bulletin* 7:6-7 (September 1976).
**Cf. *Music Cataloging Bulletin* 6:2 (November 1975); 7:2 (July 1976).

and to all keyboard works with uniform titles established per AACR that include the word "harpsichord." This was done even if these editions were edited for performance or played on the piano. This policy of subject entry has been discontinued. Subject headings for these editions now contain the word "piano" instead of "harpsichord" as in the examples below:

Bach, Johann Sebastian, 1685-1750.
    [Concerto nach italienischen Gusto, harpsichord unacc., F. major]
    Italian concerto. Edited by Hans Bischoff.
      (Kalmus piano series)
      Old subject: Suites (Harpsichord)–To 1800.
    New subject: **Piano music** (See change of subject
treatment for the Bach Italian concerto–see page 238)

Bach, Johann Sebastian, 1685-1750.
    [Inventions, harpsichord] Phonodisc.
     Glenn Gould, piano
     Old subject: Canons, fugues, etc. (Harpsichord)–To 1800.
    New subject: **Canons, fugues, etc. (Piano)**

Bach, Johann Sebastian, 1685-1750.
    [Sonata, harpsichord, S.963, D major]
    Phonodisc.
     Ruth Slenczynska, piano
     Old subject: Sonatas (Harpsichord)–To 1800.
    New subject: **Sonatas (Piano)**

Subject headings for works performed on alternative instruments. Works composed before 1800 for Baroque, Renaissance, and other early instruments (viola da gamba, recorder, oboe d'amore, etc.) which are edited for, or in recordings performed on, contemporary instruments, and works for melody instruments which are edited for or performed on alternative instruments are no longer assigned the subdivision, ", Arranged" if the key, clef, and/or notation has not been significantly changed, as in the following examples:

Bach, Johann Sebastian, 1685-1750.
    [Sonatas, viola da gamba & harpsichord, S. 1027-1029]
    Phonodisc.
     André Navarra. violoncello; Ruggero Gerlin, harpsichord.
     Old subject: Sonatas (Violoncello and harpsichord),
    Arranged.
    New subject: **Sonatas (Violoncello and harpsichord)**

(Examples continue on page 238.)

Vivaldi, Antonio, 1678-1741.
    [Concerto, flute & string orchestra, F. VI, 13, G minor]
    Phonodisc.
    Hans Martin Linde, recorder; Collegium Musicum Zürich;
    Paul Sacher, conductor.
    Old subject: Concertos (Recorder with string orchestra),
    Arranged.
    New subject: **Concertos (Recorder with string orchestra)**

Kuhlau, Friedrich, 1786-1832.
    [Sonata, violin & piano, op. 79, no.1, F major]
    Sonate en fa majeur pour flute & piano, op.79, no. 1.
    Subject: **Sonatas (Flute and piano)**
    (Classed in M242, not M244 or M219)

Bach, Johann Sebastian, 1685-1750.
    [Concerto nach italienischen Gusto, harpsichord, unacc.,
    F major]
Library of Congress no longer considers this work a suite. Editions are now
entered under subjects such as **Harpsichord music** or **Piano music**, depending on
the edition being cataloged.

Subject headings for dance forms. All headings for dance forms with specification of instruments (with the exceptions of Minuets, Polkas, Polonaises, and Waltzes,
which were not changed due to the sizes of their files) have been cancelled. They
are now entered under the name of the dance, with a second heading added for the
medium if the work is for a medium other than piano, two hands.

    Specific *see also* references have been made from **Dance music** to all of these
headings, including the four that were not changed, and from **Piano music** to all
dance headings that have piano pieces contained in their files, e.g.,

Allemandes. Cancel note and substitute:

        This heading is used without specification of instruments. A
        second heading is assigned if the work is for a medium other
        than piano (2 hands), e.g.,
        1. Allemandes. 2. **Harpsichord music.**
    xx   **Dance music**

Boleros. Cancel note and substitute:

        This heading is used without specification of instruments. A
        second heading is assigned if the work is for a medium other
        than piano (2 hands), e.g.,
        1. Boleros. 2. **Orchestral music;** 1. **Boleros.**
        2. **Piano music (8 hands).**
    xx   **Dance music**
           Piano music

ART

Catalogs of Art Collections

The catalog of an unnamed art collection which is permanently housed in an individual museum but represents only a portion of the total collection of the institution is assigned the following headings:

1) The name of the museum.* This heading is assigned even when it duplicates the main entry or an added entry.

2) A heading identifying the objects of the special collection subdivided by —Catalogs.

3) A heading for the place of the collection, normally the heading under 2) (above) used without special adjectival qualifier, and subdivided by the name of the city, which in turn is subdivided by —Catalogs.

4) A fourth heading may be added if required by the work being cataloged in order to bring out the century, subdivided by —Catalogs.

Example:

Boston. Museum of Fine Arts. *Twentieth Century American Paintings in the Museum of Fine Arts, Boston.*
1. Boston. Museum of Fine Arts.
2. Painting, American—Catalogs.
3. Painting—Massachusetts—Boston—Catalogs.
4. Painting, Modern—20th century—United States—Catalogs.

New Britain Museum of American Art. *Catalogue of the Collection, 1975*
1. Art, American—Catalogs.
2. Art, Modern—19th century—United States—Catalogs.
3. Art, Modern—20th century—United States—Catalogs.
4. Art—Connecticut—New Britain—Catalogs.
5. New Britain Museum of American Art.

If, however, the catalog in question is a general catalog to the collection of a general art museum, only the heading for the institution is assigned, since the place aspect of the collection and contents of the collection are covered by the subject-to-name references made for the particular institution.

Private Art Collections

For the catalog of a private art collection, in addition to topical headings, a heading under the name of the collection is also assigned, e.g.,

---

*When a collection of objects of any type, including works of art, is *permanently* housed in a particular building or institution, a subject entry is made under the name of the building or institution. This subject heading is not assigned if the collection is not permanently housed in the building or institution, but is only there on display or on loan temporarily, such as for an exhibition.

Title: *Bayou Bend: American Furniture, Paintings, and Silver from the Bayou Bend Collection*
1.   Bayou Bend Collection.
2.   Art, American—Catalogs.
3.   Hogg, Ima—Art collections.

Private Art Collections Belonging to a Mr. and Mrs.

For a work which discusses a private collection owned jointly by a man and his wife, subject headings under both names subdivided by **—Art collections** are assigned. Subject entry is not made under the wife's name if she is identified only by the husband's name (e.g., Mrs. John Smith) and her own name is not readily available.

Art Exhibitions

The same headings assigned to catalogs are also used for exhibitions, except that the subdivision **—Exhibitions** is used instead of **—Catalogs**.

Examples:

Title: *Art of the Six Dynasties: Centuries of Change and Innovation* [exhibition]
1.   Art, Chinese—Three kingdoms, six dynasties-Sui dynasty, 220-618—Exhibitions.
2.   Art, Chinese—Exhibitions.

Title: *Paintings, Water-Colours, and Drawings from the Hadley-Read Collection, 11th-28th June, 1974*
1.   Art, English—Exhibitions.
2.   Art, Modern—19th century—England—Exhibitions.
3.   Hadley-Read, Charles—Art collections.

For a particular named exhibition, a subject heading for the exhibition in the form of [name of exhibition, city, date], e.g., **Armory Show, New York, 1913**, is assigned.

Particular Art Movements

For a work about a particular art movement, a subject heading for the movement is assigned. A second heading for the particular medium is also assigned if the movement is commonly understood to have been represented in two or more media.

Example:

1.   Impressionism (Art)—France.
2.   Painting, Modern—19th century—France.

The second heading is not required if the work discusses the movement as a phenomenon occurring in all of the arts.

Art of Specific Time Periods*

When cataloging art publications, subject catalogers normally have at their disposal two methods of specifying time periods for art of particular places.

Library of Congress subject headings in the field of the fine arts (i.e., headings used for works classed in N-NE) represent a separate block of headings with their own traditions and special provisions. Designating the place of origin is normally accomplished by qualifying the heading for the special art form or medium, e.g., **Etching, French**. Such a heading is used for both collections of reproduction and history and criticism and is, therefore, never further subdivided by the subdivision **–History**. If a particular time period is to be specified, the chronological subdivision may be added directly to the heading:

> **Porcelain, Japanese–Edo period, 1600-1868**
> **Painting, Japanese–Edo period, 1600-1868**

These period subdivisions, however, are normally added only to headings for works on Oriental art. For Western art, two headings are assigned to bring out period and place of origin.

1. **Water-color painting–19th century–France.**
2. **Water-color painting, French.**

1. **Sculpture, Modern–19th century–France.**
2. **Sculpture, French.**

Another system of headings with wider application than fine arts headings is also used by art catalogers; namely, headings used to designate industrial products and handicrafts. Although such headings normally embrace the traditions of headings used in the field of technology, they are also assigned to works classed in NK (art industries) when the work being cataloged has an art orientation. Although some exceptions do exist, normally such objects are not qualified by the country of origin. Instead, the country is designated by a local subdivision.

> **Glass fruit jars–Canada**
> *not* Glass fruit jars, Canadian
> **Kites–Japan**
> *not* Kites, Japanese

Therefore, to bring out the history of such objects in a place, it is necessary to further subdivide by the subdivision **–History**; if warranted by the work being cataloged the heading is again further subdivided by the time period, e.g., **[object]–[place]–History–[time period]**.

---

*Cf. *Cataloging Service* 124:18-19 (Winter 1978).

> Textile fabrics—Japan—History—Edo period,
> 1600-1868.

Although most headings for objects classed in NK are considered art industry headings and are given the treatment normally accorded manufactured products, the following headings represent exceptions to this policy and are treated as fine arts headings: **Bronzes; Cut glass; Engraved glass; Porcelain; Pottery; Rugs, Oriental; Rugs, Persian; Vases.** Most, however, have not been subdivided additionally by particular time periods.

> **Cut glass, Spanish**
> **Vases, Chinese**
> **Bronzes, Chinese—To 221 B.C.**

Art Reproductions with Commentary*

When collections of paintings, drawings, engravings, etc., by an individual artist are accompanied by commentary, a subject entry under the name of the artist is made regardless of the author entry. However, the biographical heading (indicating the class of persons) is not assigned unless the accompanying text presents substantial information about the artist's personal life (at least 20 percent of the text). If the text is limited to a discussion of the artist's works and artistic ability, the biographical heading is omitted.

LAW**

General Laws (Nontopical Compilations)

A subject entry under the heading **Law** with local subdivision is made for every nontopical compilation of laws with main entry under the name of a jurisdiction followed by **Laws, statutes, etc.**, e.g.,

> Georgia. Laws, statutes, etc. *Code of Georgia: Including the Code*
> *of 1933 and All Laws of General Application Subsequently Enacted*
> 1.   **Law—Georgia.**

> Botswana. Laws, statutes, etc. *The Laws of Botswana*
> 1.   **Law—Botswana.**

---

*Cf. *Cataloging Service* 119:20 (Fall 1976).
**Cf. *Cataloging Service* 106:4 (May 1973).

General Laws (Topical Compilations)

If the compilation pertains to a particular topic, the above heading is replaced by the appropriate topical heading subdivided by the jurisdiction, e.g.,

Arkansas. Laws, statutes, etc. *Arkansas Election Code*
    1.   Election law—Arkansas.

Kansas. Laws, statutes, etc. *Income Tax Laws and Regulations*
    1.   Income tax—Kansas—Law.

Pennsylvania. Laws, statutes, etc. *Pennsylvania Code, Title 7:*
       Agriculture; Department of Agriculture; Milk Marketing Board.
    1.   Agricultural laws and legislation—Pennsylvania.
    2.   Food law and legislation—Pennsylvania.

West Virginia. Laws, statutes, etc. *West Virginia Child Labor Law and*
      Regulations
    1.   Children—Employment—West Virginia.

New York (State). Laws, statutes, etc. *New York State Thruway Authority*
      act
    1.   Express highways—Laws and legislation—New York
       (State)
    2.   New York State Thruway Authority.

Ordinances*

For the text of a published nontopical compilation of ordinances, the subject heading **Ordinances, Municipal—[place]** is used, e.g.,

Honolulu. Ordinances, etc. *The Revised Ordinances of Honolulu, 1969*
    1.   Ordinances, Municipal—Hawaii—Honolulu.

Constitution*

For the text of a published constitution, the subject heading **[jurisdiction] — Constitutional law** is used, e.g.,

France. Constitution. *Constitutional and Organic Laws of France*
    1.   France—Constitutional law.

---

*These reflect a recent change of policy. Former practice was not to assign subject headings to nontopical compilations. The new policy is similar to the practice of assigning subject headings under names of persons for autobiographies.

Charters*

For the texts of a compilation of published charters, one of the following headings is used.

> **Charters**
>
> **County charters—[place]**
>
> **Municipal charters—[place]**

Examples:

County Charters in New York State
1. **County government—New York (State)**
2. **County charters—New York (State)**

Amendments to Municipal Charters Adopted by the Several Municipal Corporations in Maryland from June 1, 1955 to December 31, 1967. Public Local Laws of Charter Counties Adopted by the Several Charter Counties in Maryland up to December 31, 1967
1. **Municipal charters—Maryland.**
2. **County charters—Maryland.**

For the text of a single charter, one of the following headings is used:

> **[city]—Charters**
> **[for an American city]**
>
> **[city]—Charters, grants, privileges**
> **[for a foreign city]**
>
> **County charters—[place]**
> **[for a county]**

Other Works of Law

Appropriate topical headings are assigned, e.g.,

Oregon. Laws, statutes, etc. *Banking Laws*
1. **Banking law—Oregon.**

Ohio. Laws, statutes, etc. *Ohio Corporation Laws Annotated*
1. **Corporation law—Ohio.**

---

*These reflect a recent change of policy. Former practice was not to assign subject headings to nontopical compilations. The new policy is similar to the practice of assigning subject headings under names of persons for autobiographies.

Arizona. Laws, statutes, etc. *Arizona Laws Pertaining to Public Libraries*
  1.   **Library legislation—Arizona.**

Claus, R. James. *Signs: Legal Rights and Aesthetic Considerations*
  1.   **Signs and sign-boards—Law and legislation—United States.**
  2.   **Landscape protection—Law and legislation—United States.**

Becker, Olga. *Index/Citator to Insurance Law*
  1.   **Insurance law—United States—Indexes.**
  2.   **Insurance law—United States—Bibliography.**

United States. District Courts. *Amendments to Rules of Civil Procedure
    for the District Courts of the United States*
  1.   **Civil procedure—United States.**
  2.   **Court rules—United States.**

*Background Material on the Fair Labor Standards Act Amendments of
    1972*
  1.   **Wages—Minimum wage—United States.**
  2.   **Overtime—United States.**

Lasser (J. K.) Institute, New York. *J. K. Lasser's How to Avoid Having
    Your Tax Return Questioned: How to Win Your Case*
  1.   **Tax protests and appeals—United States—Popular works.**

SOURCE MATERIALS IN THE FIELDS OF
GENEALOGY AND HISTORY

In the past, many publications of interest to genealogists and historians, especially local historians, were assigned headings of the type [topic]—[place]. Beginning in December 1975, such materials have been given an additional heading of the type [place]—[topic]. The topical subdivision in this case is chosen from the following list:

> —**Antiquities**
> —**Biography**
> —**Church history**
> —**Description and travel**
> —**Economic conditions**
> —**Foreign population**
> —**Genealogy**
> —**History**
>   [including the various modifications of the subdivision,
>   e.g., —**History, Military**]
> —**Industries**
> —**Religious life and customs**
> —**Social conditions**
> —**Social life and customs**

All of these are free-floating subdivisions. The subdivision —**Genealogy** or —**History** is used when none of the above seems particularly relevant to the work in hand.

The Subdivision —History*

The subdivision —**History** is a free-floating subdivision and is widely used in a variety of situations to designate a historical treatment of the topic in question. However, there are certain restrictions to its use which have developed over the years. The following information supersedes the instruction provided in the introduction to the eighth edition of the Library of Congress printed list.

General use. The subdivision —**History** is used under subjects, including names of regions, countries, cities, etc., and organizations, for descriptions and explanations of past events within a particular field of knowledge, place, or organization, e.g.,

> Aeronautics—History
> Indians—History
> Washington, D.C.—History
> Catholic Church—History
> General Motors Corporation—History

Exceptions. The subdivision —**History** is *not* used:
1) Under literary, music, or film headings. The subdivision —**History and criticism** is used instead, e.g.,

> English poetry—History and criticism
> Western films—History and criticism

2) Under subjects for which phrase headings have been provided, e.g., **Church history**; **Military history**, etc.
3) Under historical headings, or headings which have an obvious historical connotation, e.g.,

> Social history
> Migrations of nations
> Reformation
> Discoveries (in geography)
> [names of individual events or wars]

4) Under topical subdivisions which have been considered as being historical in intent. These include all subdivisions which are obviously historical in nature (e.g., —**Discovery and exploration**; —**Territorial expansion**; events such as

---

*Cf. *Cataloging Service* 120:12-14 (Winter 1977).

—Massacre; —Flood; —Riot; etc.) and subdivisions which imply history by designating special kinds of conditions (e.g., —**Economic conditions**), special customs (e.g., —**Social life and customs**), and political affairs (e.g., —**Foreign relations**; —**Politics and government**). Following is a representative list of the subdivisions of this type which are not further subdivided by —**History**:

—Administrative and political
    divisions
—Aerial exploration
—Annexation to . . .
—Anniversaries, etc.
—Antiquities
—Blizzard
—Bombardment
—Boundaries
—Capture
—Centennial celebrations, etc.
—Chronology
—Church history
—Churches
—Civilization
—Constitutional history
—Court and courtiers
—Cyclone
—Demonstration
—Description
—Description and travel
—Discovery and exploration
—Earthquake
—Economic aspects
—Economic conditions
—Economic policy
—Exiles
—Exploring expeditions
—Famines
—Festivals, etc.
—Fire
—Flood
—Foreign economic relations
—Foreign relations

—Frontier troubles
—Gold discoveries
—Heraldry
—Historical geography
—Historiography
—History
—Intellectual life
—Kings and rulers
—Landslide
—Massacre
—Origin
—Politics and government
—Popular culture
—Race question
—Relations (general) with . . .
—Relations (military) with . . .
—Religion
—Religious life and customs
—Riot
—Riots
—Rites and ceremonies
—Rural conditions
—Siege
—Sieges
—Social aspects
—Social conditions
—Social policy
—Territorial expansion
—Theater disaster

    5)   Period subdivisions. If the exceptional headings or subdivisions noted above are to be further subdivided by chronological periods, the period subdivision is assigned directly after the heading or topical subdivision, e.g.,

            Military history, Modern—20th century
            United States—Foreign relations—1783-1815
            Boston—Politics and government—1775-1865

6) Historical source materials. The subdivision —**Sources** follows directly after these exceptional headings and subdivisions without interposing the subdivision —**History**, e.g.,

> Reconstruction—Sources
> European War, 1914-1918—Sources
> China—Foreign relations—Sources
> United States—Politics and government—1783-1789—Sources

As a further subdivision under a form subdivision. In a few instances where it is necessary to designate the history of a form, and there are no alternatives, the subdivision —**History** is used to further subdivide a form subdivision, e.g.,

> Title: *Development of Medical Periodicals*
> 1.   Medicine—Periodicals—History.

Special considerations:
1)   Certain form subdivisions are not further subdivided by —**History**. The historical aspect is expressed by another division, e.g.,

Form	*History*
Medicine—Computer programs	Medicine—Data processing —History
Medicine—Indexes	Medicine—Abstracting and indexing —History

2)   By tradition, art form subdivisions are never further subdivided by —**History**, including the subdivisions —**Art**; —**Portraits**; —**Iconography**; —**Illustrations**.
3)   Under literary, music, or film form subdivisions, the subdivision —**History and criticism** is used.

History of a Discipline in a Place*

Headings of the type [name of discipline] —[place] —**History**, e.g., **Agriculture—United States—History**, are used to designate either the history of the discipline in a place or the history of conditions in a place. No attempt is usually made to distinguish the two concepts.

For a few disciplines which are not divisible by place, the history of the discipline in a place has formerly been designated by subdividing the subdivision —**History** by place, e.g., **Chemistry—History—United States**. In order to rid the system of two separate methods, i.e.,

> [name of discipline] —[place] —History
>
> [name of discipline] —History—[place]

---

*Cf. *Cataloging Service* 121:15 (Spring 1977).

Library of Congress has decided to discontinue the second type and to use the first type in all instances. All disciplines will be uniformly subdivided by place without exception. In other words, the heading

Telecommunication—United States—History

is used for either a work about the history of telecommunication in the United States or a work about the history of the discipline telecommunication in the United States.

However, there are a few special headings which provide for conditions in a particular place in an entirely different manner. For example, in the field of Economics, the economic conditions of a place are brought out by the subdivision —**Economic conditions** under the name of the place. In such instances scope notes are provided to warn the user that the heading subdivided by place refers only to the discipline in the place, including its history, and that conditions and the history of conditions are found elsewhere. Library of Congress is in the process of updating headings of this type to conform to this new decision, with scope notes added to explain the new usage. The following scope notes were recently prepared for the heading **Economics**:

Economics *(Indirect)*

Here and with local subdivision are entered works on the discipline of economics. Works on the economic conditions of particular countries, regions, cities, etc., are entered under the name of the place subdivided by **Economic conditions.**

Economics—United States

Here are entered works on the discipline of economics in the United States. Works on the economic history or conditions of the United States are entered under the heading **United States—Economic conditions.**

Economics—History

Here are entered works on the history of economics as a discipline. Works on economic history or conditions are entered under the heading **Economic history**, or the subdivision **Economic conditions** under names of countries, regions, cities, etc.

Genealogical Materials

The heading [place]—**Genealogy** is used for works of value in the study of the origin, descent, and relationship of named families, especially those works which assemble such information from family papers, deeds, wills, public records, parish registers, cemetery inscriptions, ship lists, etc. Such a heading is assigned even if the place involved is a country or larger region such as a continent.

When appropriate, a form heading is also assigned. Typical headings of this nature are:

Business records	Obituaries
Church records and registers	Probate records
Court records	Public land records
Criminal registers	Public records
Deeds	Registers of births, etc.
Heraldry	Royal descent, Families of*
Inventories of decedents' estates	Slave records
	Taxation
Land grants	Titles of honor and nobility
Marriage licenses	Trials
Mining claims	Wills
Names	

All of these may be subdivided by place except the asterisked heading.

Examples:

Title: *Wills and Their Whereabouts*
    1.   Wills—Great Britain.
    2.   Great Britain—Genealogy.

Title: *Tombstone Inscriptions and Family Records of Jefferson County*
    1.   Registers of births, etc.—Jefferson Co., Ohio.
    2.   Cemeteries—Ohio—Jefferson Co.
    3.   Jefferson Co., Ohio—Genealogy.

Title: *Index to Chester Co., Pa., Wills and Intestate Records, 1713-1850*
    1.   Probate records—Pennsylvania—Chester County—Indexes.
    2.   Chester County, Pa.—Genealogy.

Other Works of Interest to Historians

The following types of materials are also considered to be of interest to historians:
    1)   Archaeological evidence.* Typical headings:
        Earthworks (Archaeology)
        Excavations (Archaeology)
        Industrial archaeology
        Kitchen-middens
        Mounds

---

*For works on the archaeology of particular places, see the following section.

2)   Classes of persons, activities. Typical headings:
> **Buccaneers**
> **Cattle trade**
> **Cowboys**
> **Frontier and pioneer life**
> **Fur trade**
> **Gunsmiths**
> **Minorities**
>> [including individually named elements, e.g., **Swedish Americans—Minnesota**]
>
> **Physicians**
> **Pirates**
> **Printing—History**
> **Ranch life**

3)   Monuments and memorials. Typical headings:
> **Cemeteries**
> **Epitaphs**
> **Historical markers**
> **Inscriptions**
> **Memorials**
> **Monuments**
> **Sepulchral monuments**
> **Soldiers' monuments**
> **Statues**
> **Tombs**
> **War memorials**

4)   Particular uses of land, historic structures. Typical headings:
> **Bridges**
> **Churches**
> **Farms**
> **Fountains**
> **Historic sites**
> **Hotels, taverns, etc.**
> **Mines and mineral resources**
> **Parks**
> **Roads**

5)   Historic events. Typical headings:
> **Battles**
> **Earthquakes**
> **Epidemics**
> **Fires**
> **Storms**

If a work is historical in nature and requires one of the headings of the types listed above, the additional heading [**place**]—[**topic**] is usually also assigned,

Title: *Early German Printers of Lancaster*
1.   Printers—Pennsylvania—Lancaster.
2.   Lancaster, Pa.—Biography.

Title: *Sign Posts; Place Names in History of Burlington Co.*
1.   Names, Geographical—New Jersey—Burlington Co.
2.   Burlington Co., N.J.—History, Local.

Title: *Charcoal Kilns; Historic Structures Report of Santa Fe*
1.   Charcoal kilns—New Mexico—Santa Fe.
2.   Santa Fe, N.M.—Antiquities.
3.   New Mexico—Antiquities.

The prescribed extra heading [place]—[topic] is assigned to works of interest to historians and local historians only when the place in question is less than a country, e.g., a city, county, state, region of a country, etc. It is not assigned when the place in question corresponds to a country or a larger region except for works classed in D, E, and F at the Library of Congress. Neither is the extra heading required for works dealing with named entities such as parks, structures, institutions, archaeological sites, events (unless the event, such as a war, is further subdivided by place), and ethnic groups (unless further subdivided by place).

Examples of works classed in D, E, and F requiring an additional heading: [* indicates the prescribed extra heading]

Title: *National Parks and Monuments*
1.   National parks and reserves—United States.
2.   Historic sites—United States.
*3.   United States—Description and travel—1960-   —Guide-books.

Title: *Place Names of Australia*
1.   Names, Geographical—Australia.
*2.   Australia—History, Local.

Title: *The Chinese in New York*
1.   Chinese Americans—New York (City)—History.
*2.   New York (City)—History—1898-1951.

Title: *Fighting Generals*
1.   Generals—United States—Biography.
2.   United States. Army—Biography.
*3.   United States—History, Military.

Title: *Australia in the Great War*
1.   European War, 1914-1918—Australia.
*2.   Australia—History—20th century.

Title: *Who Lived to See the Day; France in Arms, 1940-1945*
1.   World War, 1939-1945—Underground movements—France.
*2.   France—History—German occupation, 1940-1945.

Examples of works where the additional heading is not assigned:

Title: *Words Like Freedom: A Multi-Cultural Bibliography*
1.   **Minorities—United States—Bibliography.**

Title: *War in the West*
1.   **World War, 1939-1945—Campaigns—Western.**

Title: *Historic Preservation: Grants-In-Aid Catalogue*
1.   **Federal aid to historic sites—United States.**
2.   **Historic buildings—United States—Conservation and restoration.**

ARCHAEOLOGICAL WORKS*

Types of Headings Used

For works on the archaeology of particular places, one or more of the following headings are used:
1)   The place with the subdivision —**Antiquities**, e.g.,

Mexico—Antiquities

Geographically the access point to the archaeology of a place is the name of the appropriate country. Access point at the country level is always provided, unless the area in question is larger than a particular country, in which case the name of the larger region (or ancient jurisdiction for which there is no modern equivalent name, e.g., **Rome**) is used.

By way of exception, the access jurisdiction in the case of Canada, Great Britain, Soviet Union, and the United States is the first order political subdivision (states, provinces, etc.) rather than the country, e.g.,

Arizona—Antiquities

England—Antiquities

If a special locality within a country (or in the first order political subdivision of the exceptional countries listed above) is the area under consideration in the work being cataloged, that locality is brought out by means of an additional heading.

The subdivision —**Antiquities** is used under the name of the place and is qualified, whenever applicable, by one of the following terms: **Buddhist, Byzantine, Celtic, Germanic, Hindu, Phenician, Roman, Slavic,** or **Turkish**, e.g.,

England—Antiquities, Roman.

If none of these terms is applicable, no qualifier is added.

---

*Cf. *Cataloging Service* 122:18-20 (Summer 1977).

2)   Name of people (or prehistoric culture or period) with local subdivision if the heading is divisible by place. Peoples who are still extant in modern times are further subdivided by —**Antiquities**, e.g.,

Mayas—Antiquities.

3)   Special aspect, if applicable. If the work focuses on a special aspect of the culture, e.g., pottery, burial practice, agriculture, etc., this is brought out by a separate heading.

4)   **Excavation (Archaeology)—[place]**. This heading is used if the work being cataloged presents facts of excavations carried out, including techniques used, and artifacts recovered, etc.

Application

The first two categories of headings (i.e., the heading for the place and the heading for the people) are required for an archaeological report if it deals with both a specific area (but not a single site) and a people. If two peoples are involved, separate headings are used to bring out the particular place and each of the peoples. If more than two peoples are involved either geographically or chronologically, or if the name of the people or peoples cannot be identified from the work being cataloged, only the heading for the place is assigned.

Headings listed under 3) and 4) above are assigned only when required by the nature of the work being cataloged.

If the name of the jurisdiction corresponds exactly to that of the people (e.g., **Rome** versus **Romans**), only the heading for the place is used. For instance, tracing 2 in each of the examples given below is superfluous:

    1.   **Egypt—Antiquities.**
    [2.   **Egyptians**]

    1.   **Greece—Antiquities.**
    [2.   **Greeks**]

    1.   **Rome—Antiquities.**
    [2.   **Romans**]

Individual sites. When a work deals with an individual site, a subject entry is made under the name of the site. Additional headings are assigned to bring out special aspects, if any. Headings listed in 1), 2), and 4) (for the place, people, and excavation) are not used, because these aspects are covered by references made to the name of the site.*

Examples of headings assigned to individual works:

Title: *Archaeological Treasures of Ancient Egypt*
    1.   **Egypt—Antiquities.**

---

*For forms of headings and references for archaeological sites, see Chapter 6.

Title: *Etruscan Painted Tombs of Tarquinia, Italy*
1.   Italy—Antiquities.
2.   Tarquinia, Italy—Antiquities.
3.   Etruscans—Italy—Tarquinia.
4.   Tombs—Italy—Tarquinia.
5.   Mural painting and decoration, Etruscan—Italy—Tarquinia.

Title: *Remains of Roman Roads in Sicily*
1.   Italy—Antiquities, Roman.
2.   Sicily—Antiquities, Roman.
3.   Romans—Italy—Sicily.
4.   Roads, Roman—Italy—Sicily.

Title: *A Complete Account of Excavations Carried Out in the Ancient Mesopotamian City of Uruk, with Emphasis on Its Pottery Sequence*
1.   Erech, Babylonia.
2.   Pottery—Iraq—Erech, Babylonia.

Title: *Excavations Carried Out in Three Anasazi Sites of Chaco Canyon, N. M.*
1.   New Mexico—Antiquities.
2.   Chaco Canyon, N.M.—Antiquities.
3.   Pueblo Indians—New Mexico—Chaco Canyon—Antiquities.
4.   Excavations (Archaeology)—New Mexico—Chaco Canyon.

"AREA STUDIES" AND "RESEARCH"*

The use of the study headings, e.g., **African studies,** and ethnic study headings, e.g., **Indian studies,** was discontinued in 1977. Instead, the type of heading **[name of area** or **ethnic group]**—Study and teaching, e.g., **Africa—Study and teaching; Indians—Study and teaching,** is used.

The heading **[name of area]**—Study and teaching is used for a work on the study of an area, including facilities, personnel, funding, projects, methodology, etc. It is not assigned to a work which presents substantive information about an area, or information obtained *as a result* of an area study program. For this type of work, a heading is assigned under the name of the area; or, if the work focuses on a special aspect of the area, including history, language, culture, etc., the heading is subdivided by the appropriate subdivision, e.g.,

> **Africa**
> **Africa—Civilization**
> **Africa—Intellectual life**

---

*Cf. *Cataloging Service* 121:15 (Spring 1977).

The use of research headings is similar. Research headings, e.g., **Engineering research; Marine biology—Research**, are assigned to works which discuss such details as the facilities, personnel, etc., for doing research in particular disciplines. Works providing the *results* of the research are assigned headings under the names of the disciplines themselves, e.g., **Engineering; Marine biology**.

ZOOLOGICAL WORKS WITH GEOGRAPHIC ASPECTS*

On page 59 of his *Subject Headings* (1951), Haykin discusses a kind of duplicate entry which is "frequently and consistently used," namely, the provision for making a duplicate entry under the next broader heading which admits of local subdivision when assigning the name of an animal which is not locally subdivided. Haykin points out further that the situation most often arises in connection with works on a particular genus or species in a place, for example:

1. **Gnatcatchers.**
2. **Birds—California.**

The additional subject entry is extremely important because it makes it possible for catalog users to carry out area surveys. Direct access to place and topic is a standard feature in the social science fields, e.g., **Ohio—Economic conditions,** but it is seldom encountered in science where greater stress is placed on topic. Without providing direct access to place this handicap may be overcome by gathering. All zoological works with a geographic aspect are gathered under a limited number of broad topical headings with local subdivision. By consulting these headings the user is able to obtain a complete array of the works on the zoology of a specific place.

General Rule

When cataloging a work on an animal of a particular place, two headings are assigned: the heading for the animal's name (family name, genus name, etc.) with local subdivision, if the heading by chance also provides for local subdivision; and the corresponding broader heading with local subdivision.

In deciding which taxonomic level constitutes the broader heading for the second heading, Library of Congress practice has varied over the years, so that different practices may be observed on Library of Congress cataloging records. The following guidelines represent current practice:

Invertebrates: Phylum level (exception: for arachnids, crustaceans, and insects of Arthropoda, use the class level).

Vertebrates: Class level

---

*Cf. *Cataloging Service* 122:16-18 (Summer 1977).

Below is a list of phyla or classes—using Library of Congress's present forms of the names—under which gathering entries are made:

Phyla of Invertebrates

Acanthocephala
Annelida
Arthropoda
Brachiopoda
Chaetognatha
Coelenterata
Ctenophora
Echinodermata
Echiuroidea
Enteropneusta
Entoprocto
Gastrotricha
Gordiacea
Kinorhyncha
Mesozoa
Molluska
Myzostomaria

Nematoda
Nemertinea
Onychophora
Pentastomida
Platyhelminthes
Pogonophora
Polyzoa
Priapulida
Protochordates
Protozoa
Pterobranchia
Rotifera
Sipunculida
Sponges
Tardigrada
Tunicata

Example:

Title: *Zwei neue interstitielle Microphthalmus-Arten (Polychaeta) von den Bermudas*
1.   Microphthalmus bermudensis.
2.   Annelida—Bermuda Islands.

Classes of Arthropoda

Arachnida
Crustacea
Insects

Example:

Title: *Beetles of Austria*
1.   Beetles—Austria.
2.   Insects—Austria.

Classes of Vertebrates

Amphibians
Birds
Fishes
Mammals
Reptiles

(Example appears on page 258.)

Example:

Title: *Squirrels of Mexico*
1.   Squirrels—Mexico.
2.   Mammals—Mexico.

Topical Subdivisions

In addition to providing geographical access to individual animals, Library of Congress also uses gathering to give access to many subdisciplines of zoology as they pertain to individual animals. In the past Library of Congress designated these special topics by gathering under broader taxonomic headings in the same manner as above, for example:

1.   Wood-rats.
2.   Mammals—Anatomy.

Because these subdisciplines, including **Anatomy, Behavior, Cytology, Evolution, Genetics, Reproduction,** etc., are now represented by the topical subdivisions found under the heading **Fishes,** the model heading for animals, they are now topics which may be used under any animal as free-floating subdivisions. Accordingly, Library of Congress will assign the topical subdivision both under the name of the specific animal (for purposes of specificity) and under the broader heading (for purposes of gathering), using the same gathering levels stated above, for example:

1.   Wood-rats—Anatomy.
2.   Mammals—Anatomy.

If a topic is more specific than any of the subdisciplines represented by subdivision under the model heading, an additional heading to bring out that topic is assigned, for example:

1.   Wood-rats—Anatomy.
2.   Cornea.
3.   Mammals—Anatomy.

APPENDICES

A—Glossáry

B—Additional Free-Floating Form and Topical Subdivisions of General
    Application

C—Free-Floating Subdivisions Used Under Names of Regions, Countries,
    Cities, etc.

D—Free-Floating Subdivisions Under Personal Names

E—Free-Floating Subdivisions Controlled by Pattern Headings

F—Subdivisions Further Subdivided by Place

G—Previous Library of Congress Practice with Regard to Geographic
    Qualifiers

H—Abbreviations

I—Capitalization

J—Punctuation

K—Filing

APPENDIX A

GLOSSARY

Alphabetical subject catalog. A catalog containing subject entries based on the principle of specific and direct entry and arranged alphabetically. Cf. **Alphabetico-classed catalog; Classed catalog; Dictionary catalog.**

Alphabetico-classed catalog. A subject catalog in which entries are listed under broad subjects and subdivided hierarchically by topics. The entries on each level of the hierarchy are arranged alphabetically. Cf. **Alphabetical subject catalog; Classed catalog; Dictionary catalog.**

Analytical subject entry. Subject entry for part of a work.

Biographical heading. A heading used with biographies which consists of the name of a class of persons with appropriate subdivisions, e.g., **Physicians—California—Biography; Poets, American—19th century—Biography.**

Biography. A special genre of works consisting of life histories of individuals, including those written by the individuals themselves, i.e., autobiographies. Cf. **Collective biography; Complete biography; Individual biography; Partial biography.**

Chronological subdivision. See Period subdivision.

Classed catalog. A subject catalog consisting of class entries arranged logically according to a systematic scheme of classification. Also called "Class catalog," "Classified subject catalog," "Systematic catalog." Cf. **Alphabetical subject catalog; Alphabetico-classed catalog; Dictionary catalog.**

Class entry. A subject entry consisting of a string of hierarchically related terms beginning with the broadest term leading to the subject in question.

Co-extensive heading. A heading which represents precisely (no more general or specific than) the subject content of a work.

Collective biography. A work consisting of two or more life histories. Cf. **Individual biography.**

Complete biography. A biography which covers the entire life story of an individual. Cf. **Partial biography.**

Cross reference. A direction from a term or a heading to another in the catalog. Cf. *See* **reference;** *See also* **reference; Refer from reference.**

Dictionary catalog. A catalog in which all the entries (author, title, subject, series, etc.) and the cross references are interfiled in one alphabetical sequence. The subject entries in a dictionary catalog are based on the principle of specific and direct entry. The term, when used in reference to the subject entries, is sometimes used interchangeably with the term, alphabetical subject catalog. Cf. **Alphabetical subject catalog; Alphabetico-classed catalog; Classed catalog.**

Direct subdivision. Geographic subdivision of subject headings by name of a local place without interposition of the name of a larger geographic entity. Previously, direct subdivision was used much more extensively than the case is now. Cf. Chapter 4.

Downward reference. A reference from a broad term to a narrow one. Cf. **Upward reference.**

Duplicate entry. 1) Entry of the same heading in two different forms, e.g., **United States—Foreign relations—France** and **France—Foreign relations— United States.**

       2) Assignment of two headings to bring out different aspects of a work. Frequently, one of the headings is a specific heading and the other a general (also called generic) heading subdivided by an aspect, e.g., **Poa** and **Grasses—Scandinavia** for a work about Poa in Scandinavia.

Explanatory reference. A reference providing explanatory statements with regard to the heading involved. It is used when a simple *see* or *see also* reference does not give adequate information or guidance to the user.

Facet analysis. The division of a subject into its component parts (facets). Each array of facets consists of parts based on the same characteristic, e.g., language facet, space facet, time facet.

Festschrift. A collection of two or more essays, addresses, or biographical, bibliographical and other contributions published in honor of a person, an institution, or a society, usually on the occasion of an anniversary or birthday celebration.

Film. A generic term for any pictorial medium intended for projection, including motion pictures, filmstrips, slides and transparencies, video tapes, and electronic video recordings.

Form heading. A heading representing the physical, bibliographical, artistic, or literary form of a work, e.g., **Encyclopedias and dictionaries; Essays; Short stories; String quartets.**

Form subdivision. A division of a subject heading which brings out the form of the work, e.g., **—Periodicals; —Bibliography; —Collected works.**

Free-floating subdivision. A subdivision which may be used by a cataloger at the Library of Congress under any existing appropriate heading for the first time without establishing the usage editorially.

General reference. A blanket reference to a group of headings rather than a particular heading. Example:
    Nicknames
        sa subdivision Nicknames *under subjects, e.g.,* Kings and
        rulers—Nicknames; *also special nicknames, e.g.,*
        Hoosier (Nickname), Uncle Sam (Nickname).
    Cf. **Specific reference.**

Geographic qualifier. The name of a larger geographic entity added to a local place name, e.g., **Cambridge, Mass.; Toledo, Spain.**

Geographic subdivision. A subdivision by the name of a place to which the subject represented by the main heading is limited. Cf. **Direct subdivision; Indirect subdivision.**

History card. *See* **Information card.**

Indirect subdivision. Geographic subdivision of subject headings by name of coun- , try, constituent country (Great Britain), state (United States), province (Canada), or constituent republic (U.S.S.R.) with further subdivision by name of state (other than United States), province (other than Canada), county, city, or other locality. Cf. **Direct subdivision.**

Individual biography. A work devoted to the life of a single individual. Cf. **Collective biography.**

Information card. A record providing information concerning the history of a heading. It is used generally with headings that have undergone changes. Also called "History card."

Jurisdictional qualifier. *See* **Political qualifier.**

Juvenile work. Works intended for children up through the age of fifteen (or through the ninth grade).

Local subdivision. *See* **Geographic subdivision.**

Model heading. A heading which serves as a model of subdivisions for headings in the same category, i.e., subdivisions listed under a model heading may be used whenever appropriate under other headings in the same category, e.g., **Shakespeare, William, 1564-1616**, as a model heading for literary authors; **Piano** as a model heading for musical instruments. Also called "Pattern heading."

Nonprint heading. A heading which is used in catalog entries but not listed in *Library of Congress Subject Headings.* Most of the headings consisting of proper names (including author headings used as subject headings) and many music headings are nonprint headings.

Partial biography. A work which presents only certain details of a person's life. Cf. **Complete biography.**

Pattern heading. *See* **Model heading.**

Period subdivision. A subdivision which shows the period or span of time treated in a work or the period during which the work appeared. Also called "Chronological subdivision."

Post-coordination. The representation of a complex subject by means of separate single-concept terms at the input stage and the retrieval of that subject by means of combining the separate terms at the search or output stage. Also called a "coordinate" system. Cf. **Pre-coordination.**

Pre-coordination. The representation of a complex subject by means of combining separate elements of the subject at the input stage. Cf. **Post-coordination.**

Political qualifier. A term (enclosed in parentheses) indicating the type of jurisdiction added to a geographic name in order to distinguish between places of the same name, e.g., **New York (State); Rome (City)**. Also called "Jurisdictional qualifier."

Qualifier. A term (enclosed in parentheses) placed after a heading for the purpose of distinguishing between homographs or clarifying the meaning of the heading, e.g., **Indexing (Machine-shop practice); PL/I (Computer program language); Mont Blanc (Freighter); Novgorod, Russia (Duchy).** Cf. **Geographic qualifier; Political qualifier.**

Refer from reference. An indication of the terms or headings *from* which references are to be made to a given heading. It is the reverse of the indication of a *see* or *see also* reference and is represented by the symbols *x* (*see* reference from) and *xx* (*see also* reference from).

Reference. *See* **Cross reference.**

See also reference. A reference from a heading to a less comprehensive or otherwise related heading. It is indicated in *Library of Congress Subject Headings* by the symbol *sa.*

See reference. A reference from a term or name not used as a heading to one that is used.

Specific entry. Entry of a work under a heading which expresses its special subject or topic as distinguished from an entry for the class or broad subject which encompasses that special subject or topic.

Specific reference. A reference from one heading to another. Cf. **General reference.**

Split files. Separate files of subject entries in a catalog under headings represented by current and obsolete terms which refer to the same subject. The device has been adopted by the Library of Congress recently to facilitate updating of terminology.

Subdivision. The device of extending a subject heading by indicating one of its aspects—form, place, period, topic. Cf. **Form subdivision; Geographic subdivision; Period subdivision; Topical subdivision.**

Subject. The theme or topic treated by the author in a work, whether stated in the title or not.

Subject analysis. The process of identifying the intellectual content of a work. The results may be displayed in a catalog or bibliography by means of notational symbols as in a classification system, or verbal terms such as subject headings or indexing terms.

Subject analytic. *See* **Analytical subject entry.**

Subject authority record. A record of a subject heading which shows its established form, cites the authorities consulted in determining the choice and form of the heading, and indicates the cross references made to and from the heading.

Subject catalog. A catalog consisting of subject entries only. The subject portion of a divided catalog.

Subject heading. The term (a word or a group of words) denoting a subject under which all material on that subject is entered in a catalog.

Subject-to-name reference. A reference from a subject heading to an author heading for the purpose of directing the user's attention from a particular field of interest to names of individuals or corporate bodies that are active or associated in some way with the field. Current Library of Congress policy requires only subject-to-corporate-name references. Also called "Red-to-Black" reference.

Syndetic device. The device used to connect related headings by means of cross references.

Synthesis. The representation of a subject by combining separate terms.

Topical subdivision. A subdivision which represents an aspect of the main subject other than form, place, or period. Cf. **Form subdivision; Geographic subdivision; Period subdivision.**

Uniform heading. Use of one heading in one form only for a given subject.

Upward reference. A reference from a narrow term to a broader term. Cf. **Downward reference.**

APPENDIX B

ADDITIONAL FREE-FLOATING FORM AND
TOPICAL SUBDIVISIONS OF GENERAL APPLICATION*

In addition to the subdivisions (with the exceptions noted below) listed in the introduction to the eighth edition of *Library of Congress Subject Headings*, the following subdivisions are also free-floating:

—Accidents—Investigation
—Archival resources *(Indirect)*
—Attitudes
—Biological control
—Comic books, strips, etc.
—Computer assisted instruction
—Congresses—Attendance
—Controversial literature
—Correspondence
—Cost effectiveness
—Data processing
—Decision making
—Energy consumption
—Energy conservation
—History—16th century
—History—17th century
—History—18th century
—History—19th century
—History—20th century
—Legal research
—Lexicography
—Library resources *(Indirect)*
—Linear programming
—Longitudinal studies
—Manuscripts—Facsimiles
—Moral and religious aspects—[religion or denomination]
—Price policy
—Rating of
—Remodeling
—Remote sensing
—Slides
—Stability
—Study and teaching—Supervision
—Study and teaching (Graduate) *(Indirect)*
—Study and teaching (Internship) *(Indirect)*
—Video tape catalogs

---

*Updated as of January 1978.

The following are free-floating "in" phrase headings:

... in fiction, drama, poetry, etc.
... in literature

The following subdivisions listed in the introduction are *not* free-floating subdivisions:

—Art collections
—Biography
[under names of disciplines]
—Coin collections
—Ethnological collections
—Interviews
[under names of disciplines]
—Law and legislation
—Library
—Photograph collections
—Private collections

The following subdivisions listed in the introduction have been deleted or revised:

—Correspondence, reminiscences, etc.
[Deleted; replaced by two subdivisions: —Correspondence;
—Biography]
—Courts and courtiers
[Changed to —Court and courtiers]
—Race question
[Deleted; replaced by —Race relations]
—Riots, [date]
[Changed to —Riots]
—Sieges, [years]
[Changed to —Sieges]
—Statistical, Medical
[Corrected to —Statistics, Medical]
—Statistical, Vital
[Corrected to —Statistics, Vital]
—Tidal wave, [year]
[Deleted; replaced by: —Tsunami, [date]]
—Tidal waves
[Replaced by —Tsunamis]

The new subdivisions which replaced the obsolete ones are free-floating.

APPENDIX C

FREE-FLOATING SUBDIVISIONS USED UNDER NAMES OF REGIONS, COUNTRIES, CITIES, ETC.

REGIONS, COUNTRIES, ETC. (CITIES EXCLUDED)*

—Abstracting and indexing
—Abstracts
—Addresses, essays, lectures
—Administrative and political divisions
—Aerial exploration
—Aerial photographs
—Air defenses
—Air defenses, Civil
—Air defenses, Military
—Altitudes
—Anecdotes, facetiae, satire, etc.
—Annexation to . . .
—Anniversaries, etc.
—Antiquities
—Antiquities—Collection and
    preservation
—Appropriations and expenditures
—Archival resources
—Armed Forces
—Bibliography
—Bio-bibliography
—Biography
—Biography—Anecdotes, facetiae,
    satire, etc.
—Biography—Portraits
—Blizzard, [date]
—Book reviews
—Boundaries
—Capital and capitol
—Census**
—Census, [date]
—Centennial celebrations, etc.
—Charters
—Charters, grants, privileges
—Church history
—Civil defense
—Civilization

—Climate
—Clubs
—Coast defenses
—Collected works
—Colonies
—Colonies—Government publications
—Colonization
—Commerce
—Commercial policy
—Commercial treaties
—Congresses
—Constitutional history
—Constitutional law
—Constitutional law—Amendments
—Court and courtiers
—Cyclone, [date]
—Defenses
—Description and travel
—Description and travel—Aerial
—Description and travel—Guide-books
—Description and travel—Tours
—Description and travel—Views
—Description, geography
—Dictionaries and encyclopedias
—Diplomatic and consular service
—Diplomatic and consular service—
    Privileges and immunities
—Directories
—Directories—Telephone
—Discovery and exploration
—Distances, etc.
—Drama
—Economic conditions
—Economic integration
—Economic policy
—Emigration and immigration
—Empresses

---

*Updated as of January 1978. Use this list for metropolitan areas.
Also special subdivisions under **United States—Census.

—Executive departments
—Executive departments—Public
    meetings
—Exiles
—Exploring expeditions
—Fairs
—Famines
—Fiction
—Foreign economic relations
—Foreign opinion
—Foreign population
—Foreign population—Housing
—Foreign relations
—Foreign relations—Treaties
—Foreign relations administration
—Forest policy
—Frontier troubles
—Full employment policies
—Gazetteers
—Genealogy
—Gentry
—Gold discoveries
—Government property
—Government publications
—Government vessels
—Governors
—Historical geography
—Historical geography—Maps
—Historiography
—History
—History—16th century*
—History—17th century*
—History—18th century*
—History—19th century*
—History—20th century*
—History—Anecdotes, facetiae,
    satire, etc.
—History—Autonomy and
    independence movements
—History—Partition, [date]
—History—Prophecies
—History—Sources
—History, Comic, satirical, etc.
—History, Local
—History, Military
—History, Naval

—Hurricane, [date]
—Hurricanes
—Imprints
—Industries
—Industries—Energy conservation
—Intellectual life
—International status
—Juvenile drama
—Juvenile fiction
—Juvenile films
—Juvenile literature
—Juvenile phonorecords
—Juvenile poetry
—Kings and rulers
—Kings and rulers—Genealogy
—Languages
—Learned institutions and societies
—Library resources
—Literary collections
—Literatures
—Manufactures
—Maps
—Maps—Bibliography
—Maps, Comparative
—Maps, Manuscript
—Maps, Outline and base
—Maps, Physical
—Maps, Pictorial
—Maps, Tourist
—Massacre, [date]
—Military policy
—Militia
—Miscellanea
—Moral conditions
—Name
—National Guard
—National security
—Native races
—Naval militia
—Navigation
—Neutrality
—Nobility
—Occupations
—Officials and employees
—Officials and employees—Appointment,
    qualifications, tenure, etc.

*Not a free-floating subdivision. It must be established editorially when used for the first time under a particular place.

Regions, Countries, etc. (Cities Excluded) (cont'd)

—Officials and employees—Pensions
—Officials and employees—Salaries, allowances, etc.
—Officials and employees—Travel regulations
—Officials and employees, Retired
—Officials and employees, Retired—Employment
—Periodicals
—Photo maps
—Poetry
—Politics and government
—Popular culture
—Population
—Population density
—Population policy
—Presidents
—Presidents—Election
—Princes and princesses
—Proclamations
—Provinces
—Public buildings
—Public lands
—Public works
—Race relations
—Registers
—Relations (general) with . . .
—Relations (military) with . . .
—Relief models
—Religion
—Religious and ecclesiastical institutions

—Religious life and customs
—Remote sensing
—Republics
—Road maps
—Royal household
—Rural conditions
—Scientific bureaus
—Seal
—Slides
—Social conditions
—Social life and customs
—Social policy
—Social registers
—Songs and music
—States
—Statistical services
—Statistics
—Statistics, Medical
—Statistics, Vital
—Surveys
—Territorial expansion
—Territories and possessions
—Tornado, [date]
—Travel regulations
—Tsunami, [date]
—Typhoon, [date]
—Voting registers
—Yearbooks
—Zoning maps

■ ■ ■ ■ ■

FREE-FLOATING SUBDIVISIONS USED UNDER NAMES OF CITIES*

—Abstracting and indexing
—Abstracts
—Addresses, essays, lectures
—Aerial photographs
—Air defenses
—Air defenses, Civil
—Air defenses, Military
—Airports

—Almshouses
—Ambulance service
—Amusements
—Anecdotes, facetiae, satire, etc.
—Anniversaries, etc.
—Antiquities
—Antiquities—Collection and preservation
—Archival resources

---

*Updated as of December 1977. Use the first list in this appendix for metropolitan areas.

—Armories
—Auditoriums, convention facili-
	ties, etc.
—Avalanche, [date]
—Bars, saloons, etc.
—Bathing beaches
—Benevolent and moral institutions
	and societies
—Bibliography
—Bio-bibliography
—Biography
—Biography—Anecdotes, facetiae,
	satire, etc.
—Biography—Portraits
—Blizzard, [date]
—Bombardment, [date]
—Bombing, [date]
—Book reviews
—Boundaries
—Bridges
—Buildings
—Buildings—Conservation and
	restoration
—Buildings—Guide-books
—Canals
—Capture, [date]
—Carnival
—Castles
—Cemeteries
—Census
—Census, [date]
—Centennial celebrations, etc.
—Charities
—Charities, Medical
—Charters
—Charters, grants, privileges
—Church history
—Churches [including cathedrals,
	chapels, basilicas, etc.]
—City planning
—Civic improvement
—Civil defense
—Civilization
—Claims
—Claims vs. . . .
—Climate
—Clubs
—Collected works
—Commerce

—Congresses
—Conservatories of music
—Convents
—Correctional institutions
—Courtyards
—Cries
—Cyclone, [date]
—Demonstration, [date]
—Description
—Description—Aerial
—Description—Guide-books
—Description—Tours
—Description—Views
—Destruction, [date]
—Dictionaries and encyclopedias
—Directories
—Directories—Telephone
—Discotheques
—Distances, etc.
—Docks, wharves, etc.
—Drama
—Dwellings
—Earthquake, [date]
—Economic conditions
—Economic policy
—Evening and continuation schools
—Executive departments
—Executive departments—Public meetings
—Exhibitions
—Explosion, [date]
—Fairs
—Ferries
—Festivals, etc.
—Fiction
—Fire, [date]
—Fires and fire prevention
—Flood, [date]
—Floods
—Foreign population
—Foreign population—Housing
—Fortifications, military installations, etc.
—Fountains
—Gates
—Gazetteers
—Genealogy
—General strike, [date]
—Gilds
—Government property
—Government publications

Cities (cont'd)

—Harbor
—Harbor–Anchorage
—Harbor–Port charges
—Harbor–Regulations
—Historical geography
—Historical geography–Maps
—Historiography
—History
—History–16th century
—History–17th century
—History–18th century
—History–19th century
—History–20th century
—History–Ancedotes, facetiae, satire, etc.
—History–Partition, [date]
—History–Prophecies
—History–Sources
—History, Comic, satirical, etc.
—History, Military
—Hospitals [including dispensaries]
—Hospitals–Outpatient services
—Hotels, motels, etc.
—Hurricane, [date]
—Hurricanes
—Imprints
—Industries
—Industries–Energy conservation
—Intellectual life
—International status
—Juvenile drama
—Juvenile fiction
—Juvenile films
—Juvenile literature
—Juvenile phonorecords
—Juvenile poetry
—Laboratories
—Landslide, [date]
—Learned institutions and societies
—Libraries [including public libraries]
—Library resources
—Lighting
—Literary collections
—Lodging-houses

—Manufactures
—Maps
—Maps–Bibliography
—Maps, Comparative
—Maps, Manuscript
—Maps, Pictorial
—Maps, Tourist
—Markets
—Massacre, [date]
—Mayors
—Miscellanea
—Monasteries
—Monuments
—Moral conditions
—Morgues
—Mosques
—Museums
—Name
—Nightclubs, dance halls, etc.
—Occupations
—Office buildings
—Officials and employees
—Officials and employees–Appointment, qualifications, tenure, etc.
—Officials and employees–Pensions
—Officials and employees–Salaries, allowances, etc.
—Officials and employees–Travel regulations
—Orphans and orphan-asylums
—Palaces
—Parks
—Periodicals
—Photo maps
—Pictorial works*
—Playgrounds
—Plazas
—Poetry
—Police
—Police–Assaults against
—Police–Attitudes
—Police–Complaints against
—Police–Height requirements
—Police–Mortality

---

*To be used only under names of ancient cities. Use "Description–Views" for all other cities.

—Police—Response time
—Politics and government
—Poor
—Poor—Health and hygiene
—Popular culture
—Population
—Population density
—Population policy
—Public buildings
—Public comfort stations
—Public laundries
—Public works
—Race relations
—Recreational activities
—Recreational facilities
—Registers
—Relations (general) with . . .
—Relations (military) with . . .
—Relief models
—Religion
—Religious and ecclesiastical
    institutions
—Religious life and customs
—Remote sensing
—Restaurants
—Riot, [date]
—Riots
—Road maps
—Schools [including public schools,
    vacation schools]
—Scientific bureaus
—Seal
—Sepulchral monuments
—Sewerage
—Shrines
—Siege, [date]
—Sieges
—Slaughter-houses
—Slides
—Social conditions

—Social life and customs
—Social policy
—Social registers
—Songs and music
—Sports facilities
—Stables
—Statistical services
—Statistics
—Statistics, Medical
—Statistics, Vital
—Statues
—Stock-yards
—Storm, [date]
—Stores, shopping centers, etc.
—Street-cleaning
—Streets [including alleys, roads, high-
    ways, etc.]
—Suburbs and environs
—Surveys
—Synagogues
—Temples
—Theater disaster, [date]
—Theaters
—Tombs
—Topes
—Tornado, [date]
—Towers
—Transit systems
—Tsunami, [date]
—Typhoon, [date]
—Underground areas
—Voting registers
—Walls
—Wards
—Water consumption
—Water-supply
—Yearbooks
—Zoning maps

APPENDIX D

FREE-FLOATING SUBDIVISIONS USED UNDER PERSONAL NAMES

Category: Founders of Religions   Model Heading: Jesus Christ

—Anthroposophical [Buddhist, Jewish, Oriental, etc.]* interpretations
—Apparitions and miracles (Modern)
—Appearances
—Appreciation *(Indirect)*
—Art
—Attitude toward [special topic]
—Baptism
—Betrayal
—Biography
   —Early life
   —History and criticism
   —Public life
   —Study and teaching
—Blessing of children
—Brethren
—Burial
—Cartoons, satire, etc.
—Character
—Childhood
—Chronology
—Conflicts
—Cult *(Indirect)*
—Date of birth
—Devotional literature
—Divinity
—Education
—Ethics
—Evangelistic methods
—Exaltation
—Example
—Family
—Friends and associates
—Genealogy

—Historicity
—History of doctrines
—Humanity
—Humiliation
—Humor
—Iconography
—Influence
—Intellectual life
—Intercession
—Journeys *(Indirect)*
—Kingdom
—Knowableness
—Knowledge and learning
—Language
—Meditations
—Miracles
—Name
—Nativity
—Natures
—Parables
—Person and offices
—Physical appearance
—Popular works
—Prayers
—Pre-existence
—Preaching
—Presentation
—Priesthood
—Primacy
—Procession
—Prophecies
—Prophetic office
—Psychology**
—Royal office

---

*Assign here the adjectival form for specific philosophies, religions, ethnic groups, or regions, making a second entry under the name of the respective philosophy, religion, ethnic group, region.

**This subdivision is assigned to works which discuss modern psychological and/or psychiatric *methods* of investigating the particular founder.

—Significance
—Similitudes
—Sinlessness
—Songs and music
—Spiritual life

—Teaching methods
—Teachings
—Temptation
—Trial
—Words

Category: Philosophers

Model Heading: Thomas Aquinas,
Saint, 1225?-1274

—Aesthetics
—Angelology
—Anthropology
—Christology
—Cosmology
—Creation
—Dictionaries, indexes, etc.
—Economics
—Education
—Ethics
—Exhibitions
—Homes and haunts *(Indirect)*
—Knowledge, Theory of
—Law
—Legends

—Logic
—Mathematics
—Metaphysics
—Methodology
—Music
—Mysticism
—Ontology
—Philosophy
—Political science
—Psychology*
—Societies, periodicals, etc.
—Sociology
—Teleology
—Theology

Category: Statesmen, politicians,
etc.**

Model Headings: Lincoln; Napoleon; or
Washington (of the 3, prefer the 1st)

—Anecdotes
—Anniversaries, etc., [date]
—Art patronage
—Assassination
—Autographs
—Birthplace
—Books and reading
—Campaigns of [date(s)]
—Captivity, [dates]
—Cartoons, satire, etc.
—Childhood and youth
—Chronology
—Coronation
—Death and burial

—Death mask
—Dictionaries, indexes, etc.
—Exhibitions
—Family
—Freemasonry
—Friends and associates
—Funeral, *see* —Death and burial
—Headquarters, [place]
—Homes *(Indirect)*
—Iconography
—Inauguration
—Journeys *(Indirect)*
—Law practice
—Library

*This subdivision is assigned to works which discuss the philosopher's views on or contributions to the discipline of psychology.

**Cf. *Cataloging Service* 124:17-18 (Winter 1978).

Category: Statesmen, politicians,
etc. (cont'd)

—Literary art
—Manuscripts
—Medals
—Military leadership
—Monuments, etc.
—Museums, relics, etc. *(Indirect)*
—Music
—Musical settings
—Oratory
—Palaces *(Indirect)*
—Personality
—Political and social views
—Political career before [date]
—Portraits, caricatures, etc.
—Postal cards
—Quotations
—Relations with [specific class of per-
son or minority group]
(When assigning this subdivision,
always assign also an additional
heading for the class of persons or
minority group.)

—Religion
—Societies, periodicals, etc.
—Songs and music
—Tomb
—Views on [specific topics]
(When assigning this subdivision,
always assign also an additional
heading for the specific
topic.)
—Views on political or social questions,
see —Political and social
views
—Will

Category: Musicians

—Aesthetics
—Anecdotes
—Anniversaries, etc. [date]
—Chronology
—Dictionaries, indexes, etc.
—Discography
—Dramaturgy
—Harmonic system
—Iconography
—Influence
—Language
—Manuscripts

Model Heading: Wagner, Richard,
1813-1883

—Monuments, etc.
—Museums, relics, etc. *(Indirect)*
—Parodies, travesties, etc.
—Performances *(Indirect)*
—Performers
—Portraits, etc.
—Religion and ethics
—Societies, periodicals, etc.
—Stories of operas
—Symbolism
—Thematic catalogs

Category: Literary authors   Model Heading: Shakespeare, William,
                                                 1564-1616*

Author. Title.
   (e.g., Shakespeare, William, 1564-1616. Hamlet.)

—Bibliography
—Concordances
—Exhibitions
—Illustrations
—Juvenile films
—Juvenile phonorecords
—Sources
   NO other subdivisions are used under author-title entries. All other
   subdivisions are used in conjunction with a second heading. (e.g.,
   2. **Shakespeare, William, 1564-1616—Characters—Women**)

—**Acting** see —**Dramatic production**;—**Stage history**
   For works on acting only of an author's plays use second heading:
   2. **Acting.**

—**Adaptations**
   To be used for discussions of adaptations as well as for collections of
   adaptations. Do NOT use for single adaptations.

—**Addresses, essays, lectures**
   Contrary to past usage, use under appropriate subdivisions. (e.g.,
   Shakespeare . . .—Religion and ethics—Addresses, essays, lectures)

—**Aesthetics**
   Discussions of the author's philosophy of art or beauty, whether explicitly
   stated or inferred from his works. Also includes the author's knowledge of
   the aesthetics of others.

—**Allegory and symbolism**
   To be used as a particular aspect of style.

—**Allusions**
   Contemporary (author's life span) and early brief references to the author.
   For author's use of allusions see —**Knowledge—[appropriate sub-subdivision]**;
   —**Style**;—**Criticism and interpretation**; etc.
   see also —**Quotations.**

—**Ancestry** see —**Biography—Ancestry**

---

*For see and see also references from other headings or subdivisions to each of these
subdivisions, consult the printed list and its supplements.

Category: Literary authors (cont'd)

—Anecdotes
see also **—Allusions**

—Anniversaries, etc. [date].
For material dealing with the celebration itself; NOT for works merely published in honor of an anniversary.

—Appreciation *(Indirect)*
Public response and reception, group opinion (positive or negative), praise, tributes, cult, etc. For scholarly reception and literary criticism prefer **—Criticism and interpretation.**

—Archives
For works dealing with any repository or collection of documentary material relating to the author. May include manuscripts, diaries, correspondence, photographs, bills, tax returns, and other items of historical interest.

—Art
To be used for authors living before 1400 A.D. For later authors use **—Portraits, etc.; —Iconography; etc.**

—Authorship
Attribution of work. (e.g., Who really wrote Shakespeare's plays?)

—Baconian [Burton, Marlowe, etc.] theory
—Collaboration

—Autobiography *see* **—Biography.**

—Autographs
Discussions of specimens of the author's handwriting.

—Facsimiles

—Autographs, Spurious *see* **—Forgeries**

—Bibliography
see also **Author. Title—Bibliography**

—Catalogs
—First editions
—Folios (1623, etc.)
—Quartos
—Theory, methods, etc. Do NOT use.
For discussions of preparing particular personal bibliographies prefer:
1. **Author.** 2. **Bibliography—Theory, methods, etc.**

Category: Literary authors (cont'd)

—Biography
To be used for autobiographies as well.

—Ancestry
—Character
Here are entered works on the interpretation of the author's personality; psychological insight into the author. For moral aspects *see* **—Religion and ethics.**
—Chronology *see* **—Chronology**
—Death and burial *see* **—Biography—Last years and death**
—Descendants
—Editing career
—Ennoblement
—Exile *(Indirect)*
(e.g., NOT **Dostoevskii . . .—Biography—Siberian exile**
but **Dostoevskii . . .—Biography—Exile—Siberia**)
—Journalistic career
—Last years *see* **—Biography—Last years and death**
—Last years and death
—London life
May be unique to Shakespeare. Used for biography of his middle years spent largely in London. Do NOT confuse with **—Homes and haunts—London.**
—Marriage
—Old age *see* **—Biography—Last years and death**
—Personality *see* **—Biography—Character**
—Political career
—Sources
—Teaching career
—Theatrical career
—Youth
For author's life to approximately 25 years of age. For Shakespeare: Includes period of education.

—Birthday books *see* **—Calendars, etc.**

—Bones *see* **—Tomb**
—Museums, relics, etc.

—Books and reading
To be used for works dealing with books which are known to have been seen by the author; his reading habits, etc. (e.g., Books borrowed from libraries, friends, etc., as well as other reading matter.)
see also **—Knowledge—[appropriate subdivision]**

—Calendars, etc.
see also **—Quotations**

Category: Literary authors (cont'd)

—**Caricatures** *see* —Portraits, etc.

—**Cartoons, satire, etc.** *see* —Portraits, etc.
                              —Humor, satire, etc.

—**Characters**
>   For groups of characters use second heading. (e.g.,
>   1.   Shakespeare . . .—Characters—Children.
>   2.   Children in literature.)

>   —Children
>   —Comic characters
>   —Criminals
>   —Dramatists
>   —Fairies
>   —Fathers
>   —Fools
>   —Ghosts
>   —Heroes
>   —Indians
>   —Irish
>   —Jews
>   —Kings and rulers
>   —Lawyers
>   —Madmen
>   —Men
>   —Messengers
>   —Monsters
>   —Physicians
>   —Rogues and vagabonds
>   —Saints
>   —Satirists
>   —Servants
>   —Teachers
>   —Villains
>   —Welshmen
>   —Women

>   —**Falstaff** [Margaret of Anjou, etc.]
>>   Particular named characters may be used at will in the running form
>>   (e.g., —**Characters—Virgin Mary**, NOT —**Characters—Mary, Virgin**)
>>   and need not be established editorially.

—**Chronology**
>   For works giving dates of author's life and works, as well as discussions
>   thereof.

Category: Literary authors (cont'd)

—Chronology of the plays *see* —Chronology

—Cipher

—Collected works *see*   —Societies, periodicals, etc.
                         —Addresses, essays, lectures

—Collections *see* —Societies, periodicals, etc.

—Comedies
    For critical works only. NOT appropriate for dramatists who principally
    write comedies (e.g., Molière).

—Commentaries *see* —Criticism and interpretation.

—Concordances
    see also —Author. Title—Concordances

—Congresses
    see also —Anniversaries, etc.; —Societies, periodicals, etc.

—Contemporaries
    see also —Friends and associates

—Contemporary England [America, France, etc.]
    Use second heading for history, social conditions, etc., of the country.
    see also —Homes and haunts

—Correspondence
    Letters from and/or to the author and discussions thereof. In case of an
    individual correspondent, use second heading for the correspondent.
        —Facsimiles
        —Indexes

—Costume *see* —Dramatic production; —Stage history
    For works on costuming only of an author's plays, use second heading:
    2. Costume.

—Criticism, Textual
    For works which aim to establish an authoritative text. (e.g., comparison
    of manuscripts and editions) NOT to be used for critical explication of text.
    NOT to be used after author-title entries.

—Criticism and interpretation
        —Congresses
        —History

Category: Literary authors (cont'd)

—Curiosa and miscellanea *see* —Miscellanea

—Dancing *see* —Knowledge—Performing arts

—Death and burial *see* —Biography—Last years and death

—Death mask

—Descendants *see* —Biography—Descendants

—Diaries

—Dictionaries, indexes, etc.
>May not be used after author-title entries.
>*see also* —Language—Glossaries, etc.

—Discography
>Equivalent to bibliography of phonorecords.

—Drama *see* . . . in fiction, drama, poetry, etc.

—Dramatic production
>To include aspects of stage presentation. (e.g., acting, costume, stage setting and scenery, etc.)

—Dramatic works
>To be used for criticism only. Not appropriate for authors who principally write drama. (e.g., Shakespeare.)

—Dramaturgy *see* —Dramatic production
> —Technique
> —Dramatic works

—Editors

—Education *see* —Knowledge and learning
> —Knowledge—Education

—Ennoblement *see* —Biography—Ennoblement

—Estate
>*see also* —Will

—Ethics *see* —Religion and ethics

—Exhibitions

Category: Literary authors (cont'd)

—Exile *see* —Biography—Exile

—Fiction *see* . . . in fiction, drama, poetry, etc.

—Film adaptations
    Discussions of motion picture productions.

—Folk-lore, mythology *see* —Knowledge—Folklore, mythology.

—Forerunners *see*   —Sources
                      —Criticism and interpretation

—Forgeries
    Use second heading for the forger.
    —Collier [Ireland, etc.]
        Use individual name for well-known forger as established by scholars.
        Do NOT establish editorially.

—Freemasonry *see* —Knowledge—Freemasons

—Friends and associates
    For author's circle of close and immediate contacts such as patrons,
    co-workers, friends, etc.

—Geology *see* —Knowledge—Earth sciences

—Glossaries *see* —Language—Glossaries, etc.

—Grammar *see* —Language—Grammar

—Grave *see* —Tomb

—Handbooks, manuals, etc.

—Handwriting *see* —Autographs

—Histories
    Discussions of Shakespeare's English Chronicle plays. Probably unique to
    Shakespeare, this is a major dramatic genre subdivision, equivalent in
    importance to —Comedies or —Tragedies.

—Homes and haunts (*Indirect*)
    For discussions of places of residence or places to which the author made
    repeated visits. For voyages and travels *see* —Journeys

Category: Literary authors (cont'd)

—Humor, satire, etc.
NOT to be used as a form subdivision; for critical works only, discussing the author's humor, irony, satire, etc.

—Iconography
Visual images pertaining to the author (e.g., photographs, medals, relics, etc., usually treated together)
see also **—Illustrations**
—Monuments, etc.
—Museums, relics, etc.
—Portraits, etc.

—Illustrations
For collections of or discussions of pictorial representations of the author's works.
see also **—Author. Title—Illustrations**

—History and criticism (Do NOT use; use **—Illustrations** only.)

—Illustrations, Comic *see* **—Illustrations**

—Influence
The author's impact on national literatures or literary movements. Use second heading for identifiable group.

—Pushkin [Scott, Eliot, etc.]
(i.e., Shakespeare's impact on Pushkin)
Use last name only for the person influenced, and make an additional subject entry for this person.

—Interviews

—Journeys *(Indirect)*
For voyages and travels actually undertaken by the author. For places of residence or repeated visits *see* **—Homes and haunts.**

—Juvenile literature
May also be used after other literary author subdivisions as appropriate.

—Knowledge—*
The subdivision **—Knowledge** is used only with a further topical subdivision from the list below to designate works dealing with the author's knowledge or treatment of a special subject. The list below is a closed list. Topics from the list are used even to the extent of assigning broader

---

*Cf. *Cataloging Service* 122:13-14 (Summer 1977).

Category: Literary authors (cont'd)

—Knowledge— (cont'd)

subdivisions for specific topics. The list was designed for use in this manner to eliminate the need to establish numerous trivial themes and to contend with overlapping categories. If a broad subdivision is assigned to a work on a specific topic, the latter is designated by means of a second heading in the form of [specific topic] in literature, e.g.,

1. Shakespeare, William, 1564-1616—Knowledge—Sports and recreation.
2. Archery in literature.

The second heading is assigned also in the case where the topic coincides with the subdivision in the first heading.

For works concerning the author's learning and scholarship in general, *see* —Knowledge and learning.

—Aesthetics *see* —Aesthetics
—America [Spain, etc.]
  Limited to countries and regions larger than countries. For a smaller geographic entity, a second heading is used, e.g., 2. **London in literature**.
—Archery *see* —Knowledge—Sports and recreation
—Architecture
—Art
—Astrology *see* —Knowledge—Occult sciences
—Astronomy
—Bible *see* —Religion and ethics
—Birds *see* —Knowledge—Zoology
—Book arts and sciences
—Books and reading *see* —Knowledge—Book arts and sciences
—Botany
—Catholic Church *see* —Religion and ethics
—Chemistry
—Classical literature *see* —Knowledge—Literature
—Commerce
—Communications
—Cosmography *see* —Philosophy; —Knowledge—Astronomy
—Costume *see* —Dramatic production
—Criticism *see* —Knowledge—Literature
—Discoveries (in geography) *see* —Knowledge—Geography
—Dreams *see* —Knowledge—Psychology
—Drinking *see* —Knowledge—Manners and customs; —Knowledge—Sports and recreation
—Dueling *see* —Knowledge—Sports and recreation
—Earth sciences
—Economics

Category: Literary authors (cont'd)

–Knowledge– (cont'd)

 –Education
 –Ethics *see* –Religion and ethics
 –Fishing *see* –Knowledge–Sports and recreation
 –Flowers *see* –Knowledge–Botany
 –Folklore, mythology
 –Food *see* –Knowledge–Manners and customs
 –Freemasons *see* –Knowledge–Manners and customs
 –Games *see* –Knowledge–Sports and recreation
 –Geography
 –Geology *see* –Knowledge–Earth sciences
 –Heraldry *see* –Knowledge–Manners and customs
 –History
 –Honor *see* –Religion and ethics
 –Insanity *see* –Knowledge–Medicine; –Knowledge–Psychology
 –Journalism *see* –Knowledge–Communications
 –Languages
 –Law
 –Literature
 –Manners and customs
 –Marriage *see* –Knowledge–Manners and customs
 –Mathematics
 –Medicine
 –Military life *see* –Knowledge–Military sciences
 –Military sciences
 –Music
 –Natural history
 –Naval art and science *see* –Knowledge–Military sciences
 –Occult sciences
 –Performing arts
 –Philosophy *see* –Philosophy
 –Physics
 –Plant lore *see* –Knowledge–Botany
 –Political sciences *see* –Political and social views
 –Printing *see* –Knowledge–Book arts and sciences; –Knowledge–Technology
 –Psychology
 –Religion *see* –Religion and ethics
 –Repentance *see* –Religion and ethics
 –Revenge *see* –Religion and ethics
 –Science
 –Social science *see* –Political and social views
 –Sports and recreation
 –Technology
 –Theater *see* –Knowledge–Performing arts
 –Zoology

Category: Literary authors (cont'd)

—Knowledge and learning
Works on the author's learning and scholarship in general.
see also **—Knowledge—appropriate subdivision and specific areas under
the author.**

—Language
Critical works dealing with the author's language in general on the linguistic
level rather than the artistic level. For language on the artistic level *see*
—Style.

    —Dialects
    —Glossaries, etc.
    —Grammar
    —Pronunciation
    —Punctuation
        For all other subdivisions prefer second heading. (e.g.,
        1. Shakespeare, William . . .—Language.
        2. English language—To 1700—Semantics.)
    —Style *see* **—Style**
    —Versification *see* **—Versification**

—Last years *see* **—Biography—Last years and death**

—Legends *see*   **—Allusions**
              —Anecdotes

—Library

—Manuscripts
   see also **—Archives**

    —Catalogs
    —Facsimiles

—Marriage *see* **—Biography—Marriage**

—Men *see* **—Relationship with men**

—Miscellanea
Used also for individual antiquarian's collection of curiosa relating to
author.

—Monuments, etc.
   see also **—Tomb**

—Moving-pictures *see* **—Film adaptations**

Category: Literary authors (cont'd)

—Museums, relics, etc.
Includes disinterred bones.
see also **—Tomb**

—Music *see* **—Knowledge—Music**

—Musical settings
Used by music catalogers only, for settings to music of words by an author.

—Mysticism *see* **—Religion and ethics.**

—Name
History, orthography, etymology, etc.

—Natural history *see* **—Knowledge—Natural history**

—Outlines, syllabi, etc. *see* **—Study and teaching—Outlines, syllabi, etc.**

Author. Paraphrases, tales, etc. *see* **—Adaptations**

—Parodies, travesties, etc.
To be used both as a form and critical heading. NOT to be used under author-title entries.

—Patriotism *see* **—Political and social views**
—Contemporary England [Spain, etc.] and/or **Patriotism in literature.**

—Periodicals *see* **—Societies, periodicals, etc.**

—Philosophy
see also **—Aesthetics**
—Political and social views
—Religion and ethics

—Plots
To be used for summaries and discussions of plot development for drama and fiction. For poetic plots *see* **—Summaries, arguments, etc.**

—Poetic works
To be used for criticism only. NOT appropriate for authors who principally write poetry. (e.g., Robert Frost.)

—Poetry *see* ... **in fiction, drama, poetry, etc.**

—Political and social views

Category: Literary authors (cont'd)

—Political science *see* —Political and social views for books classed in literature.

—Portraits, caricatures, etc. *see* —Art; —Portraits, etc.

—Portraits, etc.
> Also includes cartoons, criticism of caricatures, etc.
> *see also* —Art

—Prohibited books. Do NOT use. Use instead:
> 1. Author. 2. Censorship.

—Pronunciation *see* —Language—Pronunciation

—Prose
> To be used only for criticism of prose works or passages. NOT appropriate for authors who principally write prose.

—Psychological studies *see* —Biography—Character

—Psychology *see* —Biography—Character

—Quotations
> For collections of and discussions about the author's quotations.
> *see also* —Calendars

—Radio and television plays

—Relations with contemporaries *see* —Friends and associates

—Relationship with men
> For works on intimate associations.
> *see also* —Friends and associates
> —John Doe [Harry Smith, etc.]
>> Names may be used at will in the running form and need not be established editorially. Use second subject for the person.

—Relationship with women
> For works on intimate associations.
> *see also* —Friends and associates
> —Charlotte von Stein [Charlotte Buff, etc.]
>> Names may be used at will in the running form and need not be established editorially. Use second subject for the person.

—Religion and ethics

—Romances (Tragicomedies) *see* —Tragicomedies

Category: Literary authors (cont'd)

—Satire *see* —Humor, satire, etc.

—Scholia
Marginal annotations, explanatory comments or remarks, especially on the text of a classic by an early grammarian.

—Social views *see* —Political and social views

—Societies, periodicals, etc.
see also —Congresses

—Songs and music
For books classed in M. For literary aspects *see* —Knowledge—Music

—Discography
—History and criticism

—Sources
see also —Author. Title—Sources

—Bibliography

—Spiritualistic interpretations (BF subdivision)

—Spurious and doubtful works *see* —Author. Spurious and doubtful works.

—Authorship; —Forgeries.

Author. Spurious and doubtful works.
This author form heading may be used as subject heading when Descriptive Cataloging has used it as a main or secondary entry. (Usually for voluminous authors.)
EXAMPLES: 1. Shakespeare, William, 1564-1616.
Spurious and doubtful works.
Has been used for collections, studies and bibliographies of Shakespearean apocrypha.

* * *

1. Shakespeare, William, 1564-1616. Spurious and doubtful works.
Double falsehood.
For criticism of this play of disputed authorship.

—Stage history *(Indirect)*

—To 1625
—1625-1800
—1800-

Category: Literary authors (cont'd)

—Stage presentation *see*   —Stage history
  —Dramatic production

—Stage-setting and scenery *see* —Dramatic production; —Stage history
  For works on stage setting and scenery only of an author's plays use second
  heading: **2. Theaters—Stage setting and scenery,** or **2. Moving pictures—
  Setting and scenery,** or **2. Television—Stage setting and scenery.**

—Study and teaching
  (FORMERLY —Study)
  —Outlines, syllabi, etc.

—Style
  Rhetoric, figures of speech (imagery, metaphor, simile, etc.) artistic use of
  language in general. —**Technique** is a larger concept. For specific aspects of
  language (nouns, verbs, adjectives, syntax, pronunciation, etc.)
  see —**Language**
  see also —**Allegory and symbolism**

—Summaries, arguments, etc.
  For summaries and discussions of action in poetic works. For drama and
  fiction *see* —**Plots**

—Supernatural element *see* —Knowledge—Occult sciences

—Symbolism *see* —Allegory and symbolism

—Technique
  Structural and formal elements in drama, fiction, and narrative poetry;
  the art of writing. (e.g., general construction, asides, soliloquies, unities,
  dramatic irony, scene structure, stream-of-consciousness, etc.)
  see also —**Style**
    —**Versification**

—Television and radio plays *see* —Radio and television plays

—Theology *see* —Religion and ethics

—Tomb
  To include grave, interred bones, etc. For disinterred bones *see*
  —**Museums, relics, etc.**

—Tragedies
  For critical works only. Not appropriate for dramatists who principally write
  tragedies (e.g., Racine).

Category: Literary authors (cont'd)

—Tragicomedies
> For critical works only. Not appropriate for dramatists who principally write tragicomedies.

—Translations
> For history and criticism and collections of translations. Not to be used as a form heading for single translations.

—Translations, French [German, etc.]

—Translators *see* —Translations

—Versification
> The technique of writing verse; the structural composition of poetry, including rhythm, rhyme, alliteration, etc.
> *see also* —Style

—Will
> *see also* —Estate

—Women *see* —Relationship with women

—Yearbooks *see* —Societies, periodicals, etc.

APPENDIX E

FREE-FLOATING SUBDIVISIONS CONTROLLED
BY PATTERN HEADINGS*

Category: Musical instruments   Model Heading: Piano

—Catalogs and collections
—Chord diagrams
—Construction
—Dictionaries
—History
—Instruction and study
   —Juvenile
—Juvenile literature
—Maintenance and repair
—Methods
   —Group instruction
   —Juvenile
   —Self-instruction
—Methods (Bluegrass)
—Methods (Blues)

—Methods (Boogie woogie)
—Methods (Country)
—Methods (Jazz)
—Methods (Ragtime)
—Methods (Rock)
—Orchestra studies
—Performance
—Practicing
—Studies and exercises
   —Juvenile
—Studies and exercises (Bluegrass)
—Studies and exercises (Blues)
—Studies and exercises (Jazz)
—Studies and exercises (Rock)
—Tuning

Category: Music compositions**   Model Heading: Operas

—Analysis, appreciation
—Analytical guides
—Bibliography
   —Catalogs
   —Graded lists
—Discography
—Excerpts
   [used after form headings only]
—History and criticism***
—Instructive editions
—Interpretation (Phrasing, dynamics,
   etc.)
—Librettos

—Parts
—Parts (solo)
—Piano scores
—Piano scores (4 hands)
—Programs
—Scenarios
—Scores
—Scores and parts
—Scores and parts (solo)
—Stage guides
—Stories, plots, etc.
—Teaching pieces
—Thematic catalogs

---

*For subdivisions under model headings other than the ones listed here, consult *Library of Congress Subject Headings* and its supplements.

**For music compositions published either in collections (including headings for form, medium, style, music for special seasons and occasions, music settings of special texts, etc.) or as separate works.

***Not used under the model heading **Operas**, since the heading **Opera** is assigned to works about the form. The same is true in other cases where headings for form exist in the singular and the plural, e.g., **Symphony, Symphonies; Suite (Music), Suites** [but **Suites (Piano)**— History and criticism]; **Sonata, Sonatas; Sonata (Piano), Sonatas (Piano).**

Category: Music compositions (cont'd)

—Vocal scores
—Vocal scores with continuo
—Vocal scores with guitar
—Vocal scores with organ
—Vocal scores with piano
—Vocal scores with piano (4 hands)
—Vocal scores with piano and organ
—Vocal scores with pianos (2)

, Arranged
    [used after medium and form headings for instrumental music, e.g.,
    Piano music, Arranged.

Subdivisions for musical format, e.g., **—Parts; —Piano scores; —Scores; —Vocal scores with piano,** are not used after headings for music of special seasons, occasions, styles, etc., where the medium is not directly stated or implied, e.g., **Christmas music; Country music; Te Deum laudamus (Music),** and after headings for categories of works which are generally published in one format only, e.g., compositions for one instrument, hymns, and songs and choruses with accompaniment of one instrument or two keyboard instruments, or without accompaniment.

Category: Legislative bodies (Including individual chambers)	Model Heading: United States. Congress.
—Alabama [Illinois, Texas, etc.] delegation	—Elections, [date]
—Anecdotes, facetiae, satire, etc.	—Expulsion
—Appropriations and expenditures	—Food service
—Archives	—Freedom of debate
—Biography	—Handbooks, manuals, etc.
—Calendars	—Information services
—Caricatures and cartoons	—Officials and employees
—Censures	—Officials and employees—Salaries, allowances, etc.
—Centennial celebrations, etc.	—Powers and duties
—Chaplains	—Private bills
—Committees	—Privileges and immunities
—Committees—Indexes	—Public relations
—Committees—Rules and practice	—Qualifications
—Committees—Seniority system	—Reform
—Conference committees	—Registers
—Contested elections	—Reporters and reporting
—Directories	—Resolutions
—Discipline	—Rules and practice
—Election districts	—Salaries, pensions, etc.
—Elections	—Travel regulations
	—Voting

Category: Educational institutions (Types)

Model Heading: Universities and colleges*

—Accounting
—Accreditation
—Administration
—Admission
—Anecdotes, facetiae, satire, etc.
—Alumni
—Archives
—Buildings
—Buildings—Energy conservation
—Business management
—Chapel exercises
—Curricula
—Data processing
—Directories
—Employees
—Entrance requirements
—Evaluation
—Examinations
—Faculty
—Faculty—Terminology
—Finance
—Food service
—Graduate work

—Graduate work—Examinations
—Graduate work of women
—Handbooks, manuals, etc.
—History
—Honors courses
—Insignia
—Law and legislation *(Indirect)*
—Literary collections
—Names
—Planning *(Indirect)*
—Prayers
—Privileges and immunities *(Indirect)*
—Registers
—Religion
—Safety measures
—Sanitary affairs
—Sermons
—Societies, etc.
—Statistics
—Taxation *(Indirect)*
—Terminology
—Yearbooks

Category: Educational institutions (Individual)

Model Heading: Harvard University

—Addresses, essays, lectures
—Administration
—Admission
—Alumni
—Alumni—Directories
—Anniversaries, etc.
—Archives
—Athletics
—Basketball
—Bibliography
—Biography
—Buildings
—Curricula
—Degrees

—Description
—Description—Aerial
—Description—Guide-books
—Description—Views
—Directories
—Directories—Telephone
—Dissertations
—Employees
—Employees—Political activity
—Endowments
—Entrance requirements
—Entrance requirements—[subject]
—Examinations
—Examinations—[subject]

*The heading **Universities and colleges** will be used as the model heading for types of educational institutions at all levels (primary, secondary, higher, etc.). The heading **Schools** will no longer be used as a model heading.

Category: Educational institutions (Individual) (cont'd)

—Faculty
—Faculty—Salaries, pensions, etc.
—Finance
—Football
—Freshmen
—Funds and scholarships
—Graduate students
—Graduate work
—Heraldry
—History
—History—Revolution, 1775-1783
—History—Civil War, 1861-1865
—History—Bibliography
—History—Sources
—Insignia
—Libraries
—Maps
—Museums
—Orchestras and bands
—Periodicals

—Planning *(Indirect)*
—Poetry
—Portraits
—Presidents
—Prizes
—Public relations
—Registers
—Religion
—Riot, [date]
—Sanitary affairs
—Societies, etc.
—Songs and music
—Statistics
—Students
—Students—Caricatures and cartoons
—Students—Yearbooks
—Track athletics
—Wrestling

SUBDIVISIONS FURTHER SUBDIVIDED BY PLACE

If both local subdivision and topical or form subdivision are to be applied in cataloging a work, the customary practice is to interpose the geographic name between the heading and the topical or form subdivision (see page xii of the introduction to *Library of Congress Subject Headings*). However, for a few specifically designated subdivisions, the geographic name is added to the subdivision, e.g.,

Construction industry—Law and legislation—Poland

Below is a complete list of the subdivisions which the Library of Congress is now consistently establishing with the provision for further subdivision by place. There may be examples of subdivision practice in the eighth edition of *Library of Congress Subject Headings* which are in conflict with this list. However, these exceptions will be corrected on a continuing basis when new works are cataloged. All subdivisions below are further subdivided indirectly. In addition, some of the subdivisions listed are free-floating subdivisions and therefore will not appear in *Library of Congress Subject Headings* under any particular subject heading (see *Cataloging Service*, bulletin 114, p. 9).

—Appreciation
—Care and hygiene
—Care and treatment
—Censorship
—Certification
—Civil rights
—Collectors and collecting*
—Colonization
—Competitions
—Conservation and restoration
  [only when used under fine arts headings other than architecture]
—Contracts and specifications
—Control
—Cost of living adjustments
—Cult
—Dental care
—Dialects
—Diseases
—Diseases and hygiene

—Diseases and pests
—Dislocations
—Documentation*
—Economic aspects
—Education
  [when used under classes of persons]
—Employment
—Environmental aspects
—Estimates
—Forgeries*
—Government ownership
—Health and hygiene
—Homes
—Homes and haunts
—Hospital care
—Hospitals
—Hospitals and asylums
—Hospitals and sanitariums
—Housing
—Hygienic aspects
—In-service training

---

*May also interpose place.

297

—Information services*
—Institutional care
—Labeling
—Law and legislation
—Legal status, laws, etc.
—Library resources*
—Licenses
—Malpractice
—Medical care
—Missions
—Mutilation, defacement, etc.
—Pensions
—Planning
—Political aspects
—Prices
—Private collections*
—Production standards
—Protection
—Psychiatric care
—Publishing
—Rehabilitation
—Reporting
—Research*
—Research grants
—Safety regulations
—Salaries, pensions, etc.
—Scholarships, fellowships, etc.

—Social aspects
—Specifications
—Standards
—Study and teaching*
—Study and teaching
   (Continuing education)*
—Study and teaching
   (Elementary)*
—Study and teaching
   (Graduate)*
—Study and teaching
   (Higher)*
—Study and teaching
   (Internship)*
—Study and teaching
   (Preschool)
—Study and teaching
   (Primary)*
—Study and teaching
   (Secondary)*
—Taxation
—Teacher training
—Tournaments
—Toxicology
—Valuation
—Vocational guidance*

---

*May also interpose place.

APPENDIX G

PREVIOUS LIBRARY OF CONGRESS PRACTICE*
WITH REGARD TO GEOGRAPHIC QUALIFIERS

The following is based on Haykin's discussion:**
    1)   The geographic qualifier is added when the name of the place alone is not sufficient to identify it clearly in the mind of the user of the catalog, particularly in the case of foreign places, and when there are two or more places bearing the same name. This means that headings for well-known places contain the local place names only. However, whether a place is well-known or not is, in many cases, a subjective judgment. This has become a source of uncertainty on the part of catalogers outside of the Library of Congress. In his *Guide*, Haykin includes two lists of cities for which the Library of Congress omits the geographic qualifier. These are reproduced below.

LIST OF CITIES IN THE UNITED STATES AND CANADA
FOR WHICH THE LIBRARY OF CONGRESS OMITS
THE DESIGNATION OF STATE OR PROVINCE***

Albany	Hartford
Annapolis	. Indianapolis
Atlanta	Jersey City
Atlantic City	Los Angeles
Baltimore	Memphis
Boston	Milwaukee
Brooklyn	Minneapolis
Buffalo	Montreal
Chattanooga	Nashville
Chicago	New Haven
Cincinnati	New Orleans
Cleveland	New York
Colorado Springs	Oklahoma City
Dallas	Omaha
Denver	Ottawa
Des Moines	Philadelphia
Detroit	Pittsburgh
Duluth	Providence
Fort Wayne	Quebec
Grand Rapids	Richmond

(List continued on page 300.)

---

    *Current practice is described in Chapter 6.
    **David Judson Haykin, *Subject Headings: A Practical Guide* (Washington: Government Printing Office, 1951), pp. 51-52, 105-108.
    ***In indirect subdivision by place the name of the state or province is nevertheless interpolated.

CITIES IN THE UNITED STATES AND CANADA (cont'd)

St. Augustine
St. Louis
St. Paul
Salt Lake City
San Antonio
San Francisco
Savannah
Scranton

Seattle
Spokane
Tacoma
Tallahassee
Toledo
Toronto
Trenton
Wheeling

LIST OF CITIES OUTSIDE THE UNITED STATES AND CANADA FOR WHICH THE LIBRARY OF CONGRESS OMITS THE DESIGNATION OF COUNTRY*

Aachen
Addis Ababa
Adelaide
Aleppo
Algiers (City)
Amsterdam
Ankara
Antwerp
Asunción
Athens
Augsburg
Bagdad
Baku
Barcelona
Basel
Beirut
Belfast
Belgrad
Berlin
Bern
Bogotá
Bologna
Bolzano (City)
    [also known as
    Bozen]
Bombay
Bonn
Bordeaux

Bratislava
    [also known as
    Pressburg]
Bremen
Brescia
Breslau
Brisbane
Brünn
    [also known as
    Brno]
Brunswick (City)
Brussels
Bucharest
Budapest
Buenos Aires
Cairo
Calcutta
Cape Town
Caracas
Ciudad Trujillo
    [also known as
    Santo Domingo]
Cluj
    [also known as
    Kolozsvár]
Coimbra
Cologne

Copenhagen
Cremona
Czernowitz
    [also known as
    Cernăuţi]
Damascus
Danzig
Delhi
Dresden
Dublin
Düsseldorf
Durazzo
Edinburgh
Erivan
Essen
Florence
Frankfurt am Main
Freiburg i.B.
Geneva
Genoa
Ghent
Glasgow
Graz
Guatemala (City)
Haarlem
Hague
Hamburg

---

*In indirect subdivision by place the name of the country is nevertheless interpolated.

CITIES OUTSIDE THE UNITED STATES AND CANADA (cont'd)

Hanover (City)
Havana
Helsingfors
Istanbul
Jaffa
Jassy
Jerusalem
Johannesburg
Kaunas
   [also known as
   Kovno]
Kazan
Kharkov
Kiel
Kiev
Kishinev
Koblenz
Königsberg
Krakow
   [also known as
   Cracow]
Kyoto
Lahore
Leghorn
Leipzig
Lemberg
   [also known as Lwów]
Leningrad
   [also known as Petro-
   grad and St.
   Petersburg]
Lhasa
Liège
Lille
Lima
Lisbon
Liverpool
London
Lübeck
Luxemburg (City)
Lyons
Madras
Madrid
Mainz
Managua
Manila
Maracaibo

Marseille
Melbourne
Mexico (City)
Milan
Minsk
Monte Carlo
Montevideo
Moscow
Mosul
Munich
Nagasaki
Nancy
Naples
Nice
Nuremberg
   [also known as
   Nürnberg]
Odessa
Osaka
Oslo
   [also known as
   Christiania]
Oxford
Padua
Panama (City)
Paris
Peking
   [also known as
   Peiping]
Prague
Pretoria
Quito
Rangoon
Reims
Reykjavik
Riga
Rio de Janeiro
Rome (City)
Rotterdam
Rouen
San Salvador
Santiago de Chile
Sevastopol
Seville
Shanghai
Smyrna
Sofia

Stalingrad
Stockholm
Strassburg
   [also known as
   Strasbourg]
Stuttgart
Sydney
Tallinn
   [also known as
   Reval]
Tartu
   [also known as
   Dorpat]
Tashkend
Tegucigalpa
Teheran
Thessalonike
   [L.C. form; also
   known as
   Saloniki]
Tokyo
Toulouse
Treves
   [also known as
   Trier]
Tunis (City)
Turin
Uppsala
Utrecht
Valencia (City)
Valparaiso (City)
Venice
Vienna
Vilna
Warsaw
Wiesbaden
Zagreb
Zürich
Zutphen

(Text continues on page 302.)

It should be noted that these lists were compiled in the early 1950s. There are other cities which fall into these categories but do not appear in these lists. Furthermore, the lists are for cities only, and do not include many other local places which are also used without geographic qualifiers. More up-to-date or comprehensive lists have not been compiled by the Library of Congress. Subject catalogers usually rely on authority cards as guides.

2)   For places that require geographic qualifiers, the name of the country or its usual abbreviation is added. For cities in the United States, Canada, and Great Britain, the names of the states or provinces are used as geographic qualifiers.

> **Saint-Dizier, France**
> **Smolensk, Russia**
> **Beatrice, Neb.**
> **Victoria, B.C.**
> **Dundee, Scot.**

3)   In cases where there are two or more places bearing the same name, the largest and best-known city by the name is entered without qualification, on the assumption that most readers seek information about well-known cities; using the name without qualification places it in the catalog ahead of other cities of the same name.

> **Athens** [for the city in Greece]
> **Athens, Ga.**
> **Athens, Ohio**
>
> **London** [for the city in England]
> **London, Ont.**

4)   Names of counties in the United States and Canada are followed by the name of the state or province, elsewhere by the name of the country.

> **Charlotte Co., N.B.**
> **Durham Co., Ont.**
> **East Feliciana Parish, La.**
> [The parish in Louisiana corresponds to the county in other states]
> **Washington Co., Ohio**
> **Limerick, Ire. (County)**

Where two or more places of the same name exist in the same country, state, province, or other similar jurisdiction which has been used as the geographic qualifier, the name is further qualified by adding the name of a lesser distinguishing jurisdiction in parentheses. See examples on page 303.

Washington, Ohio (Fayette Co.)
Washington, Ohio (Guernsey Co.)

Bradford, Eng. (Devonshire)
Bradford, Eng. (Northumberland: Berwick-upon-Tweed Div.)
Bradford, Eng. (Northumberland: Wansbeck Div.)

Templemore, Ire. (Co. Mayo)
Templemore, Ire. (Co. Tipperary)

Athies, France (Aisne)
Athies, France (Pas-de-Calais)

APPENDIX H

ABBREVIATIONS*

Subject headings make very little use of abbreviations in their formation. Current policy requires that, in establishing new subject headings, no abbreviations be used except in the following cases:

1)   Etc.

[topic] —Handbooks, manuals, etc.

2)   Mr. and Mrs.

Rickey, George—Art collections
x **Collection of Mr. and Mrs. George Rickey**

3)   Qualifiers to geographic headings. Most geographic headings established by the Subject Cataloging Division at the Library of Congress are qualified by the names of the larger geographic units. For such qualifiers, the provisions for abbreviations in *Anglo-American Cataloging Rules* are generally followed. These are listed below.

Abbreviations of the names of states of the United States, and names not abbreviated:

Ala.	Hawaii	Mass.	N. M.	S. D.
Alaska	Idaho	Mich.	N. Y.	Tenn.
Ariz.	Ill.	Minn.	N. C.	Tex.
Ark.	Ind.	Miss.	N. D.	Utah
Calif.	Iowa	Mo.	Ohio	Vt.
Colo.	Kan.	Mont.	Okla.	Va.
Conn.	Ky.	Neb.	Or.	Wash.
D.C.	La.	Nev.	Pa.	W. Va.
Del.	Me.	N. H.	R. I.	Wis.
Fla.	Md.	N. J.	S. C.	Wyo.
Ga.				

---

*Cf. *Cataloging Service* 121:17 (Spring 1977).

Abbreviations of other place names:

Name	Abbreviation	Name	Abbreviation
Alberta	Alta.	Puerto Rico	P. R.
British Columbia	B. C.	Quebec	Que.
England	Eng.	Russian Soviet Fed-	
Germany	Ger.*	erated Socialist	
Ireland	Ire.**	Republic	use: Russia
Manitoba	Man.	Saskatchewan	Sask.
New Brunswick	N. B.	Scotland	Scot.
New Zealand	N. Z.	Union of Soviet	
Newfoundland	Nfld.	Socialist Republics	use: Russia
Northwest Territories	N.W.T.	Virgin Islands	V. I.
Nova Scotia	N. S.	Yukon Territory	Yukon
Ontario	Ont.		
Prince Edward Island	P.E.I.		

4)   Name headings. When name headings established by the Descriptive Cataloging Division at the Library of Congress are used as subject headings, any abbreviations appearing in the established headings are retained, e.g.,

United States. Dept. of Agriculture
Labour Party (Gt. Brit.)
U. S. East-West Trade Center
St. Mary's Church, Fairfax Station, Va.

5)   Initialisms as subject headings. Initials are used in the construction of individual headings if the concept is commonly referred to in the abbreviated form, e.g.,

C.O.D. shipments
DDT (Insecticide)

Past practice varied slightly. Following are some of the recent changes:

1)   All topical and form subdivisions, some of which used to be abbreviated in the tracings previously, are now spelled out, e.g., **United States—Politics and government**, not **United States—Pol. & govt.**

2)   The jurisdictions **United States** and **Great Britain** which used to be abbreviated are now spelled out, regardless of their location in the heading, e.g.,

---

*Used for both East and West Germany.
**Used for both the Republic of Ireland and Northern Ireland.

United States–Periodicals
Water-supply–United States
Children in the United States
Progressivism (United States politics)

3) Ampersands are not used.

4) The word "Saint" and its foreign equivalents are spelled out, e.g.,

Altdorfer, Albrecht, 1480 (ca.)-1538. Sankt
Florian Altar.

5) Names of the months are spelled out, e.g.,

Washington, D.C.–Demonstration, 1969 (November 15)

APPENDIX I

CAPITALIZATION

COMMON NOUNS AND ADJECTIVES

Common nouns and adjectives are *not* capitalized *except* in the following cases:

1) The first letter of the first word in a heading is always capitalized.

2) In an inverted heading, the first letter of the first word in the inverted element which would have been the initial word in the natural word order is capitalized, e.g.,

> Medicine, *P*reventive
> Medicine, *S*tate
> Medicine, *M*agic, mystic, and spagiric
> Medicines, *A*ntagonism of
> Medicines, *P*atent, proprietary, etc.
> Educational law and legislation, *C*olonial

3) The first letter of the first word in a qualifier is capitalized unless the word is a preposition, e.g.,

> Channels (*H*ydraulic engineering)
> Shuttle cars (*M*ine haulage)
> Sicilianas (*B*assoon, clarinet, flute, oboe)
> Distance measuring equipment (*A*ircraft to ground station)
> Flowers (in religion, folk-lore, etc.)

4) The first letter in the first word of each subdivision is always capitalized, e.g.,

> Airplanes—*M*odels—*R*adio control
> Shakespeare, William, 1564-1616—*K*nowledge—*M*ilitary sciences

PROPER NAMES

Personal and corporate name headings which also serve as author headings are established by the Descriptive Cataloging Division at the Library of Congress. The rules for descriptive cataloging are followed.

For proper names used in subject entries only, the following guidelines are provided. With the exceptions noted below, proper names, including common nouns and adjectives which form an integral part of the name, are capitalized, e.g.,

Cape Hatteras National Seashore
Carabost State Forest, Australia
Grandfather Mountain, N. C.
Hortus Cave, France
Rio de la Plata Valley, Brazil-Argentine Republic
Powder River Basin, Wyo. and Mont.
Middle Atlantic States
Islamic Empire
Longfellow National Historic Site, Mass.
St. Louis—Plazas—Lafeyette Square
Ringfield Plantation, Va.
Ickmeld Way, Eng.
Forth Bridge
Heart Mountain Relocation Center, Wyo.
Southern Pacific Railroad
Ballots Project
MARC System
Jesus People
Jean Hersholt Film Collection
Washington, D. C. Morris Statue (Capitol)
Russo-Polish War, 1919-1920
East African Safari Rally
Saint Valentine's Day
Antwerp—Longshoremen's Strike, 1907
Cuban Missile Crisis, October, 1962

Exceptions:

1)   Certain kinds of proper names conventionally have never been established in accordance with the above policy. The same patterns are followed in establishing new headings in the same categories. Examples:

China—History—Ming dynasty, 1368-1644
Veitch family
Peking metropolitan area, China
Vera Cruz region, Mex.
Spercheios River watershed, Greece
Schultz site, Mich.

2)   Names of individual movements are not capitalized, e.g.,

Women's liberation movement

AUTHOR-TITLE SUBJECT HEADINGS AND UNIFORM TITLES

The practice of descriptive cataloging is followed, e.g.,

Milton, John, 1608-1674. Paradise regained.
Rembrandt Harmenszoon van Rijn, 1606-1669. Night watch.
Arabian nights.
Bible. O. T. Five scrolls—Commentaries.
Bible. O. T. Minor prophets—Commentaries.
Bible. N. T. Apocryphal books. Epistle of Barnabas
—Commentaries.

APPENDIX J

PUNCTUATION

The following punctuation marks are used in Library of Congress subject headings:

Apostrophe. Standard practice is followed.

Brackets. Brackets are used in the printed list to indicate multiple headings, e.g., **Authors, American [English, French, etc.]**, but are not used in subject entries.

Comma. A comma is used
1) to separate parallel terms in a heading, e.g., **Hotels, taverns, etc.**,
2) to separate the noun from the modifier in an inverted heading, e.g., **Hospitals, Naval and marine; Plants, Effect of soil acidity on,**
3) to separate the surname or family name from the forename or given name, and to separate the name from the dates, e.g., **Shakespeare, William, 1564-1616,**
4) to separate a place name from its geographic qualifier, e.g., **Cambridge, Mass.**

Dash. An "m" dash is used to signify a subdivision, e.g., **New York (City)–Police –Statistics–Periodicals.**

Hyphen. *Webster's Third New International Dictionary* is followed as far as feasible.

Parentheses. Parentheses are used
1) to enclose a qualifier, e.g., **Meteor (Fighter planes); Nassau (Duchy),**
2) to enclose the specification of musical instruments in certain music headings, e.g., **Quartets (Piano, oboe, violin, violoncello).**

Period. A period is used
1) as an abbreviation mark, e.g., **United States. Dept. of Agriculture,**
2) to separate a name heading from a subheading in the case of corporate headings and from the title in the case of an author-title subject entry, e.g., **New York (City). Police Dept. Warrant Division; Shakespeare, William, 1564-1616. Hamlet.**
3) at the end of every tracing, with the exception of a tracing ending in a closing parenthesis which makes the period unnecessary.

APPENDIX K

FILING

MANUALLY-PRODUCED CATALOGS

At the Library of Congress, entries in manually-produced catalogs, including its card catalogs, are arranged according to the *Filing Rules for the Dictionary Catalogs of the Library of Congress* (1956). The rules related directly to subject entries are reproduced below. Note that many of the examples used to illustrate these rules contain abbreviations (e.g., **U. S.** for **United States;** —**For. rel.** for —**Foreign relations;** —**Hist.** for —**History**) which are no longer used. For current practice regarding abbreviations, see Appendix H.

FILING RULES

Library of Congress filing rules follow on page 312.

Preliminary note.

Throughout this manual the correct position of subject entries has been indicated in various examples. If the rules for the arrangement of author entries (both personal and corporate) are thoroughly understood, subject entries will not cause much difficulty. Certain fundamental rules, however, must always be remembered, as follows:

I. The proper order of entries when the names of a person, place and thing are identical is:

A. Person

B. Place

C. Subject [other than a specific subject that is arranged after its own author and added entries]

D. Title

> *Example:*
> Stone, Samuel
> Stone, Thomas
> *Stone, *Pa.*   [name of a place]
> STONE   [name of an object]
> Stone   [a title beginning with the word]

II. Any author entry (either personal or corporate) may have its own subject entry. When this is the case the subject entry follows directly after its own author and added entries. Often there will be a subject entry before there is a corresponding author entry, but, in such cases, the subject entry is filed in the same position where the author entry would be filed. As an exception, general subject entries for a place, both with and *without* subject subdivisions, are arranged after all of the official and unofficial author entries for the place.

> *Example:*
> Stone, Thomas   [person as author]
> Stone, Thomas   [added entry]
> STONE, THOMAS   [person as subject]
> *Stone, *Pa.*   [place alone as corporate author]
> *Stone, Pa.*   [added entry]
> *Stone, *Pa. Dept. of Education*   [place as corporate author with
>   official subheading]
> *Stone, Pa. Dept. of Education*   [added entry]
> *STONE, PA. DEPT. OF EDUCATION*   [subject]
> *Stone, *Pa. Fire Dept.*   [corporate author]
> *STONE, PA. WATER COMMISSIONERS*   [subject]
> *STONE, PA. [place as general subject without subject subdivision]
> *STONE, PA.—BIOG.
> *STONE, PA.—HIST.
> *STONE, PA.—WATER SUPPLY
> STONE   [i. e., a thing as subject]
> STONE, *see also* BUILDING STONES
> STONE, ARTIFICIAL
> The Stone age in North America   [title of a book]
> Stone and Webster, *Boston*
> STONE AND WEBSTER, BOSTON

III. Summary of rules for SUBJECT ARRANGEMENT.

Arrange by groups in the following order:

A. The subject without subdivision.

B. Subject with form or subject subdivisions, separated from the subject by a dash, *e. g.*, ART—HISTORY; ART—PERIODICALS.

C. Subject with period subdivisions, separated from the subject by a dash, *e. g.*, ENGLISH LITERATURE—17TH CENTURY; FRANCE—HISTORY—REVOLUTION.

D. Subject with geographical subdivisions, separated from the subject by a dash, *e. g.*, ART—ITALY.

E. Subject followed by a parenthetical term, *e. g.*, ANALYSIS (MATHEMATICS); MASS (CANON LAW); MASS (CHEMISTRY).

F. Inverted subject headings, *e. g.*, ART, ANCIENT; ART, ITALIAN; BIRDS, PROTECTION OF.

G. Phrase headings beginning with the subject word, *e. g.*, ART AND STATE.

Note. See the following rules for exceptions to the arrangement of subjects under Groups E and F, the principal variation being in **PLACE ARRANGEMENT**. In **PLACE ARRANGEMENT,** following the general rule that a place precedes a thing, an inverted heading entered under a place name *precedes* an entry for an object or thing entered under the same name and followed by a parenthetical term, *e. g.*, BALTIMORE, BATTLE OF, 1814 *precedes* BALTIMORE (SLOOP OF WAR). In **SUBJECT ARRANGEMENT,** aside from places, the parenthetical term usually precedes the inverted subject heading, *e. g.*, LOVE (THEOLOGY) precedes LOVE, MATERNAL.

IV. Details of arrangement:

A. Subject without subdivision.

Arrange entries for the same subject heading alphabetically by the main entry of the book; or, if the entry is a subject analytic for a part of a book written by an author other than the author of the whole book, arrange by the author of the analytic.

> *Example:*
> **MARBLE**
> **Adams, Frank Dawson.**
>> An experimental investigation into the flow of marble. By Frank D. adams . . . and John T. Nicolson. 1901.
>> **MARBLE**
>> **Afbeelding** der marmor soorten, volgens hunne natuurlyke koleuren. 1776.
>> **MARBLE**
>> **Bowles, Oliver.**
>>> The technology of marble quarrying. 1916.
>>> **MARBLE**
>>> **Kessler, Daniel William.**
>>>> A study of problems relating to the maintenance of interior marble. 1927.
>>>> **MARBLE**
>>>> **Merrill, George Perkins.**
>>>>> Report on some carbonic acid tests on the weathering of marbles and limestones.
>>>>> (*In* **U. S. National Museum. Proceedings. Washington, 1916.** 23½ᶜᵐ. **v. 49, p. 347–349**)
>>>>> **MARBLE**

Renwick, William George.
◦ Marble and marble working. 1909.

B. Form or subject subdivisions, separated from the subject by a dash.
Arrange alphabetically by the subdivisions.   For a list of abbreviations of form and
subject subdivisions, *see* **Abbreviations III.**

Example:
CHEMISTRY
CHEMISTRY—ABSTRACTS
CHEMISTRY—ADDRESSES, ESSAYS, LECTURES
CHEMISTRY—BIBL.
CHEMISTRY—DICTIONARIES
CHEMISTRY—EARLY WORKS TO 1800.[1]
CHEMISTRY—EXPERIMENTS
CHEMISTRY—HIST.

C. Period subdivisions, separated from the subject by a dash.

1. Arrange chronologically, but if a subject like U. S.—FOREIGN RELATIONS
has form and subject divisions as well as period divisions, the form and subject
divisions, arranged alphabetically, come first, followed by the period divisions,
arranged chronologically.

2. Periods of time beginning with the same year but extending to different years
are arranged so as to bring the longest period first.   If a period subdivision is left
open (*e. g.*, 1898–   ), it precedes all other period subdivisions beginning with the
same or later years.

3. Period subdivisions in the form of phrases (*e. g.*, U. S.—HIST.—COLONIAL
PERIOD; U. S.—HIST.—CIVIL WAR) are arranged chronologically, not alphabetically.   For the proper filing of such phrases in the chronological arrangement
consult *Subject headings used in the dictionary catalogs of the Library of Congress.*

4. Under LANGUAGE and LITERATURE subjects, such subdivisions as OLD
FRENCH; EARLY MODERN (TO 1700); 18TH CENT., etc., are regarded as
period subdivisions.   The divisions ANCIENT, MEDIEVAL, RENAISSANCE
and MODERN are filed as period divisions only when used as further divisions of
the subdivisions HISTORY or HISTORY & CRITICISM.   Otherwise they are
treated as adjectival inversions and filed with the inverted subject headings.

Examples:
U. S.—FOR. REL.
U. S.—FOR. REL.—BIBL.
U. S.—FOR. REL.—SPEECHES IN CONGRESS
U. S.—FOR. REL.—TREATIES
U. S.—FOR. REL.—REVOLUTION
U. S.—FOR. REL.—1783–1865
U. S.—FOR. REL.—CONSTITUTIONAL PERIOD, 1789–1809
U. S.—FOR. REL.—1789–1797
U. S.—FOR. REL.—ALGERIA
U. S.—FOR. REL.—SPAIN
U. S.—HISTORIC HOUSES, ETC.
U. S.—HIST.
U. S.—HIST.—BIBL.
U. S.—HIST.—PERIODICALS

---

[1] EARLY WORKS TO 1800, in this example, is considered as a form division, not a period division.

SUBJECT ARRANGEMENT   **Sub—IV. C.**

U. S.—HIST.—SOURCES
U. S.—HIST.—STUDY AND TEACHING
U. S.—HIST.—COLONIAL PERIOD
U. S.—HIST.—KING WILLIAM'S WAR, 1689–1697
U. S.—HIST.—QUEEN ANNE'S WAR, 1702–1713
U. S.—HIST.—KING GEORGE'S WAR, 1744–1748
U. S.—HIST.—FRENCH AND INDIAN WAR, 1755–1763
U. S.—HIST.—REVOLUTION
U. S.—HIST.—REVOLUTION—AMERICAN FORCES
U. S.—HIST.—REVOLUTION—BIOG.
U. S.—HIST.—REVOLUTION—SOURCES
U. S.—HIST.—1783–1865
U. S.—HIST.—CONFEDERATION, 1783–1789
U. S.—HIST.—CONSTITUTIONAL PERIOD, 1789–1809
U. S.—HIST.—WAR WITH FRANCE, 1789–1800
U. S.—HIST.—TRIPOLITAN WAR, 1801–1805
U. S.—HIST.—WAR OF 1812
U. S.—HIST.—1815–1861
U. S.—HIST.—WAR WITH ALGERIA, 1815
U. S.—HIST.—WAR WITH MEXICO, 1845–1848
U. S.—HIST.—1849–1877
U. S.—HIST.—CIVIL WAR
U. S.—HIST.—1865–
U. S.—HIST.—1865–1898
U. S.—HIST.—1898–
U. S.—HIST.—WAR OF 1898
U. S.—HIST.—20TH CENTURY
U. S.—HIST.—1933–1945

U. S.—HISTORY, JUVENILE
U. S.—HISTORY, LOCAL
U. S.—HISTORY, MILITARY

MUSIC—HIST. & CRIT.

MUSIC—HIST. & CRIT.—ANCIENT
MUSIC—HIST. & CRIT.—MEDIEVAL
MUSIC—HIST. & CRIT.—16TH–17TH CENT.
MUSIC—HIST. & CRIT.—MODERN

MUSIC—INSTRUCTION AND STUDY

GERMAN LITERATURE
GERMAN LITERATURE (COLLECTIONS)
GERMAN LITERATURE (SELECTIONS: EXTRACTS, ETC.)

GERMAN LITERATURE—ADDRESSES, ESSAYS, LECTURES
GERMAN LITERATURE—AUSTRIAN AUTHORS
GERMAN LITERATURE—BIBL.
GERMAN LITERATURE—CATHOLIC AUTHORS
GERMAN LITERATURE—HIST. & CRIT.
GERMAN LITERATURE—JEWISH AUTHORS
GERMAN LITERATURE—STUDY AND TEACHING
GERMAN LITERATURE—SWISS AUTHORS
GERMAN LITERATURE—YEAR BOOKS

GERMAN LITERATURE—OLD HIGH GERMAN
GERMAN LITERATURE—MIDDLE HIGH GERMAN
GERMAN LITERATURE—EARLY MODERN (TO 1700)
GERMAN LITERATURE—18TH CENT.
GERMAN LITERATURE—19TH CENT.
GERMAN LITERATURE—20TH CENT.

GERMAN LITERATURE—ANSBACH
GERMAN LITERATURE—AUSTRIA
GERMAN LITERATURE—BAVARIA
GERMAN LITERATURE—HESSE
GERMAN LITERATURE—SWABIA

In the above example, note that the subjects followed by the parenthetical terms (COLLECTIONS) and (SELECTIONS: EXTRACTS, ETC.) precede all other divisions.

Note, too, that the subject divisions AUSTRIAN AUTHORS, CATHOLIC AUTHORS, etc. are not treated as geographical subdivisions but are interfiled with the other form and subject divisions.

5. A grouping of subject cards by periods under a person's name is sometimes considered advisable if there are many cards under his name.

Example:

NAPOLEON I, EMPEROR OF THE FRENCH
—ADDRESSES, SERMONS, ETC.
—ANECDOTES
—BIBL.
—CORONATION
—DRAMA
—FICTION
—POETRY
—PORTRAITS, CARICATURES, ETC.
—SATIRE

—AT BRIENNE, 1779–1784
—ITALIAN CAMPAIGN, 1796–1797
—EGYPTIAN CAMPAIGN, 1798–1799
—CONSULATE AND EMPIRE, 1799–1814
—CONSULATE, 1799–1804
—CAMPAIGNS OF 1799
—ITALIAN CAMPAIGN, 1800
—ATTEMPT ON THE LIFE OF, DEC. 24, 1800
—EMPIRE, 1804–1814
—GERMAN AND AUSTRIAN CAMPAIGN, 1805
—CAMPAIGNS OF 1806–1807
     [etc., etc.]

D. Geographical subdivisions, separated from the subject by a dash.

Arrange alphabetically by the subdivisions.

NOTE: Inverted subject headings formed with a racial or linguistic adjective, *e. g.*, ART, AMERICAN; ART, ENGLISH, etc., are not regarded as geographical divisions but are to be filed with the other inverted subject headings. Occasionally a subject will be found where some filer has inadvisedly interfiled these inverted subject headings with the geographical divisions. When such arrangements are discovered they should be called to the attention of the Senior Filer so that the correction can be made.

Example:

LEGENDS—ARABIA
LEGENDS—ARGENTINE REPUBLIC
LEGENDS—AUSTRALIA
LEGENDS—BOHEMIA
LEGENDS—CALIFORNIA
LEGENDS—CHINA
LEGENDS—EGYPT
LEGENDS—ENGLAND
LEGENDS—IRELAND
LEGENDS—PORTUGAL

SUBJECT ARRANGEMENT   **Sub—IV. E.**

LEGENDS—SWITZERLAND
LEGENDS—ZULULAND
LEGENDS, ARABIC
LEGENDS, BOHEMIAN
LEGENDS, BUDDHIST
LEGENDS, CELTIC
LEGENDS, EGYPTIAN
LEGENDS, GERMAN
LEGENDS, GERMANIC
LEGENDS, GREEK
LEGENDS, JEWISH
LEGENDS, NORSE
LEGENDS, SWISS

E. Subject followed by a parenthetical term.

Arrange *after* subjects with form, subject, period and geographical divisions but *before* the inverted subject headings beginning with the same word.[1] If there are several subjects with parenthetical terms, arrange alphabetically by those terms.

Examples:

COOKERY

COOKERY—BIBL.
COOKERY—DICTIONARIES
COOKERY—EARLY WORKS TO 1800
COOKERY—HIST.
COOKERY—JUVENILE LITERATURE
COOKERY—LABORATORY MANUALS
COOKERY—STUDY AND TEACHING

COOKERY—YEAR-BOOKS
COOKERY (APPLES)
COOKERY (CHEESE)
COOKERY (FISH)
COOKERY (MEAT)
COOKERY (OYSTERS)
COOKERY (VEGETABLES)
COOKERY (WINE)

COOKERY, AMERICAN
COOKERY, CHINESE
COOKERY, CREOLE
COOKERY, ENGLISH
COOKERY, MEXICAN
COOKERY, SWEDISH
COOKERY, SYRIAN

Cookery and dining in imperial Rome
The cookery book
Cookery for beginners
COOKERY FOR INSTITUTIONS, ETC.
COOKERY FOR THE SICK
Cookery, foreign and domestic
Cookery in the public schools

---

[1] Under **SUBJECT ARRANGEMENT** the *A. L. A. Filing Code* recommends filing subjects followed by **parenthetical** terms *after* the inverted subject headings. This is probably a better arrangement, as the Library of Congress practice **sometimes** introduces an entirely different subject between another subject and its subdivisions and the same subject followed by an **inverted** word or phrase. *See* The **APPENDIX** for the recommended alternate rule which agrees with the A. L. A. rule. Note, however, that under **PLACE ARRANGEMENT** the Library of Congress files an inverted heading beginning with the **place** name *before* the same name followed by a parenthetical term, if that name represents a thing, *e. g.*, FLORENCE, SYNOD OF, 1478 before FLORENCE (SCHOONER).

```
INFANTS
INFANTS—CARE AND HYGIENE
INFANTS—DISEASES
INFANTS—MORTALITY
INFANTS—NUTRITION
INFANTS (NEW-BORN)
INFANTS PREMATURE)
INFANTS STILL-BORN) see STILL-BIRTH
INFANTS, FOODS FOR, see INFANTS—NUTRITION
Infants and children; their feeding and growth
Infants' wool knit outerwear

Mass, Konrad                                            [person]
MASS                                                   [subject]
MASS—HIST.
MASS (CANON LAW)
MASS (CANON LAW) see also LORD'S SUPPER (CANON LAW)
MASS (CHEMISTRY)
MASS, STANDARDS OF, see STANDARDS OF MASS
The Mass and the life of prayer
Mass-clocks
The Mass explained to children
Mass production equipment
```

Exceptions:

For the arrangement of place names, either author or subject, followed by administrative designations or ecclesiastical jurisdictions in parentheses, such as (*Archdiocese*), (*Bishopric*), (*City*), (*Colony*), (*Diocese*), (*Province*), (*State*), (*Territory*), etc., *see* **Place Arrangement III.**

In literature subject headings, the subject followed by the parenthetical terms (COLLECTIONS) or (SELECTIONS: EXTRACTS, ETC.) follows the subject used alone but *precedes* all subdivisions of the subject. On the other hand, a subject followed by a parenthetical term indicating a form or branch of literature, *e. g.*, (COMEDY) or (TRAGEDY) follows all subdivisions of the general subject. The same principle is followed in arranging a subject heading like MUSIC (COLLECTIONS), which precedes all subdivisions of MUSIC.

Examples:
```
FRENCH DRAMA
FRENCH DRAMA, see also MORALITIES, FRENCH
FRENCH DRAMA (COLLECTIONS)
FRENCH DRAMA (SELECTIONS: EXTRACTS, ETC.)
FRENCH DRAMA—ADDRESSES, ESSAYS, LECTURES
FRENCH DRAMA—BIBL.
FRENCH DRAMA—HIST. & CRIT.
FRENCH DRAMA—TRANSLATIONS INTO ENGLISH
FRENCH DRAMA—MEDIEVAL
FRENCH DRAMA—16TH CENT.
FRENCH DRAMA—17TH CENT.
FRENCH DRAMA—20TH CENT.
FRENCH DRAMA—20TH CENT.—HIST. & CRIT.
FRENCH DRAMA (COMEDY)
FRENCH DRAMA (COMEDY)—HIST. & CRIT.
FRENCH DRAMA (TRAGEDY)
FRENCH DRAMA (TRAGEDY)—HIST. & CRIT.
```

SUBJECT ARRANGEMENT   Sub—IV. F.

MUSIC
MUSIC (COLLECTIONS)
MUSIC—ACOUSTICS AND PHYSICS
MUSIC—ANALYTICAL GUIDES
MUSIC—BIBL.

But note that the non-parenthetical subdivisions COLLECTED WORKS and COLLECTIONS are always interfiled
with the other subdivisions of the same subject.

Example:

CHEMISTRY
CHEMISTRY—ADDRESSES, ESSAYS, LECTURES
CHEMISTRY—APPARATUS, *see* CHEMICAL APPARATUS
CHEMISTRY—BIBL.
CHEMISTRY—COLLECTED WORKS
CHEMISTRY—COLLECTIONS
CHEMISTRY—CONGRESSES
CHEMISTRY—DICTIONARIES

F. Inverted subject headings.

1. Arrange alphabetically by the word following the comma.

2. The divisions ANCIENT, MEDIEVAL, RENAISSANCE and MODERN, following a comma, are treated as adjectival inversions and arranged here with the inverted headings, not with the period subdivisions. When they are used, however, as further divisions of HISTORY and HISTORY & CRITICISM, and are separated from those subdivisions by a dash, they are then treated as period divisions.

3. Inverted subject headings formed with a racial or linguistic adjective, *e. g.,* ART, AMERICAN; ART, GREEK, etc., belong in this group rather than with the geographical subdivisions.

4. Inverted subject headings formed with a racial or linguistic adjective are interfiled with those formed with an adjective denoting style, in order to avoid the confusion of separate alphabets.

Example:

ART
ART—ADDRESSES, ESSAYS, LECTURES
ART—BIBL.
ART—GALLERIES AND MUSEUMS
ART—HIST.
ART—STUDY AND TEACHING
ART—YEAR-BOOK
ART—AFRICA
ART—ANTWERP
ART—BOSTON
ART—FRANCE
ART—GREECE
ART—LONDON
ART—PORTUGAL
ART—U. S.
ART, AFRICAN
ART, AMERICAN
ART, ANCIENT
ART, CHINESE
ART, DECORATIVE
ART, EGYPTIAN
ART, FRENCH

ART, GRECO-ROMAN
ART, GREEK
ART, MEDIEVAL
ART, MODERN
ART, MUNICIPAL
ART, RENAISSANCE
ART, ROMAN
Art activities in the modern world
ART AND STATE

LIGHT
LIGHT *see also* OPTICS
LIGHT—ADDRESSES, ESSAYS, LECTURES
LIGHT—BIBL.
LIGHT—EFFECT ON PLANTS
LIGHT—LABORATORY MANUALS
LIGHT—PHYSIOLOGICAL EFFECT
LIGHT—STUDY AND TEACHING
LIGHT—VELOCITY
LIGHT—WAVE-LENGTH
LIGHT (EASEMENT) *see* LIGHT AND AIR (EASEMENTS)
LIGHT, COLORED
LIGHT, CORPUSCULAR THEORY OF
LIGHT, ELECTRIC, *see* ELECTRIC LIGHTING
LIGHT, INVISIBLE, *see* SPECTRA, INFRA-RED
LIGHT, WAVE THEORY OF
LIGHT, ZODIACAL, *see* ZODIACAL LIGHT
Light   [*i. e.*, a periodical]
Light, a guide thru life
The light above the cross roads
The light that failed

Exception:

Under **Place Arrangement** an inverted heading entered under the place name, *e. g.*, AFRICA, BRITISH EAST; CALIFORNIA, SOUTHERN; TENNESSEE, MIDDLE, is to be regarded as a different subject. It is arranged after all of the subdivisions of the general place name and after that name followed by an administrative designation in parentheses, but *before* the same word followed by a non-administrative designation in parentheses, such as (CRUISER), (STEAM-SHIP), etc. This follows the general rule that a place precedes a thing.

Example:

Africa, Bernabe   [person]
Africa, J. Simpson   [person]
AFRICA
AFRICA—COLONIZATION
AFRICA—RACE QUESTION
AFRICA—ZOOLOGY
Africa (*City*) *see* Mahedia, *Tunis*
AFRICA, BRITISH EAST
AFRICA, BRITISH EAST —DESCR. & TRAV.
AFRICA, CENTRAL
AFRICA, EAST
AFRICA, NORTH
AFRICA, NORTH—HIST.
AFRICA, NORTHWEST
AFRICA, SOUTH

SUBJECT ARRANGEMENT   Sub—IV. G.

> AFRICA, WEST
> *AFRICA (STEAMSHIP)
> Africa; journal of the International Institute of African Languages and
>   Cultures
> Africa   [*i. e.*, title of a book]
> Africa and peace
> Africa speaks

G. Phrase subject headings.

Interfile alphabetically with titles and other long headings beginning with the same word.

> *Example:*
> French, William Riley
> French-Matheu, Victor
> French-Sheldon, M., *see* Sheldon, M   French-
> FRENCH FAMILY [1]
> French à la mode
> FRENCH-AMERICAN NEWSPAPERS
> French and American Claims Commission
> The French army from within
> FRENCH BALLADS AND SONGS
> French Book of the Month Club, *New York*
> FRENCH BULLDOGS
> French by sound
> FRENCH-CANADIAN DIALECT
> The French-Canadian in prose and verse
> FRENCH-CANADIAN LITERATURE
> FRENCH-CANADIANS
> FRENCH CLOVER, *see* ALFALFA
> French cook book
> FRENCH DRAMA
> French Equatorial Africa
> FRENCH FARCES
> French for beginners
> FRENCH IN OHIO

[1] Note that the subject FRENCH FAMILY does not belong in this group of phrase subject headings but is arranged after all of the single and compound surnames.

149

COMPUTER-PRODUCED CATALOGS

Entries in computer-produced catalogs* of the Library of Congress are arranged according to the rules set forth in the document entitled "Filing Arrangement in the Library of Congress Catalogs" (1971) prepared by John C. Rather. The following excerpts from the document contain rules related to subject entries.

■ ■ ■

General Rules

1. **Basic Filing Order**
    Fields in a filing entry are arranged word by word, and words are arranged character by character. This procedure is continued until one of the following conditions occurs:
    a. A prescribed filing position is reached.
    b. The field comes to an end (in which case placement is determined by another field of the entry or by applying one of the rules given hereafter).
    c. A mark of punctuation showing a subarrangement intervenes.

1.1. Order of Letters
    Letters are arranged according to the order of the English alphabet (A-Z).

1.1.1. Modified Letters
    Modified letters are treated like their plain equivalents in the English alphabet. Thus all diacritical marks and modifications of recognizable English letters are treated as if they did not exist; e.g., ä, á, å, ø, ł, ñ are filed as a, o, l, n.
    Example
    Hand blows
    Hand book for Prospect Park
    Hand in glove
    Håndbok for sangere
    Handbook for adventure
    Hände am Pflug
    Hands on the past
    Handu   [Indic surname]

1.2. Placement of Numerals
    Numbers expressed in digits or other notation (e.g., roman numerals) precede letters and, with few exceptions, they are arranged according to their numerical

---

*To date these are the *Library of Congress Subject Headings* and *Library of Congress Catalogs: Film and Other Materials for Projection.*

value. According to this rule, all filing entries beginning with numerals appear before entries beginning with the letter A. Numbers expressed as words are filed alphabetically. Detailed instructions for filing numerals are given in Rule 16.

Example

1, 2, 3, and more
1, 2, buckle my shoe
3 died variously
10 ways to become rich
13 jolly saints
112 Elm Street
838 ways to amuse a child
1000 spare time money making ideas
1984
10,000 trade names
1,000,000 delinquents
A is for anatomy
A4D desert speed run
Aa, Abraham
Longitude 30 west
Longitude and time
Nineteen eighty-four
Oberlin College
One, two, three for fun
Rubinstein, Akiba
Ten thousand miles on a bicycle
Three 14th century English mystics
Three by Tey
Thucydides

1.3 Signs and Symbols

Nonalphabetic signs and symbols within a field are generally ignored in filing and the following letters or numerals are used as the basis of arrangement.

1.3.1. Punctuation

Punctuation as such has no place in the collating sequence of characters considered in filing arrangement. A mark of punctuation is taken into account, however, in two situations: 1) when it signals the end of an element or field and indicates the need for subarrangement as described in the following rules; and 2) when it serves as the sole separator between two discrete words (e.g., Mott-Smith; 1951/1952; 1:3) and so must be treated as equivalent to a space.

* * * *

3. Identification of Elements in a Field

3.3.5 Topical Subject Heading Fields

The following examples show the leading elements of various types of topical subject headings and also illustrate cases of nonsignificant punctuation. In topical subject headings, a comma followed by a space and an uppercase letter is significant. When the following letter is lowercase, the comma is nonsignificant.

Examples

Amblyopia
Death in literature
Flute, saxophone, harp with string orchestra

Death—Causes
Government business enterprises—Accounting
Hotels, taversn, etc.—Austria

Death, Apparent
Forestry law and legislation, Colonial
Lasers, Effect of radiation on
Necessity, Fort, Battle of, 1754

Authority (Religion)
Charitable uses, trusts, and foundations (Hindu law)

* * * *

5. **Order of Subordinate Filing Elements**

5.6. Topical Subject Headings
When the leading elements of two or more topical subject headings are identical but they are qualified by different means, the fields are grouped in the following order:

a. Leading element alone
b. Leading element followed by a comma and qualifying word(s)
c. Leading element followed by parenthetical qualifier

Subarrangement within any group is by succeeding subordinate elements.

Example

Children
Children, Adopted
Children, Vagrant
Children (International law)
Children (Roman law)

5.7. Subject Subdivisions
In any subject heading field, subordinate elements that follow a dash (that is, subject subdivisions) are grouped in the following order:

a. Period subdivisions
b. Form and topical subdivisions
c. Geographical subdivisions

These distinctions are maintained at every level of subject subdivision. The treatment of subject subdivisions in relation to other subdivisions of the same heading is described in Rule 6.2.

Examples
> German literature
> German literature–17th century
> German literature–20th century
> German literature–Addresses, essays, lectures
> German literature–History and criticism
> German literature–Yearbooks
> German literature–Alsace
> German literature–Zürich
> German literature in foreign countries
>
> Catholic Church–Government
> Catholic Church–History–16th century
> Catholic Church–History–20th century
> Catholic Church–History–1965-
> Catholic Church–History–Bibliography
> Catholic Church–History–Text-books
> Catholic Church–Hymns
>
> Protestant Episcopal Church in the U.S.A.
> [abbreviated hereafter as P.E.C.]
> P.E.C.–Missions
> P.E.C.–Sermons
> P.E.C.–Alabama
> P.E.C.–North Carolina
> P.E.C.–Texas
> P.E.C. General convention

* * * *

6. Placement of Certain Types of Fields

To obtain coherent groupings of filing entries relating to the same entity, the following rules must be observed in arranging three types of fields: 1) author-title fields; 2) fields containing subject subdivisions; 3) personal name fields containing form subheadings.

6.1. Author-Title Fields

A field comprising a personal or corporate author and a title (e.g., Aristoteles. *Metaphysica*; Society for Pure English. *Tract no. 36*) is treated as if it consisted of two separate fields containing the same information. Thus, with respect to this consideration, no distinction is made between a filing entry containing separate fields for an author and a title and a filing entry containing an author-title added or subject entry for the same work. See Rule 8 for instruction on the arrangement of entries under the name of an author.

6.2. Fields Containing Subject Subdivisions

A field containing a subject subdivision is treated as if it consisted of at least two parts: the heading proper and the subject subdivision(s). In the case of author-title fields with subject subdivisions, the field is treated as if it consisted of three parts (author, title, subject subdivision) to satisfy the requirements of Rule 6.1. In both circumstances, the subject heading field is grouped with main and added entry fields containing the heading proper. After the functional order of the fields has been taken into account (see Rule 7), arrangement is by subject subdivision.

6.3. Personal Name Fields Containing Form Subheadings
A personal name field containing a form subheading (e.g., Spurious and doubtful works) is treated as an entirely different entity from the personal name on which it is based. Such a heading is arranged after all main, added, and subject entries relating to that particular person.
Examples

Aristoteles
    Ethica
Aristoteles
    Metaphysica
Aristoteles. Metaphysica   [author-title added entry]
ARISTOTELES. METAPHYSICA   [author-title subject entry]
ARISTOTELES. METAPHYSICA—BIBLIOGRAPHY
Aristoteles
    Poetica
Aristoteles
    Rhetorica
Aristoteles. Rhetorica
ARISTOTELES
ARISTOTELES—BIBLIOGRAPHY
ARISTOTELES—TRANSLATIONS
Aristoteles. **Spurious and doubtful works**

Philadelphia   [main entry]
PHILADELPHIA
PHILADELPHIA—DESCRIPTION
PHILADELPHIA—POLITICS AND GOVERNMENT
PHILADELPHIA—WATER-SUPPLY
Philadelphia. Athenaeum
PHILADELPHIA. ATHENAEUM
Philadelphia. Board of Health
Philadelphia. Centennial Exhibition, 1876
PHILADELPHIA. CENTENNIAL EXHIBITION, 1876
PHILADELPHIA. CENTENNIAL EXHIBITION, 1876—GUIDE-BOOKS
PHILADELPHIA. CENTENNIAL EXHIBITION, 1876—SONGS
    AND MUSIC
PHILADELPHIA. CENTENNIAL EXHIBITION, 1876—BRAZIL
PHILADELPHIA. CENTENNIAL EXHIBITION, 1876
    —SWITZERLAND
Philadelphia. City Planning Commission
Philadelphia. Free Library.
    Decade of growth, 1951-1960   [bibliographic title]
Philadelphia. Free Library. **Research bulletin**
            [series added entry]

(List continues on next page.)

Philadelphia. Free Library
   Rules and regulations . . .
PHILADELPHIA. FREE LIBRARY
Philadelphia. Free Library. Rare Book Dept.
PHILADELPHIA. FREE LIBRARY. THOMAS HOLME BRANCH
Philadelphia. Free Quaker Meeting House

* * * *

7.   **Functional Order of Fields**
    When the first fields of two or more filing entries are identical and the fields denote the same entity, the entries are grouped according to the cataloging function of these fields (that is, their relationship to the work cataloged or their use in the catalog) in the following order:
    a.   Main entry, added entry, see reference
    b.   See-also reference from main or added entry
    c.   Subject entry
    d.   See-also reference from a subject entry

Example
    Roosevelt, Franklin Delano, Pres. U.S., 1882-1945
                         [main entry]
    Roosevelt, Franklin Delano, Pres. U.S., 1882-1945
                         [added entry]
    Roosevelt, Franklin Delano, Pres. U.S., 1882-1945
       see also
    New York (State) Governor, 1929-1932 (Franklin D. Roosevelt)
    U.S. President, 1933-1945 (Franklin D. Roosevelt)
    ROOSEVELT, FRANKLIN DELANO, PRES. U.S., 1882-1945
                      [subject entry]
    ROOSEVELT, FRANKLIN DELANO, PRES. U.S., 1882-1945
       see also
    PRESIDENTIAL CRUISE TO THE GALAPAGOS ISLANDS, 1938

* * * *

8.   **Subarrangement of Identical Fields That Have the Same Function**
    When the first fields of two or more filing entries denote the same entity and they are functionally identical, the entries are arranged according to their subordinate fields. The selection of subordinate fields for a filing entry must conform to one of four basic patterns:
    a.   Type 1:   (1)   Main or added entry for a person or corporate body
                       (2)   Title
                       (3)   Imprint date
    b.   Type 2:   (1)   Author-title added entry
                       (2)   Imprint date
    c.   Type 3:   (1)   Main or added entry under title
                       (2)   Imprint date
    d.   Type 4:   (1)   Subject entry (including author-title entries)
                       (2)   All fields of Type 1 or Type 3 filing entry for catalog record in question

8.1. Choice of Title

Filing entries of Types 1, 2, and 3 can contain only one title. In the case of Types 1 and 3, if more than one kind of title is present in the catalog record, the order of preference is: 1) uniform title heading; 2) uniform filing title; 3) romanized title; 4) bibliographic title. In the case of a Type 2 filing entry, the title to be used occurs as part of the first field.

8.1.1. Uniform Title Headings and Filing Titles

Some of the elements necessary to arrange a uniform title heading properly may appear in a uniform filing title field. For example, the uniform title heading Arabian nights may be made more specific by giving the language of the edition in a filing title field. When this occurs, the uniform title heading and the filing title are treated as one field which is used in the filing entry.

Examples

> Shaw, George Bernard, 1856-1950
>> Arms and the man. 1913
>
> Shaw, George Bernard, 1856-1950
>> Arms and the man. 1958
>
> Shaw, George Bernard, 1856-1950
>> Arms and the man. Chinese
>
> Shaw, George Bernard, 1856-1950
>> Arms and the man. French
>
> SHAW, GEORGE BERNARD, 1856-1950. ARMS AND THE MAN
>> Alexander, Nigel
>>> A critical commentary on . . . 'Arms and the man'
>
> SHAW, GEORGE BERNARD, 1856-1950. ARMS AND THE MAN
>> Carrington, Norman Thomas
>>> G. Bernard Shaw: Arms and the man
>
> Shaw, George Bernard, 1856-1950
>> Caesar and Cleopatra. 1913
>
> Shaw, George Bernard, 1856-1950. Caesar and Cleopatra. 1934
>> [main entry under Ketchum]
>
> Shaw, George Bernard, 1856-1950
>> Caesar and Cleopatra. 1952
>
> SHAW, GEORGE BERNARD, 1856-1950. CAESAR AND CLEOPATRA
>> Deans, Marjorie
>>> Meeting at the Sphinx
>
> Shaw, George Bernard, 1856-1950
>> The complete plays of Bernard Shaw
>
> Shaw, George Bernard, 1856-1950
>> Do we agree?
>>> [main entry under Chesterton]
>
> Shaw, George Bernard, 1856-1950
>> Dramatic criticism, 1895-98
>
> Shaw, George Bernard, 1856-1950
>> Ellen Terry and Bernard Shaw
>>> [main entry under Terry]

(List continues on next page.)

Shaw, George Bernard, 1856-1950
 Forecasts of the coming century
  [main entry under Carpenter]
Shaw, George Bernard, 1856-1950
 Die heilige Johanna, *see his* Saint Joan. German
Shaw, George Bernard, 1856-1950
 Le héros et le soldat, *see his* Arms and the man. French
Shaw, George Bernard, 1856-1950
 On language
Shaw, George Bernard, 1856-1950
 Saint Joan. 1924
Shaw, George Bernard, 1856-1950. Saint Joan. 1964
 [main entry under Swander]
Shaw, George Bernard, 1856-1950
 Saint Joan. 1966
Shaw, George Bernard, 1856-1950
 Saint Joan. German
Shaw, George Bernard, 1856-1950
 Selected works. 1956   [uniform title]
Shaw, George Bernard, 1856-1950
 Selected works. Russ. 1946 [uniform title]
Shaw, George Bernard, 1856-1950
 Selected works. Russ. 1956 [uniform title]
Shaw, George Bernard, 1856-1950
 Works   [uniform title]
Shaw, George Bernard, 1856-1950
 Yin hsiung yü mei jen, *see his* Arms and the man. Chinese
Shaw, George Bernard, 1856-1950
 You never can tell. 1906
Shaw, George Bernard, 1856-1950
 see also
 Shaw Society of America
SHAW, GEORGE BERNARD, 1856-1950
 Adam, Ruth
  What Shaw really said
SHAW, GEORGE BERNARD, 1856-1950
 Bab, Julius, 1880-
  Bernard Shaw
SHAW, GEORGE BERNARD, 1856-1950
 Henderson, Archibald, 1877-
  Bernard Shaw: playboy and prophet
SHAW, GEORGE BERNARD, 1856-1950
 Henderson, Archibald, 1877-
  European dramatists
SHAW, GEORGE BERNARD, 1856-1950
 Henderson, Archibald, 1877-
  Interpreters of life and the modern spirit

(List continues on page 330.)

SHAW, GEORGE BERNARD, 1856-1950
The Heretics
[main entry under title]

The light. 1856	[monograph; main entry under Hurley]
Light. 1881	[serial]
Light. 1890	[serial]
Light. 1896	[serial]
The light. 1907	[monograph; main entry under Gorst]
The Light. 1909	[serial]
Light. 1923	[serial]
Light. 1930	[monograph; main entry under Rutherford]
Light. 1931	[serial]
The Light. 1938	[serial; main entry under another title]
Light. 1942	[monograph; main entry under Hotchkiss]
The light. 1943	[monograph; main entry under Young]
The light. 1958	[monograph; main entry under Saint-Marcoux]
Light. 1965	[monograph; main entry under Kohn]
Light. 1968	[monograph; main entry under Waller]

CHESS
　Abrahams, Gerald, 1907-
　　The chess mind
CHESS
　Abrahams, Gerald, 1907-
　　Technique in chess
CHESS
　Academie universelle des jeux
　　[main entry under title]
CHESS
　Agnel, Hyacinth R　　1799-1871
　　The book of chess
CHESS
　Agostini, Orfeu Gilberto d'
　　Xadrez básico
CHESS
　Alatortsev, Vladimir Alekseevich
　　Problemy sovremennoĭ teorii shakmat
　　　[romanized title]
CHESS
　Alatortsev, Vladimir Alekseevich
　　Vzaimodeĭstvie figur i peshek
　　　[romanized title]

9.   **Treatment of Identical Filing Entries**

When two or more filing entries are identical, no effort need be made to arrange them within their group. In a manual file, the new entry can simply be placed after those already there. This situation occurs most commonly with filing entries for titles of various kinds (see Type 3 filing entry in Rule 8).

Example

      Light (Motion picture) 1957
      Light (Motion picture) 1965
      Light (Motion picture) 1968
      Light (Motion picture) 1969
      Light (Motion picture) 1969
      Light (Motion picture) 1969

* * * *

16. **Numerals**

16.7.1. Incompletely Expressed Dates

A historic time period that is generalized or expressed only in words is treated as if it consisted of the full range of dates for the period. For example, 16th century is arranged as 1500-1599 and under **U.S.—History, Civil War** is arranged as 1861-1865. A period subdivision in the form of "To [date" is treated as if it were 0-[date] (e.g., To 1517 is arranged as 0-1517). Period subdivisions are arranged chronologically even when the dates do not appear first. Geologic time periods are arranged alphabetically.

Examples

      U.S.—Foreign relations—Revolution [1776-1782]
      U.S.—Foreign relations—1783-1865
      U.S.—Foreign relations—1789-1797
      U.S.—Foreign relations—Constitutional period, 1789-1809

      Egypt—History—To 332 B.C. [0-332 B.C.]
      Egypt—History—Ancient to 640 A.D. [0-640 A.D.]
      Egypt—History—332-30 B.C.
      Egypt—History—Graeco-Roman period, 332 B.C.-640 A.D.
      Egypt—History—30 B.C.-640 A.D.
      Egypt—History—640-1250
      Egypt—History—640-1882

      India—History—Early to 324 B.C. [0-324 B.C.]
      India—History—324 B.C.-1000 A.D.
      India—History—1000-1526
      India—History—1500-1765
      India—History—18th century [1700-1799]
      India—History—British occupation, 1765-1947
      India—History—Rohilla War, 1774
      India—History—19th century [1800-1899]
      India—History—Mutiny, 1809

(Examples continue on page 332.)

English fiction—Middle English (1100-1500)
English fiction—Early modern (to 1700) [1501-1700]
English fiction—18th century [1700-1799]
English fiction—19th century [1800-1899]
English fiction—20th century [1900-1999]

BIBLIOGRAPHY

American Library Association. Division of Cataloging and Classification. Committee on Subject Headings. "Bibliography of Subject Headings Lists 1938-1952," *Journal of Cataloging and Classification* 8:159-70 (December 1952).

Angell, Richard S. "Library of Congress Subject Headings—Review and Forecast," *Subject Retrieval in the Seventies: New Directions: Proceedings of an International Symposium.* Edited by Hans (Hanan) Wellisch and Thomas D. Wilson. Westport, Conn.: Greenwood Publishing Company, 1972, pp. 143-63.

Angell, Richard S. "Standards for Subject Headings: A National Program," *Journal of Cataloging and Classification* 10:191-97 (October 1954).

Austin, Derek. "The Development of PRECIS: A Theoretical and Technical History," *Journal of Documentation* 30:47-102 (March 1974).

Austin, Derek, and Jeremy A. Digger. "PRECIS: The Preserved Context Index System," *Library Resources & Technical Services* 21:13-30 (Winter 1977).

Bates, Marcia J. "Factors Affecting Subject Catalog Search Success," *Journal of the American Society for Information Science* 28:161-69 (May 1977).

Berman, Sanford. *Prejudices and Antipathies: A Tract on the LC Subject Heads Concerning People.* Metuchen, N.J.: Scarecrow, 1971. 249pp.

Bishop, William Warner. "Subject Headings in Dictionary Catalogs," *Library Journal* 31:C113-C123 (August 1906).

Black, Henry. "An Approach to a Theory of Subject Headings," *College & Research Libraries* 7:244-48, 255 (July 1946).

Brinkler, Bartol. "The Geographical Approach to Materials in the *Library of Congress Subject Headings*," *Library Resources & Technical Services* 6:49-63 (Winter 1962). "Comment from the Library of Congress," by John W. Cronin, Ibid. 6:63-64 (Winter 1962).

Cataloging Service 1- , June 1945- (Washington: Library of Congress, Processing Dept.).

Chan, Lois Mai. "Alphabetical Arrangement and Subject Collocation in Library of Congress Subject Headings," *Library Resources & Technical Services* 21:156-69 (Spring 1977).

Chan, Lois Mai. " 'American Poetry' but 'Satire, American': The Direct and Inverted Forms of Subject Headings Containing National Adjectives," *Library Resources & Technical Services* 17:330-39 (Summer 1973).

Chan, Lois Mai. "The Period Subdivision in Subject Headings," *Library Resources & Technical Services* 16:453-59 (Fall 1972).

Christ, John M. *Concepts and Subject Headings: Their Relation in Information Retrieval and Library Science.* Metuchen, N.J.: Scarecrow Press, 1972. 174pp.

Clack, Doris. *Black Literature Resources: Analysis and Organization.* New York: Marcel Dekker, 1975. 207pp.

Coates, E. J. *Subject Catalogues: Headings and Structure*. London, Library Association, 1960. 186pp.

Coen, James A. "An Investigation of Indirect Subdivision by Place in Library of Congress Subject Headings," *Library Resources & Technical Services* 13:62-78 (Winter 1969).

Coetzee, P. C. "Syntactics and Semantics of the Subject Heading: An Essay in Catalogistics," *Mousaion* 21:1-41; 22:1-30; 23:1-30 (1957).

Colby, Robert A. "Current Problems in the Subject Analysis of Literature," *Journal of Cataloging and Classification* 10:19-28 (January 1954).

Cranshaw, J. "The Alphabetico-Classed Catalogue and Its Near Relatives," *Library Assistant* 30:202-211 (1937).

Cutter, Charles A. *Rules for a Dictionary Catalog*. 4th ed. rewritten. Washington: Government Printing Office, 1904. 146pp.

Daily, Jay E. "The Grammar of Subject Headings: A Formulation of Rules for Subject Heading Based on a Syntactical and Morphological Analysis of the Library of Congress List," Diss. Columbia Univ., 1957. 234pp.

Daily, Jay E. "Many Changes, No Alteration: An Analysis of Library of Congress Subject Headings, Seventh Edition," *Library Journal* 92:3961-63 (November 1, 1967).

Daily, Jay E. "Subject Headings and the Theory of Classification," *American Documentation* 8:269-74 (October 1957).

Daniels Ganning, Mary Kay. "The Catalog: Its Nature and Prospects," *Journal of Library Automation* 9:48-66 (March 1976).

Dunkin, Paul S. *Cataloging U.S.A.* Chicago: American Library Association, 1969. 159pp.

Eaton, Thelma. *Cataloging and Classification: An Introductory Manual*. 4th ed. Ann Arbor: distributed by Edwards Brothers, 1967. 231pp.

Foskett, A. C. *The Subject Approach to Information*. 2nd ed. revised and enlarged. Hamden, Conn.: Linnet Books & Clive Bingley, 1972. 429pp.

Frarey, Carlyle J. "Developments in Subject Cataloging," *Library Trends* 2:217-35 (October 1953).

Frarey, Carlyle J. "Practical Problems in Subject Heading Work: A Summary," *Journal of Cataloging and Classification* 8:154-58 (December 1952).

Frarey, Carlyle J. "The Role of Research in Establishing Standards for Subject Headings," *Journal of Cataloging and Classification* 10:179-90 (October 1954).

Frarey, Carlyle J. "Studies of Use of the Subject Catalog: Summary and Evaluation," *The Subject Analysis of Library Materials*. Ed. Maurice F. Tauber. New York: School of Library Service, Columbia University, 1953, pp. 147-65.

Frarey, Carlyle J. *Subject Headings*. (The State of the Library Art, vol. 1, part 2). New Brunswick, N.J.: Graduate School of Library Science, Rutgers–The State University, 1960. 92pp.

Frarey, Carlyle J., ed. "Symposium on Subject Headings," *Journal of Cataloging and Classification* 8:131-58 (December 1952). Eleven papers containing remarks of speakers at the DCC meeting at the ALA Conf., N.Y., July 1-2, 1952.

Gjelsness, Rudolph H. "The Classified Catalog *vs.* The Dictionary Catalog," *Library Journal* 56:18-21 (January 1, 1931).

Gull, C. D. "Some Remarks on Subject Headings," *Special Libraries* 40:83-88 (March 1949).

Hanson, J. C. M. "The Subject Catalogs of the Library of Congress," *Bulletin of the American Library Association* 3:385-97 (1909).

Hardy, May G. "The Library of Congress Subject Catalog: An Evaluation," *Library Quarterly* 22:40-50 (January 1952).

Harris, Jessica Lee. *Subject Analysis: Computer Implications of Rigorous Definition.* With a preface by Maurice F. Tauber and Theodore C. Hines. Metuchen, N.J.: Scarecrow Press, 1970. 279pp.

Haykin, David Judson. "Let's Get Down to Fundamentals!" *Medical Library Association Bulletin* 36:82-85 (April 1948).

Haykin, David Judson. "Project for a Subject Heading Code: Revised." Washington, 1957. 10pp.

Haykin, David Judson. *Subject Headings: A Practical Guide.* Washington: Government Printing Office, 1951. 140pp.

Haykin, David Judson. "Subject Headings: Principles and Development," *The Subject Analysis of Library Materials.* Edited by Maurice F. Tauber. New York: School of Library Service, Columbia University, 1953, pp. 43-54.

Hickey, Doralyn J. "Subject Analysis: An Interpretive Survey," *Library Trends* 25:273-91 (July 1976).

Holmes, Robert R. "Introduction to the Seventh Edition of Subject Headings Used in the Dictionary Catalogs of the Library of Congress," *Library Resources & Technical Services* 12:323-29 (Summer 1968).

Horner, John. *Cataloguing.* London: Association of Assistant Librarians, 1970. 479pp.

Immroth, John Phillip. *Analysis of Vocabulary Control in Library of Congress Classification and Subject Headings.* Littleton, Colo.: Libraries Unlimited, 1971. 172pp.

International PRECIS Workshop. *The PRECIS Index System: Principles, Applications, and Prospects: Proceedings.* Edited by Hans H. Wellisch. New York: H. W. Wilson Company, 1977. 211pp.

Jackson, Sidney L. *Catalog Use Study: Director's Report.* Edited by Vaclav Mostecky. Chicago: American Library Association, 1958. 86pp.

Jackson, Sidney L. "Sears and LC Subject Headings: A Sample Comparison," *Library Journal* 86:755-56, 775 (February 15, 1961).

Lancaster, F. W. *Vocabulary Control for Information Retrieval.* Washington: Information Resources Press, 1972. 233pp.

Lancaster, F. W. "Vocabulary Control in Information Retrieval Systems," *Advances in Librarianship* 7:1-40 (1977).

Langridge, Derek. "Subject Headings," *Training in Indexing.* Norman Knight, ed. Cambridge, Mass.: M.I.T. Press, 1969, pp. 75-85.

Lilley, Oliver L. "Evaluation of the Subject Catalog: Criticisms and a Proposal," *American Documentation* 5:41-60 (1954).

Lilley, Oliver L. "How Specific Is Specific?" *Journal of Cataloging and Classification* 11:3-8 (January 1955).

Lilley, Oliver L. "Terminology, Form, Specificity and the Syndetic Structure of Subject Headings for English Literature." Diss. New York: Columbia University, 1958. 503pp.

Lipetz, Ben-Ami. "Catalog Use in a Large Research Library," *Library Quarterly* 42:129-39 (January 1972).

Lubetzky, Seymour. "Titles: Fifth Column of the Catalog," *Library Quarterly* 11:412-30 (1941).

McKinlay, John. "Concerning Subject Authority Catalogues," *Library Resources & Technical Services* 16:460-65 (Fall 1972).

MacNair, Mary W. "The Library of Congress List of Subject Headings," *Bulletin of the American Library Association* 23:301 (1929).

Mann, Margaret. *Introduction to Cataloging and the Classification of Books.* 2nd ed. Chicago: American Library Association, 1943. 276pp.

Metcalfe, John. *Alphabetical Subject Indication of Information.* (Rutgers Series on Systems for the Intellectual Organization of Information, Vol. 3). New Brunswick, N.J.: Graduate School of Library Service, Rutgers University, 1965. 148pp.

Metcalfe, John. *Information Indexing and Subject Cataloging: Alphabetical: Classified: Coordinate: Mechanical.* New York: Scarecrow Press, 1957. 338pp.

Metcalfe, John. *Information Retrieval, British & American, 1876-1976.* Metuchen, N.J.: Scarecrow Press, 1976. 243pp.

Metcalfe, John. *Subject Classifying and Indexing of Libraries and Literature.* New York: Scarecrow Press, 1959. 347pp.

Mostecky, Vaclav. "Study of the See-Also Reference Structure in Relation to the Subject of International Law," *American Documentation* 7:294-314 (1956).

Needham, C. D. *Organizing Knowledge in Libraries: An Introduction to Information Retrieval.* 2nd rev. ed. London: A. Deutsch, 1971. 448pp.

Norris, Dorothy May. *A History of Cataloguing and Cataloguing Methods 1100-1850: With an Introductory Survey of Ancient Times.* London: Grafton, 1939. 246pp.

Olding, R. K. "Form of Alphabetico-Specific Subject Headings, and a Brief Code," *Australian Library Journal* 10:127-37 (July 1961).

Osborn, Andrew D. *Serial Publications: Their Place and Treatment in Libraries.* 2nd ed. rev. Chicago: American Library Association, 1973. 434pp.

Pettee, Julia. "The Philosophy of Subject Headings," *Special Libraries* 23:181-82 (April 1932).

Pettee, Julia. *Subject Headings: The History and Theory of the Alphabetical Subject Approach to Books.* New York: H. W. Wilson Company, 1947. 191pp.

Prevost, Marie Louise. "An Approach to Theory and Method in General Subject Headings," *Library Quarterly* 16:140-51 (April 1946).

"Principles of the *Sears List of Subject Headings*," *Sears List of Subject Headings*. 11th ed. Edited by Barbara M. Westby. New York: H. W. Wilson Company, 1977, pp. xi-xxxiv.

Quattlebaum, Marguerite V., comp. *LC Period Subdivisions under Names of Places.* 2nd ed. Washington: Library of Congress, 1975. 111pp.

Ramakrishnan, M. N. "Adjectives in Subject Headings," *Herald of Library Science* 1:139-41 (July 1962).

Ranganathan, S. R. "Subject Heading and Facet Analysis," *Journal of Documentation* 20:109-119 (September 1964).

Rather, John C. "Filing Arrangement in the Library of Congress Catalogs: An Operational Document." Provisional Version. Washington: Library of Congress, 1971. 79pp.

Richmond, Phyllis Allen. "Cats: An Example of Concealed Classification in Subject Headings," *Library Resources & Technical Services* 3:102-112 (Spring 1959).

Richmond, Phyllis Allen. "A Divided Catalog—Then What?" *American Documentation* 7:315-19 (1956).

Richmond, Phyllis Allen. "Research Possibilities in the Machine-Readable Catalog: Use of the Catalog to Study Itself," *Journal of Academic Librarianship* 2:224-29 (November 1976).

Schaeffer, Rudolf F. "Delights and Pitfalls of Subject Cataloging," *Library Resources & Technical Services* 14:98-108 (Winter 1970).

Scheerer, George. "The Subject Catalog Examined," *Library Quarterly* 27:187-98 (July 1957).

Schwartz, Jacob. "A Dozen Desultory Denunciations of the Dictionary Catalogue, with a Theory of Cataloguing," *Library Journal* 11:470-77 (December 1886).

Seely, Pauline A. "Subject Headings Today," *Library Journal* 78:17-22 (January 1, 1953).

Sharp, Henry A. "Cataloguing: Some New Approaches. The Dictionary Subject Approach," *Library World* 57:92-94 (December 1955).

Shera, Jesse H., and Margaret E. Egan. *The Classified Catalog: Basic Principles and Practices.* With a Code for the Construction and Maintenance of the Classified Catalog by Jeannette M. Lynn and Zola Hilton. Chicago: American Library Association, 1956. 130pp.

Sinkankas, George M. *A Study in the Syndetic Structure of the Library of Congress List of Subject Headings.* Pittsburgh: University of Pittsburgh Graduate School of Library and Information Sciences, 1972. 116pp.

Steinweg, Hilda. "Thought on Subject Headings," *Journal of Cataloging and Classification* 6:40-45 (Spring 1950).

"Subject Access Project," *Occasional Newsletter* (Syracuse University School of Information Studies), No. 3, May 1977. 4pp. Project Director: Pauline Atherton.

The Subject Analysis of Library Materials: Papers presented at an Institute, June 24-28, 1952, under the sponsorship of the School of Library Service, Columbia University, and the A.L.A. Division of Cataloging and Classification. Edited by Maurice F. Tauber. New York: School of Library Service, Columbia University, 1953. 235pp.

"Subject Heading Code in Preparation," *College & Resource Libraries* 14:216 (April 1953).

Subject Retrieval in the Seventies: New Directions: Proceedings of an International Symposium Held at the Center of Adult Education, University of Maryland, College Park, May 14 to 15, 1971. Edited by Hans (Hanan) Wellisch and Thomas D. Wilson. (Contributions in Librarianship and Information Science, No. 3). Westport, Conn.: Greenwood Publishing, 1972. 180pp.

Taube, Mortimer. "Specificity in Subject Headings and Coordinate Indexing," *Library Trends* 1:219-23 (October 1952).

Taylor, Jed H. "Classification and Subject-Headings in the Small College Library," *Library Resources & Technical Services* 5:87-90 (Winter 1961).

Taylor, Kanardy L. "Subject Catalogs *vs.* Classified Catalogs," *The Subject Analysis of Library Materials.* Edited by Maurice F. Tauber. New York: School of Library Service, Columbia University, 1953, pp. 100-113.

United States. Library of Congress. *Departmental & Divisional Manuals, No. 3: Subject Cataloging Division.* Washington. 1950.

United States. Library of Congress. Processing Department. *Filing Rules for the Dictionary Catalogs of the Library of Congress.* Washington: Processing Department, 1956. 187pp.

United States. Library of Congress. Subject Cataloging Division. *Library of Congress Subject Headings.* 8th ed. Washington: Library of Congress, 1975. 2 v. with supplements.

United States. Library of Congress. Subject Cataloging Division. *Library of Congress Subject Headings in Microform.* Washington: Library of Congress, 1976- . (Microfiche).

Van Hoesen, H. B. "Perspective in Cataloging with Some Applications," *Library Quarterly* 14:100-107 (April 1944).

Vatican Library. *Rules for the Catalog of Printed Books.* Trans. from the 2nd. Italian ed. by The Very Rev. Thomas J. Shanahan, Victor A. Schaefer, and Constantin T. Vesselowsky. Edited by Wyllis E. Wright. Chicago: American Library Association, 1948. 426pp.

White, John B. "On Changing Subject Headings," *Library Resources & Technical Services* 16:466-69 (Fall 1972). Comment by Edward J. Blume (letter). *Library Resources & Technical Services* 17:268 (Spring 1973).

Williams, James G. *Classified Library of Congress Subject Headings.* New York: Marcel Dekker, 1972. 2v.

Woods, William Edward. "Headings, Subject. See SUBJECT HEADINGS," *Library Resources & Technical Services* 16:79-81 (Winter 1972).

Wright, Wyllis E. "Standards for Subject Headings: Problems and Opportunities," *Journal of Cataloging and Classification* 10:175-78 (October 1954).

Wright, Wyllis E. "The Subject Approach to Knowledge: Historical Aspects and Purposes," *The Subject Analysis of Library Materials.* Edited by Maurice F. Tauber. New York: School of Library Service, Columbia University, 1953, pp. 8-15.

INDEX